ST ANTONY'S/MACMILLAN SERIES
General editors: Archie Brown (1978–85) and Rosemary Thorp (1985–   ), both Fellows of St Antony's College, Oxford

Roy Allison FINLAND'S RELATIONS WITH THE SOVIET UNION, 1944–84
Said Amir Arjomand (editor) FROM NATIONALISM TO REVOLUTIONARY ISLAM
Anders Aslund PRIVATE ENTERPRISE IN EASTERN EUROPE
Omer Bartov THE EASTERN FRONT, 1941–45, GERMAN TROOPS AND THE BARBARISATION OF WARFARE
Archie Brown (editor) POLITICAL CULTURE AND COMMUNIST STUDIES
Archie Brown (editor) POLITICAL LEADERSHIP AND THE SOVIET UNION
Archie Brown and Michael Kaser (editors) SOVIET POLICY FOR THE 1980s
S.B. Burman CHIEFDOM POLITICS AND ALIEN LAW
Renfrew Christie ELECTRICITY, INDUSTRY AND CLASS IN SOUTH AFRICA
Robert O. Collins and Francis M. Deng (editors) THE BRITISH IN THE SUDAN 1898–1956
Wilhelm Deist THE *WEHRMACHT* AND GERMAN REARMAMENT
Guido di Tella ARGENTINA UNDER PERÓN, 1973–76
Guido di Tella and D.C.M. Platt (editors) THE POLITICAL ECONOMY OF ARGENTINA 1880–1946
Simon Duke US DEFENCE BASES IN THE UNITED KINGDOM
Julius A. Elias PLATO'S DEFENCE OF POETRY
Ricardo Ffrench-Davis and Ernesto Tironi (editors) LATIN AMERICA AND THE NEW INTERNATIONAL ECONOMIC ORDER
David Footman ANTONIN BESSE OF ADEN
Bohdan Harasymiw POLITICAL ELITE RECRUITMENT IN THE SOVIET UNION
Neil Harding (editor) THE STATE IN SOCIALIST SOCIETY
Richard Holt SPORT AND SOCIETY IN MODERN FRANCE
Albert Hourani EUROPE AND THE MIDDLE EAST
Albert Hourani THE EMERGENCE OF THE MODERN MIDDLE EAST
J.R. Jennings GEORGES SOREL
A. Kemp-Welch (translator) THE BIRTH OF SOLIDARITY
Paul Kennedy and Anthony Nicholls (editors) NATIONALIST AND RACIALIST MOVEMENTS IN BRITAIN AND GERMANY BEFORE 1914
Richard Kindersley (editor) IN SEARCH OF EUROCOMMUNISM
Bohdan Krawchenko SOCIAL CHANGE AND NATIONAL CONSCIOUSNESS IN TWENTIETH-CENTURY UKRAINE
Gisela C. Lebzelter POLITICAL ANTI-SEMITISM IN ENGLAND, 1918–1939
Nancy Lubin LABOUR AND NATIONALITY IN SOVIET CENTRAL ASIA
C.A. MacDonald THE UNITED STATES, BRITAIN AND APPEASEMENT, 1936–1939
Robert H. McNeal TSAR AND COSSACK, 1855–1914
David Nicholls HAITI IN CARIBBEAN CONTEXT
Patrick O'Brien (editor) RAILWAYS AND THE ECONOMIC DEVELOPMENT OF WESTERN EUROPE, 1830–1914
Amii Omara-Otunna POLITICS AND THE MILITARY IN UGANDA, 1890–1985

Roger Owen (*editor*) STUDIES IN THE ECONOMIC AND SOCIAL HISTORY OF PALESTINE IN THE NINETEENTH AND TWENTIETH CENTURIES

D.C.M. Platt and Guido di Tella (*editors*) ARGENTINA, AUSTRALIA AND CANADA: STUDIES IN COMPARATIVE DEVELOPMENT, 1870–1965

Irena Powell WRITERS AND SOCIETY IN MODERN JAPAN

Alex Pravda (*editor*) HOW RULING COMMUNIST PARTIES ARE GOVERNED

T.H. Rigby and Ferenc Fehér (*editors*) POLITICAL LEGITIMATION IN COMMUNIST STATES

Hans Rogger JEWISH POLICIES AND RIGHT-WING POLITICS IN IMPERIAL RUSSIA

Marilyn Rueschemeyer PROFESSIONAL WORK AND MARRIAGE

A.J.R. Russell-Wood THE BLACK MAN IN SLAVERY AND FREEDOM IN COLONIAL BRAZIL

Nurit Schleijman UNDERCOVER AGENTS IN THE RUSSIAN REVOLUTIONARY MOVEMENT

Amnon Sella and Yael Yishai ISRAEL THE PEACEFUL BELLIGERENT, 1967–79

Aron Shai BRITAIN AND CHINA, 1941–47

Lewis H. Siegelbaum THE POLITICS OF INDUSTRIAL MOBILIZATION IN RUSSIA, 1914–17

David Stafford BRITAIN AND EUROPEAN RESISTANCE, 1940–1945

Nancy Stepan THE IDEA OF RACE IN SCIENCE

Marvin Swartz THE POLITICS OF BRITISH FOREIGN POLICY IN THE ERA OF DISRAELI AND GLADSTONE

Rosemary Thorp (*editor*) LATIN AMERICA IN THE 1930s

Rosemary Thorp and Laurence Whitehead (*editors*) INFLATION AND STABILISATION IN LATIN AMERICA

Rosemary Thorp and Laurence Whitehead (*editors*) LATIN AMERICAN DEBT AND THE ADJUSTMENT CRISIS

Rudolf L. Tökés (*editor*) OPPOSITION IN EASTERN EUROPE

Toshio Yokoyama JAPAN IN THE VICTORIAN MIND

Series Standing Order

If you would like to receive future titles in this series as they are published, you can make use of our standing order facility. To place a standing order please contact your bookseller or, in case of difficulty, write to us at the address below with your name and address and the name of the series. Please state with which title you wish to begin your standing order. (If you live outside the UK we may not have the rights for your area, in which case we will forward your order to the publisher concerned.)

Standing Order Service, Macmillan Distribution Ltd, Houndmills, Basingstoke, Hampshire, RG21 2XS, England.

Japan in the Victorian Mind

A Study of Stereotyped Images of a Nation 1850−80

Toshio Yokoyama
Associate Professor of the History of Modern Japanese Culture, Kyoto University

© Toshio Yokoyama 1987

All rights reserved. No reproduction, copy or transmission of this publication may be made without written permission.

No paragraph of this publication may be reproduced, copied or transmitted save with written permission or in accordance with the provisions of the Copyright Act 1956 (as amended), or under the terms of any licence permitting limited copying issued by the Copyright Licensing Agency, 33-4 Alfred Place, London WC1E 7DP.

Any person who does any unauthorised act in relation to this publication may be liable to criminal prosecution and civil claims for damages.

First published 1987
Reprinted 1989

Published by
THE MACMILLAN PRESS LTD
Houndmills, Basingstoke, Hampshire RG21 2XS
and London
Companies and representatives
throughout the world

Printed in Great Britain by
Antony Rowe,
Chippenham, Wilts

British Library Cataloguing in Publication Data
Yokoyama, Toshio
Japan in the Victorian mind: a study of
stereotyped images of a nation, 1850-80.
—(St Antony's/Macmillan series)
1. Public opinion—Great Britain—
History—19th century 2. Japan—
Foreign opinion, British
I. Title II. St Antony's College
III. Series
952   D5881.3
ISBN 0-333-40472-6

In memory of Richard Storry, 1913–82

*This book has been published
with the help of a grant from
the Suntory Foundation, Osaka*

Contents

Chronological Table		viii
List of Plates		xii
List of Abbreviations		xiii
Map of Japan and the Asian Continent		xiv
Preface		xv
Introduction		xix
1	'This Singular Country'	1
2	Japan and the Edinburgh Publishers	21
3	Britain, the Happy Suitor of a Fairyland	46
4	Britain, the Suitor Disillusioned	67
5	In Quest of the Inner Life of the Japanese	88
6	'The Strange History of this Strange Country'	109
7	The Expanding Gulf	134
8	Victorian Travellers in the Japanese 'Elf-land'	150
Conclusion		170
Notes and References		176
Select Bibliography		208
Index		220

Chronological Table

Year	Britain & other Western countries	Inter-continental events	Japan & other Far Eastern countries
1840		The Anglo-Chinese Opium War (1840–42)	
41			The Tempô Reform in Japan (1841–43)
43		Shanghai opened to the West	
48	The February Revolution (France) The March Revolution (Germany)		
1850			The Taiping Rebellion in China (1850–64)
51	Louis Napoleon's coup d'état	The Great Exhibition, London	
53		Commodore Perry's Expedition to Japan (1853–54) The Crimean War (1853–56)	
54	Exhibition of Japanese applied art in London	The Anglo-Japanese Covention	
56	The print maker Felix Bracquemond discovered *Hokusai Manga* in Paris	The *Arrow* War in China (1856–58)	
57		The Elgin Mission to China & Japan (1857–59) The Indian 'Mutiny' (1857–59)	

58		The Tientsin Treaty The Anglo-Japanese Commercial Treaty	
59	Charles Darwin's *Origin of Species* (London) Laurence Oliphant's *Lord Elgin's Mission to China & Japan* (Edinburgh & London)		Rutherford Alcock arrived in Japan as British Consul General
1860	Thackeray's *Cornhill Magazine* founded in London	The Peking Treaty	
61	Victor Emanuel II became King of Italy The American Civil War (1861–65)		
62		The first Tokugawa Mission to Europe The London International Exhibition	The British Legation in Edo (Tokyo) attacked by samurai
63	Rutherford Alcock's *Capital of the Tycoon* (London) Thomas Huxley's *Zoological Evidences as to Man's Place in Nature* (London)	Kagoshima bombarded by the Royal Navy	
64		Shimonoseki bombarded by a combined fleet of western warships The First International Workingmen's Association, London (1864–76)	
65			Harry Parkes arrived in Japan as British Minister

67	The Second Reform Bill in Britain	The Paris Universal Exposition	
	The Austro-Hungarian Empire established		The Tokugawa Shogun resigned
68	The First Disraeli Cabinet		The Meiji Restoration of Imperial Rule
	The First Gladstone Cabinet		The Kobe Incident
	Friedrich Max Müller became Professor of Comparative Philology at Oxford		
	Charles Dilke's *Greater Britain* (London)		
69	Transcontinental railway system opened in the USA	The Suez Canal opened	
1870	The Franco-Prussian War (1870–71)		
	The Education Act in Britain		
71	The German Empire established	Telegraphic communication opened between London & Shanghai	The abolition of feudal domains in Japan
	The Paris Commune	The Iwakura Mission to the USA & Europe (1871–73)	
	Bertram Mitford's *Tales of Old Japan* (London)		
72		The Japanese Government abandoned its traditional anti-Christian policy	The General Education Law in Japan
			The first Japanese railway opened
			The Asiatic Society of Japan established in Yokohama

Chronological Table

73	Baron de Hübner's *Promenade autour du monde* (Paris)	The Vienna Universal Exhibition	
74	The economic depression increasingly serious in Britain The Second Disraeli Cabinet		The Japanese Expedition to Formosa
76			The Japanese-Korean Commercial Treaty
77		Queen Victoria became Empress of India	The Satsuma Rebellion
78		The Paris Universal Exposition	
1880	The Second Gladstone Cabinet Isabella Bird's *Unbeaten Tracks in Japan* (London)		
85	Gilbert & Sullivan's *Mikado* first performed in London		

List of Plates

1. Japanese Buddhist Temple
2. Japanese Lady Painting
3. Japanese Villages near Nagasaki
4. Japanese Tea-Gardens
5. Japanese Children's Gymnastics (from a Japanese drawing)
6. Japanese Astronomers and Mount Fuji, or Fujiyama (from a Japanese drawing)
7. Japanese Ambassadors at the London International Exhibition
8. The Japanese Court in the London International Exhibition
9. Japanese Gnomes' Picnic (from a Japanese drawing)
10. Japanese Court Dress (from a Japanese drawing)
11. Ceremonial Trousers for Samurai (from a Japanese drawing)
12. Sumô Wrestling in the Great Amphitheatre of Edo (from a Japanese drawing)
13. Samurai Attack on the British Legation in Edo
14. Seppuku, or Hara-Kiri (from a Japanese drawing)
15. Japanese Sermon (by a Japanese artist commissioned by Mitford)
16. Nihonbashi, or Japan Bridge, Edo (from a Japanese drawing)
17. Public Bath-House in Edo (from a Japanese drawing)
18. The Japanese Women in the Paris International Exposition
19. Fashionable Costumes of Modern Japanese Officers
20. Occupations of Ministers to Japan
21. Opening of the First Railway in Japan: Arrival of the Mikado at Yokohama Station
22. Worcester 'Japanese' Porcelain at the Vienna Exhibition
23. *Daibutsu,* or the Great Image of Buddha, at Kamakura
24. Globe-trotters in Rickshaws
25. *Miyako Odori,* or the Kyoto Dance, at the Minamiza Theatre

These plates have been reproduced with the kind permission of the following libraries and museum: Kyoto University Library: Plates 3, 7, 8, 13, 16, 18, 19, 21, 22 and 25; Research Institute for Humanistic Studies Library, Kyoto University: Plates 1, 2, 5, 6, 9, 10, 11, 12, 14, 15, 20, 23 and 24; Faculty of Law Library, Kyoto University: Plate 17; Kobe City Museum: Plate 4.

List of Abbreviations

Asiatic Jour.	The *Asiatic Journal and Monthly Register for Britain and Foreign India, China, and Australasia*
BL, Addit. MSS.	The British Library, Additional Manuscripts
Blackw.	*Blackwood's Edinburgh Magazine*
Contem. Rev.	The *Contemporary Review*
Cornhill.	The *Cornhill Magazine*
Dubl. Rev.	The *Dublin Review*
Edin. Rev.	The *Edinburgh Review*
Fort. Rev.	The *Fortnightly Review*
Fraser.	*Fraser's Magazine for Town and Country*
House. Words	*Household Words*
Macmillan.	*Macmillan's Magazine*
New Monthly Mag.	The *New Monthly Magazine and Humorist*
New Quar. Mag.	The *New Quarterly Magazine*
New Quar. Rev.	The *New Quarterly Review*
NLS, BP	The Blackwood Papers at the National Library of Scotland
North Brit. Rev.	The *North British Review*
PRO, FO	The Foreign Office Papers at the Public Record Office
Quar. Rev.	The *Quarterly Review*
RU, LA	The Longman's Archive at the University of Reading
Saturday Rev.	The *Saturday Review*
Wellesley Index	The *Wellesley Index to Victorian Periodicals 1824–1900*
Westmin. Rev.	The *Westminster Review*

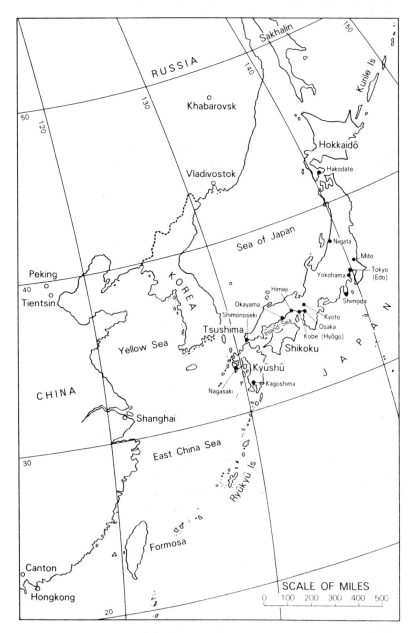

Japan and the Asian Continent

Preface

There is little room for doubting that, in most countries of the world, life has been acquiring an increasingly international flavour. The word 'internationalisation' itself has become more fashionable and even in some cases become something of a shibboleth. The result of these trends is that it is no longer as easy as it once was to resort to notions of 'national character' to explain why certain patterns of behaviour should be common among the inhabitants of any given country.

No country can now pretend to be free of the global net of cause-and-effect relations. Patterns of behaviour that seem at first sight to be distinctly Japanese or distinctly English turn out on careful examination to be the complex products of manifold international influences. Furthermore, conditions of urban life in the late twentieth century demand the same sort of adaptability of people throughout the world. Thus the life of a family living in a flat in Tokyo may well have more in common with that of a family living in a flat in London or an apartment in Paris than with that of another Japanese family living in a village in rural Japan.

Perhaps we are now coming to a stage in human history where nationality is becoming a less emotional issue, a stage, in other words, that marks the end of the age of intense nationalism. If so, the *dramatis personae* of this book may seem to the late twentieth-century reader to be naïvely nationalistic. And their earnest beliefs in the 'national defects' of the Japanese and the Chinese may invite complacent smiles.

Nevertheless, it would be premature to say that the habit of perceiving people in terms of 'national characteristics' has become a thing of the past. On the contrary, it often seems to be very much alive and tends to obscure a more objective understanding of the late twentieth-century world. This is particularly true in the case of economic relationships. When international trade conflicts arise, it is comforting for both parties to attribute disagreements to supposed national differences, or, where Japan is concerned, to 'national characteristics' that are supposedly unique to Japan. In this sense, one might say that the Victorian perceptions of Japan and the Japanese have not entirely lost their influences.

This work is based on my Oxford modern history thesis, which I completed in 1982. I would like to acknowledge the kind help of my supervisors, the late Professor Richard Storry and Dr Ann Waswo. My thanks are also due to Dr Theodore Zeldin and Dr James McMullen of St Antony's College, Oxford, Emeritus Professor Yoshida Mitsukuni of Kyoto University and Dr Kumakura Isao of Tsukuba University. Their encouragement enabled me to complete my thesis.

My endnotes indicate all too briefly how much I am indebted to the work of other scholars. Furthermore, I owe much to Dr Bonnie McMullen, Mrs Dorothie Storry, and Col. and Mrs Hugh Toye for their stylistic advice on drafts of my thesis. I am also grateful to the British Council for awarding me a scholarship to enable me to study in Oxford during the academic year 1976–77.

I received help from so many libraries and archives that I cannot hope to acknowledge them all here. However, I should like to mention particularly the help given to me by the staff of the following institutions: the Bodleian Library; the National Registers of Archives in London and Edinburgh; the National Library of Scotland; the British Library; the Public Record Office; the Gloucestershire County Record Office; Kyoto University Library; the National Diet Library, Tokyo; and the Archives of the Japanese Foreign Ministry. At the same time, I would like to express my thanks to Dr J. A. Edwards, Keeper of Archives and Manuscripts at Reading University Library; Dr Thomas Rae, Keeper of the Department of Manuscripts of the National Library of Scotland; Mrs Virginia Murray of the John Murray Archives; Mr Gordon Phillips, Archivist of *The Times*, and his successor Mrs Ann Piggott; Miss Rosamund Campbell, Librarian of St Antony's College, Oxford; and Ms Itô Hisako, Assistant Archivist of Yokohama Archives of History.

Dr Zeldin and Professor Ian Nish of the London School of Economics and Political Science provided most useful criticisms to my completed thesis. Dr Zeldin and Professor Arthur Stockwin of St Antony's College, Oxford, took the initiative in suggesting publication of my work in the St Antony's/Macmillan Series. In Japan, Professor Haga Tôru of Tokyo University also took a deep interest in the publication of my research.

Converting a thesis into a book is always a difficult task. In this process, I owe much to my friends, Dr Gordon Daniels of Sheffield University and Dr and Mrs Peter Kornicki of Cambridge University, without whose assistance my work would not have reached its present form.

Many of my friends and colleagues in Britain, Japan and France have given me help in various ways. I am no less grateful because I cannot list them all; but I should particularly like to mention the following individuals and groups; Mr Louis Allen, Dr Carmen Blacker, Professor George Elison, Ms Jill Haas, Mr Hagihara Nobutoshi, Emeritus Professor Hayashiya Tatsusaburô, Ms Sue Henny, Emeritus Professor Kawano Kenji, Dr Jean-Pierre Lehmann, Emeritus Professor Ôta Takeo, Mr Keith Povey, Dr and Mrs Brian Powell, Ms Nina Raj, Emeritus Professor Ueyama Shumpei, Professor Umesao Tadao, Dr Richard Ware; members of St Antony's College, Oxford; also members of Emeritus Professor Sakata Yoshio's seminar in Kyoto, and my colleagues at the Research Institute for Humanistic Studies, Kyoto University.

The following institutions and corporations have kindly given me formal permission to reproduce quotations from documents either in their custody or whose copyright they own: the British Library (Macmillan Archive); the Archives of the Japanese Foreign Ministry (Marshall File); John Murray; the Trustees of the National Library of Scotland and Messrs William Blackwood & Sons (Blackwood Papers); the Controller of Her Majesty's Stationary Office and the Public Record Office (Crown-copyright Foreign Office Papers); Reading University Library and the Longman Group Limited (Longman Archives); the Gloucestershire County Record Office (Redesdale Papers). Grateful thanks are extended also to the Royal General Theatrical Fund Association, the owner of the subsisting copyright in Sir William S. Gilbert's unpublished writings, and the association's lawyer Mr C.G. Prestige of Lawrence Graham, Lincoln's Inn, for having given me permission to include in this book one of Sir William's letters in the above mentioned Redesdale Papers.

Finally, I would particularly like to express my gratitude both to the Editorial Board of this series, including the Warden, Dr Raymond Carr, Mr Archie Brown and Mrs Rosemary Thorp, of St Antony's College, and Mr T.M. Farmiloe of the Macmillan Press, and to the Suntory Foundation, for their harmonious joint endeavours.

Shugakuin, Kyoto   TOSHIO YOKOYAMA

Introduction

More than a century has passed since 14 March 1885. On that night, the Savoy Theatre almost shook to its foundations: Gilbert and Sullivan stood and bowed before the curtain and the applause seemed neverending. The première of *The Mikado* was over amidst great excitement. This new work was to establish an unprecedented record in the history of operetta of 672 successive performances. It was also to win enormous popularity not only in the British Empire, but in America, Holland, Germany and Scandinavia. It remains the most popular English operetta of all time.

Why such success? Admirers of the Savoy Operas tend to attribute this phenomenon simply to the 'genius' of the author Gilbert, or to the music of the composer Sullivan. But why this quasi-Japanese piece in particular? Perhaps because there was at the time a cult of Japan in London, which had been stirred by an exhibition in Knightsbridge entitled 'The Japanese Village'. But why such long-lasting popularity, particularly among the British? It is true that the operetta contained many satirical points expressed in metaphors drawn from Japan, which reminded the audience of their own world. Gilbert is said to have spent only six months writing this operetta, but to make it as 'authentically Japanese' as possible, he was assisted during rehearsals by some of the Japanese who had been employed in the Knightsbridge exhibition. However, judging from the substantial variety of British ideas and images of Japan which were so effectively used in *The Mikado*, one wonders whether Gilbert himself intensively studied much contemporary and earlier literature on Japan, or if he was assisted by some knowledgeable British individual perhaps?

Most of the Japanese officials and businessmen who were staying in London at that time resented *The Mikado*, feeling that their sovereign was being ridiculed every evening in a performance based on fantasy. Among them, however, was a journalist who expressed quite a different opinion. A former official of Japan's *ancien régime*, Fukuchi Gen'ichirô (1841–1906), who had ample experience of Europe, asserted that the operetta was not altogether fantastic but showed a good understanding of traditional samurai society.[1] Whether Fukuchi was right or not will not be discussed here, but he might have found some supporters among Europeans. Here is a letter Gilbert sent to a certain gentleman three days after the première:

It would have given us sincere pleasure to dine with you on Wednesday but unhappily we have a dinner party at home on that day.
I must thank you again for your invaluable help. I have received two letters from Europeans recently resident in Japan (both strangers to me) complimenting us on the fidelity with which the local characteristics are reproduced.

Very truly yours,
W.S. Gilbert[2]

The favourable comments on 'the local characteristics' made by recent residents of Japan could well have implied something deeper than the Japanese styles of bowing and using fans which the 'Villagers' of Knightsbridge had taught the actors and actresses. Thus Gilbert could have been thanking the gentleman for his special help. If the recipient of this letter of gratitude had provided Gilbert with important concepts about traditional Japan, and given him selected articles and books on things Japanese, every detail of the plot of *The Mikado* seems to gain fresh significance. This formative influence may also give us an insight into the secret of the lasting popularity of the operetta. The identity of the man who gave Gilbert this 'invaluable help' will be revealed at the end of this book, once some of his earlier writings on Japan have been introduced.

Victorian writers and the reading public had first encountered Japan thirty years before the appearance of Gilbert and Sullivan's *The Mikado* in London. To them it was a country on the easternmost boundary of the world, which had been closed to Englishmen for more than two centuries. This book is a short history of the image of Japan which resulted from that encounter. By examining what was written about Japan at the time and noting the continuities and subtle changes in the views and images conveyed, one comes to understand not only the nature of Anglo-Japanese relations in the latter half of the nineteenth century, but also the minds of Victorian writers. The latter is the chief concern of this book, which seeks to trace these writers' changing consciousness towards the outside world and of themselves as members of the most powerful empire in the world.

The main focus of our attention will be monthly and quarterly reviews and magazines of national circulation and influence. In contrast to reporting in *The Times,* which stressed the latest news from Japan, articles in these periodicals tended to offer background information and interpretation, and in contrast to scholarly books on Japan written by a small number of specialists, these articles were aimed at a

Introduction

more general public. As will be shown, both the authors of these articles and their editors believed that concessions had to be made to their readers, who were assumed to be curious but ignorant about Japan. Authors consciously strove to make Japan comprehensible, and at the same time to increase their readership and sales. Therefore, a study of ideas and images of Japan which appeared in their articles, a genre which has been little analysed,[3] will help to reveal the approximate perception of Japan which prevailed among literate Victorians.

The period to be considered is from 1850 to 1880, three decades of profound social and intellectual change in both Britain and Japan. At the beginning of the period, Britain, detached from the revolutionary Continent, boasted of its civilising mission, and many people naïvely extolled the benefits which vigorous manufacture, free trade, individualism and self-help would bring to other nations. At the same time, increasing numbers of newly literate people as well as the middle class became obsessed by morality, which proved to be one of the stabilising forces of society and the backbone of an immense sense of national superiority. However, after the rise of Bismarck's Germany in the early 1870s and the Depression from 1874, the ideal of *laissez faire* and open-mindedness towards the outside world began to fade in Britain. At the same time, the rise of the common people during the 1860s and the early 1870s was inevitably accompanied by increasing state responsibility for social welfare and social regulation. This was implied in such laws as the Reform Bill of 1867, the Education Act of 1870, and the Trade Union Act of 1871. The shift in mood was rapid, as W.W. Rostow has observed:

> ... the mid-century hopes of permanent peace and of universal free trade with the countries of the Empire dropping like ripe fruit from the tree, hardened into a more exclusive conception of Empire and a defensive British nationalism vis-à-vis Germany.[4]

Japan also saw immense social changes in this period. In 1854, the long seclusion policy of the Tokugawa Shogunate came to an end after direct pressure from Commodore Perry's American squadron. At the turn of the 1850s, trade with the West began, which caused serious instability in the domestic economy. During the early 1860s, a strong nationalist movement among the samurai class was expressed in violent attacks on foreigners. However, the bombardment of Kagoshima by Britain in 1863 and of Shimonoseki the following year by a fleet of British, French, American and Dutch warships drastically changed the outlook of many samurai. They recognised the power of the West and saw the urgent necessity of mastering its military technology. The traditional fear of national dishonour which was widely shared among Japan's ruling elites gave impetus to an anti-Shogunate movement as the inability of the Tokugawa to govern and protect the country became clear. In addition, from the late eighteenth century an increasing desire for self-importance among well-to-do commoners had promoted a new notion of their country: *Shinkoku* – the divine land. Support for the emperor as the nation's legitimate ruler grew rapidly,[5] and during the years 1868 and 1869 the restoration of imperial rule was confirmed by a short civil war. The main objective of the new Meiji government was to strengthen the economic and military power of the country to make it competitive with the Western powers. Feudal domains were abolished in 1871 and various egalitarian measures were adopted in education, the economy and military organisation so as to create a strong sense of national unity.

From the beginning of the 1850s, Japan's value as a potential market for Britain was never regarded highly by the British authorities, as China dominated their conception of the Far East.[6] Yet British intellectuals continued to show an interest in Japan throughout this period, though their pursuit of accurate information was not always consistent. On the other hand, the new Japanese government regarded Britain as the apex of Western civilisation and employed many British advisers to assist in its programme of modernisation. The number of Japanese intellectuals who admired Britain increased throughout the period, and in the 1870s many of them were studying such contemporary British works as John Stuart Mill's *On Liberty* and Samuel Smiles' *Self Help* in an effort to fathom the secrets of the British Empire's success. The British were thus the objects of increasingly respectful attitudes on the part of the Japanese. Of course, there were exceptions, not only fanatical patriots but the journalist Murata Fumio (1833–91), and the politician Nakai Ôshû (1838–94), who knew Britain well but were not altogether enthusiastic about it.[7] However, there was a general tendency in Japan to idealise Great Britain. This was the broad background in Britain and Japan against which Victorian writers published their many articles and reviews.

This study does not pretend to cover all the hundreds of magazines and reviews which were published during the period under consideration. On the contrary, it is based on a limited survey of about twenty national periodicals which showed comparatively strong interest in Japan at one time or another, and which seem to have established the standard patterns for writing about Japan in such fields as international relations, politics, economics, religion, society and arts and crafts.[8]

Books, newspapers and other sources of information about Japan, such as international exhibitions, the records of Japanese visitors to Britain and Japanese goods imported into Europe, have been consulted when they seem to have had some influence on ideas about Japan expressed in the articles in these periodicals.

In my analysis, emphasis has been laid on the language which the authors of articles employed when introducing Japan to their readers, since it was their key means of putting raw information in a more acceptable form for the British public. Where possible, the role of editors in publishing articles on Japan has also been traced. For editors were often responsible for producing certain images of Japan in their publications. In particular, the archive of the Edinburgh publishers, William Blackwood & Sons, in the National Library of Scotland, has been extensively used because of the significance to this study of *Blackwood's Edinburgh Magazine*, and of the rich information about the magazine's editorship which the archive contains. In fact, this magazine, which ended its life of more than a century and a half in December 1980,[9] was one of the most prominent magazines of the British Empire. Besides being an organ for the conservative – not necessarily highly educated – landed gentry of the British establishment,[10] the magazine proved to be a notable forum for many Scottish and English officials and merchants who were active on the frontiers of empire. In it they expressed, both consciously and unconsciously, their ideas of self-identity on the basis of their personal experiences abroad.

Whenever feasible, this study will attempt to explain the Japanese customs and behaviour which British visitors to the country observed and which they often misinterpreted. As will be demonstrated, the gap between Japanese reality and British perception was often large, and provides an important clue to understanding the role of subjectivity – of the observer's own expectations and values – in generating images of others.

In this book, a considerable amount of space will be devoted to quotations which allow Victorian writers to speak for themselves. This is probably the most effective way of presenting a true picture of the almost forgotten world of magazine and review articles on nineteenth-century Japan.

Note. In this book, Japanese personal names are written in the usual Japanese order with the family name first. Circumflex accents are added to mark the long vowels in Japanese words, except on the well-known place names Kyoto, Tokyo, Osaka and Kobe, and on these nouns: Shogun, daimyo and Shinto, as they appear in this form in English dictionaries.

Pl. 1 Japanese Buddhist Temple. Reproduced from MacFarlane's *Japan* (London, 1852), p. 203. Note pigtails and palm trees. These were also exotic to most Japanese. See pp.16, 180n 113.

Pl. 2 Japanese Lady Painting. Reproduced from *ibid*., p. 329. Note her features unusual for a Japanese of the time.   See pp. 16, 180n, 113.

Pl. 3 Japanese Villages near Nagasaki. Reproduced from *The Illustrated London News* (27 January 1855). A sketch by a correspondent of *The I.L.N.* who accompanied Admiral Stirling's expedition to Japan in 1854.   See pp. 16, 130n, 113.

Pl. 4 Japanese Tea-Gardens. Reproduced from Oliphant's *Narrative of Earl of Elgin's Mission to China and Japan* (Edinburgh & London, 1859), vol. 11, facing p. 167. 'A tasteful tea-garden where visitors are attended by nymphs': a popular image of Japan in the early 1860s.   See pp. 23, 43, 48, 154.

Pl. 5 Japanese Children's Gymnastics (from a Japanese drawing). Reproduced from *ibid*., vol. ii, p. 217. 'The happy & chubby Japanese children': another popular image of the time.   See pp. 46, 49, 152, 155.

Pl. 6 Japanese Astronomers and Mount Fuji, or Fujiyama (from a Japanese drawing). Reproduced from *ibid*., vol. ii, p. 218. 'The amiable people in the beautiful country': another popular image of the time. See pp. 25–6, 47–8, 65, 154–5.

Pl. 7 Japanese Ambassadors at the London International Exhibition. Reproduced from *The Illustrated London News* (24 May 1862). At the Exhibition, 'their Excellencies' were intrigued by the movements of a European music conductor, and amused themselves, imitating him. (MacDonald's *Cornhill* article of May 1863). See p. 76.

Pl. 8 The Japanese Court in the London International Exhibition. Reproduced from *ibid*. (20 September 1862). About the Japanese Court was 'a quaint picturesqueness', wrote a reporter of *The I.L.N.* See p. 75.

Pl. 9 Japanese Gnomes' picnic (from a Japanese drawing). Reproduced from Alcock's *The Capital of the Tycoon* (London, 1863), vol. ii, p. 300.

Pl. 10 Japanese Court Dress (from a Japanese drawing). Reproduced from *ibid.*, vol. i, p. 386.

Pl. 11 Ceremonial Trousers for Samurai (from a Japanese drawing). Reproduced from *ibid.*, vol. ii, p. 290.

Plates 9, 10, 11 Alcock selected these Japanese drawings to illustrate 'the grotesqueness of Japan'. See pp. 82, 157.

Pl. 12 Sumō Wrestling in the Great Amphitheatre of Edo (from a Japanese drawing). Reproduced from J.M.W. Silver's *Sketches of Japanese Manners and Customs* (London, 1867), facing p. 30.
Silver wrote: 'From constant practice they attain a muscular development that would eclipse that of our prize-ring champions; but their paunchy figures and sluggish movements render any further comparison impossible.'   See pp. 32, 162.

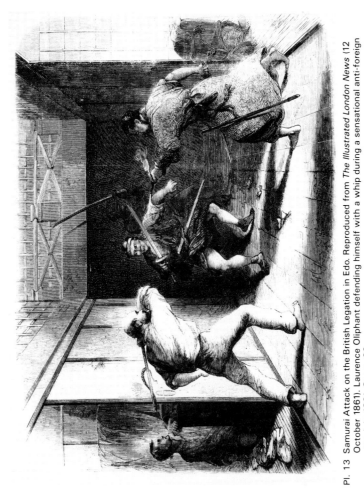

Pl. 13 Samurai Attack on the British Legation in Edo. Reproduced from *The Illustrated London News* (12 October 1861). Laurence Oliphant defending himself with a whip during a sensational anti-foreign attack in 1861. See p. 66.

1 'This Singular Country'

On a bright spring day in 1851 when Japan was still secluded from the outer world except for a small number of Dutch and Chinese merchants, an English ship approached the harbour of Nagasaki unnoticed. The picturesque bay was surrounded by green hills, and among the cedars white houses reflected the bright sun. Seeing the Japanese coast, those on board cried out: 'Surely we shall like Japan.'

The name of the vessel was the *Phantom Ship*, but it was only an imaginary ship invented by the popular writer, Henry Morley (1822–94). Since 1850, Morley had been working on Charles Dickens' literary weekly *Household Words*, a two-penny family journal of instruction and entertainment,[1] for a middle-class audience. The story of the ship's visit to Japan appeared in this periodical as a part of a series on lesser known countries of the world.[2]

Through the eyes of visitors clad in 'phantom cloaks', Morley introduced his readers to the peaceful world of a well-to-do Nagasaki gentleman and his wife, who lived surrounded by 'the strangeness of all things'.[3] Although at that time no one in London could predict what would happen in relations between the West and Japan, Morley was vaguely expecting a happy encounter with this 'acute race'.[4] He was certainly aware that internal peace in Japan was kept by 'strong mutual restrictions' among the inhabitants, which he called a 'tyranny of custom'. Yet he could not help expressing a liking for the Japanese:

> They have original and thinking minds; with a dash of Asiatic fierceness, they are generous, joyous, sympathetic.[5]

The expectation of a joyful meeting with Japan grew stronger among British writers during the 1850s, and the cry on board the *Phantom Ship* proved a general omen for their later attitudes towards Japan. Most of them were willing to be pleased by Japan. Had they become so tired of Britain's difficult relations with China since the turn of the 1830s that they looked for a more pleasurable meeting with another country in the Far East? Or had it been a long-cherished dream of Europeans, from the time of Jonathan Swift – or even further back, from the times of Christopher Columbus or Marco Polo – to find an interesting people there? However, one must not overlook the fact that their optimistic mood was connected with their ideas about the quaintness of things Japanese.

Japanese manners and customs, such as the samurai's *hara-kiri* and the married lady's blackening of her teeth, which Morley had mentioned in passing, were to attract much attention from British writers during the 1850s. The idea that Japan was a 'strange and singular country' – which implied uniqueness or bizarre qualities – was to persist in British magazine and review articles not only in the 1850s, but throughout most of the following thirty years. This, of course, does not mean that these writers relied on the same unchanged information about Japan during that period. On the contrary, Japan underwent rapid social changes and British knowledge and understanding of Japanese history and culture also developed. But the general view of Japan not only survived but even reinforced itself on many occasions. Why did this persistence of the image occur? To what extent was this phenomenon the result of random historical factors? Or is it possible to conclude that this image world was naturally self-perpetuating and broadly independent of reality?

In the earlier half of the 1850s, the basic mode of describing Japan seems to have already been established, being helped by various historical factors. Although fresh information about Japan was yet to reach Britain, a newly aroused public curiosity – following news of the future American expedition (1853) – was so strong that it had to be satisfied at all costs.

It was in the early spring of 1852 that popular British interest in Japan entered its first excited stage as information spread in Europe of the United States' plan for a powerful expedition to Japan. In March, *The Times* published the news.[6] In April, May and June, the *China Mail* of Hong Kong,[7] and in Britain, magazines such as *Bentley's Miscellany*, *Lawson's Merchant's Magazine* and the *New Monthly Magazine and Humorist* began discussing possible American attitudes towards Japan. It was not only secular circles in Britain that showed interest in the news, there was some from religious groups also. In the same year, Charles Russell (1812–80), Professor of Ecclesiastical History at St Patrick's College, Maynooth, and one of the most prolific Catholic authors of the time, contributed an article on Japan to the Catholic monthly *Dublin Review*, the editorship of which Russell shared with Nicholas Wiseman, former Rector of the English College in Rome.[8] Russell wrote that the 'limits of the Terra Incognita' of the old geographers were 'narrowing fast'.[9] His view was strengthened by the account of Évariste Régis Huc, the French Catholic Missionary, of his journey into Tibet.[10] But in Russell's eyes the news about Japan seemed more exciting to the public than that of Tibet:

> The expedition to Japan recently fitted out by the government of the United States, and the circumstances which have led to it, have opened a new page in the history of the Eastern World; and in the interest which this prospect of a glimpse into Japan has excited, the public have almost begun to forget the kindred wonders of Chinese Tartary and Tibet.[11]

Several books on Japan were published in Britain in 1852 and 1853, but they were only reprints, abridgements or compilations of former publications. Among these new editions, Engelbert Kaempfer's *History of Japan* (originally published in London in 1727 in John Gasper Scheuchzer's translation from the author's German manuscripts) became particularly popular. For example, an abridged and edited edition was published in *Blackwood's Universal Library of Standard Authors* in 1852, as well as in Nathaniel Cooke's *Universal Library of Standard Authors* in 1853. About the same time Richard Griffin also published an anthology entitled *Popular Voyages and Travels* which contained Kaempfer's 'Account of Japan'.

Besides Kaempfer, the early-nineteenth-century work of a Russian naval officer, Captain Wasily Mikhailowich Golownin, also attracted much attention. In 1818, Golownin had published in London *Narrative of My Captivity in Japan during the Years 1811, 1812 and 1813*, and the next year, *Recollections of Japan*, to which his editor had added much supplementary information from Kaempfer and other old travellers' accounts of the country. The publisher of these books, Henry Colburn, was shrewd enough to perceive the new curiosity about Japan and reissued the two works in 1852, combining them under the new title, *Japan and the Japanese: Comprising the Narrative of a Captivity in Japan, and an Account of British Commercial Intercourse with that Country. Manners and Customs of the Japanese* – Mrs William Busk's anonymous compilation of works by Philipp Franz von Siebold and by other people of the Dutch factory at Nagasaki, which had been published in a ten-part serial in the *Asiatic Journal and Monthly Register for Britain and Foreign India, China, and Australasia* in 1839 and 1840,[12] and reprinted in a volume by John Murray in 1841 – appeared in a new edition by Murray in 1852.

Before the arrival of fresh information from Japan, magazine and review articles were naturally obliged to be dependent on these old sources. For example, Alexander Knox (1818–91), 'a master of terse argument' and one of the leader writers of *The Times* during the early years of John Delane's editorship,[13] published an article on Japan in the *Edinburgh Review* in October 1852.[14] This quarterly, then edited by William Empson, 'professor in general polity and laws of England' at East India College, Haileybury, had been and was the most influential Whig periodical from the beginning of the nineteenth century.[15] Knox's major sources ranged from the seventeenth century to the nineteenth century: the French edition of Kaempfer's *History of Japan*,[16] Golownin's *Narrative*, von Siebold's *Nippon*,[17] Stamford Raffles' *History of Java*,[18] Pierre François Xavier de Charlevoix's *Histoire et description générale du Japon*[19] and *Astley's Collection of Voyages and Travels*,[20] which contained the records of the early British navigators to Japan: William Adams, Richard Cocks and John Saris. As regards Charles Russell's article mentioned above, it was based on Golownin's *Japan and the Japanese* as well as the popular author Charles MacFarlane's *Japan: An Account, Geographical and Historical*[21] which was also one of 'the first fruits of the newly aroused interest' in Japan.[22] This book was a compilation of a 'well-stored, choice library' about Japan collected by a military officer James Drummond, who had been in Nagasaki when a boy. MacFarlane had had access to this library for twenty years.[23] In the case of Henry Morley's article in *Household Words,* from its contents it is obvious that he had used at least Mrs Busk's *Manners and Customs of the Japanese*, works by Golownin, and Kaempfer's *History.*

This style of writing articles about Japan based on a mixture of old sources, including even Jesuits' reports from the sixteenth century, was seldom questioned. On the contrary, there was a rather firm conviction that Japan had not changed for centuries and that writers could therefore use almost any old account to describe contemporary Japan. For example, the editor of Kaempfer's account of Japan in Cooke's *Universal Library* wrote in his preface to the account:

> Having thus been cut off from almost all intercourse with foreign nations for such a long period, it is not to be expected that, considering that circumstance and the stationary character of eastern civilisation, the manners, habits, customs, etc., of the Japanese should have materially altered during that time.[24]

It thus did not matter what piece of information, however old, was chosen for articles about Japan so long as it satisfied the curiosity of the reading public. This tendency was strong enough to last even after the mid-1850s, when news of the success of the American expedition began to appear in British popular magazines.[25]

So what images of Japan were presented in British magazines and reviews in the early 1850s? As the two lengthy articles by Alexander Knox and Charles Russell seem to have been intended as a standard introduction of Japan to their readers, let us focus our attention on these. Knox first expressed his general concept of Japan in these words: 'Japan remains to us a vague and shadowy idea'.[26] The Japanese people, in Knox's mind, had 'remained a mystery for two centuries'.[27] He then started attaching the labels 'strange' and 'singular' to various pieces of information about the country:

> Strange and singular as every thing we have heard about Japan undoubtedly is, nothing is so strange or so singular as the determination of the inhabitants to resist all intercourse with their fellow-creatures, except it be the fact that they have been able to act upon the resolution with effect during upwards of two centuries.[28]

'This singular people', 'the Forbidden Land', and 'a sealed book' were the words for Japan and the Japanese which Knox conspicuously used in his writing. Russell also emphasised 'the mystery and uncertainty' which lingered about his information concerning certain aspects of Japan,[29] and used the general label 'extraordinary' for the country and the people.[30]

In Kaempfer's *History of Japan,* on which the two writers directly or indirectly depended, words such as 'singular' or 'extraordinary' had rarely been used. Certainly, Charles Peter Thunberg, the naturalist who had become a physician at the Dutch factory of Nagasaki in 1775, had once called Japan 'a singular country' in a rather sweeping way.[31] Also, one can find the words 'extraordinary' and 'singular' in some parts of Golownin's *Recollections* and of Mrs Busk's *Manners and Customs.*[32] However, the use of those adjectives in books on Japan published before the mid-nineteenth century was less conspicuous and more often confined to certain particular aspects of Japan than was the case in the writings of Knox and Russell. In fact, earlier writers did not indulge in the notion of the singularity of Japan to the extent Knox and Russell did. It seems that during the early 1850s there emerged a strong tendency among British contributors to magazines and reviews not only to emphasise the uncertainty of their knowledge about Japan but also to attach to the country the general labels, 'singular' or 'extraordinary', and to emphasise the difficulty in understanding Japan and the Japanese.

In spite of their emphasis on the singularity of Japan, however, these writers seemed confident that they knew the country fairly well. It was a paradox. Of course, familiarity with a country can coexist with the view that the country is singular or mysterious, but usually an increase in knowledge about others tends to help one understand them and to modify at least one's general mystification. Look at Russell's confidence:

> Yet it is really surprising, considering the strict and jealous isolation so long maintained by the Japanese authorities, how abundant and how trustworthy are the materials for a history of this extraordinary people.[33]

This point had also been clear in one of the sources for Russell's writing, MacFarlane's *Japan*. MacFarlane mentioned the existence of many books on Japan in 'Latin, Portuguese, Spanish, Italian, French, Dutch, German and English', and maintained:

> Taking all these works as a fund of information, we may safely be said to know more of the Japanese than we knew of the Turks a hundred years ago.[34]

Knox was rather more careful in judging the validity of the information which each book on Japan contained:

> When we come to ask ourselves what we really do know of Japan, we find that we know both more and less than we had supposed until we sat down to express our information in a precise form.[35]

He, too, insisted, however, that there was a good stock of knowledge about Japan which had been kept in Britain.

Among the variety of topics of Japan they covered in their articles, there were three major fields to which they drew attention: first, the people and their manners and customs; second, governmental institutions; third, religious customs. With regard to the character of the Japanese people, Russell wrote:

> They are still gentle, courteous, obliging, and respectful in their intercourse with one another, and even with foreigners, in so far as intercourse with them is permitted.[36]

He also mentioned the rarity of quarrelling in public, children's respect for and obedience to their parents, and parents' affection for their children.[37] There are two characteristic points to note in his generalisation: one is the stress on the unchanging nature of the Japanese, and the other is the emphasis on their amiability.

Russell wrote confidently, on the basis of sources which were out of date, that the Japanese 'still' possessed these characteristics. Of course, one cannot deny that there was a general belief in Britain in 'the stationary character of the eastern civilisation', as the editor of Kaempfer's account in Cooke's *Universal Library* expressed it. As regards China, adjectives such as 'old' and 'ancient' were frequently used in order to emphasise its unchanging nature. For example, Whitwell Elwin, priest and the then editor of the powerful Tory periodicial, the *Quarterly Review,* discussed recent travel accounts of China and expressed this idea about the Chinese:

> . . . the most ancient and unchangeable nation in the world, they are themselves the records of the past.[38]

Knox was impressed that Japan should have enjoyed peace for more than two centuries under its government's uncompromising policy of secluding the country from the outside world. He wanted to understand this fact, which contrasted greatly with the recent history of Europe. A simple way was to resort to the stereotyped idea of the stationary East. He found that Thunberg's writings had shown 'a marvellous correspondence' with Kaempfer's.[39] This point seems to have been sufficient for Knox to conclude:

> Every thing . . . is so immutable in this empire that things remain at the present moment in Japan pretty much as they were in Kaempfer's time.[40]

In the case of Russell, he was chiefly interested in the future reintroduction of Christianity to Japan.[41] His language may therefore have been coloured by his hope that the Japanese had still maintained the good nature which St Francis Xavier had encountered in the past:

> The national character of the Japanese does not seem to have deteriorated since the days of St. Francis Xavier and his companions, by whom it was depicted in the most amiable colours.[42]

The second point, the emphasis on the amiability of the Japanese, was particularly conspicuous in Russell's article. The idea about the chastity of Japanese women played a decisive role in promoting his image of an amiable people. Russell assured his readers:

> Instances of violation of conjugal chastity on the part of the females, are said to be almost absolutely unknown.[43]

Russell could have modified his statement by using the somewhat contradictory report of Father de Angelis, the seventeenth-century Jesuit missionary to Japan, whom Golownin's editor had quoted in a footnote attached to the Russian captain's memoirs.[44] But Russell seems to have been determined to praise Japanese women. MacFarlane's book was probably responsible for Russell's attitude. MacFarlane was, as he himself admitted, under the strong influence of his 'accomplished old friend', the late James Drummond, who used to say, 'The Japanese are the most fascinating, elegant ladies that I ever saw in any country in the world'.[45] MacFarlane tried to introduce his readers to the cultivated and lively characteristics of Japanese ladies.[46] When he quoted from Mrs Busk's account of Japanese women's 'fair station in society' and the 'fidelity of the wife' and the 'purity of the maiden',[47] he completely omitted what Mrs Busk had added about the Japanese wife's 'complete dependence' on her husband, sons and other relatives. Mrs Busk had also maintained subsequently that the Japanese wife had been treated 'rather as a toy for her husband's recreation, than as the rational, confidential partner of his life'.[48] In Russell's readers' eyes, Japanese women were bound to appear very independent and responsible by themselves.

Knox was also in a mood to be pleased by Japanese women. He confessed that the Japanese beauty described in von Siebold's *Nippon* was 'a far more comely personage in European eyes than any Mongolian belle'.[49] He also mentioned that there was 'considerable delicacy and dignity' about the portrait of the man engraved on the same page.[50] Knox, admitting that the Japanese belonged to the Asiatics, asserted 'But amidst Asiatics the Japanese stand supreme'.[51] He felt it necessary to mention their chivalry, obedience to authorities, conjugal faith, gentleness and courtesy, and thirst for knowledge.[52]

However, both Russell and Knox's favourable views of the Japanese character were counterbalanced by some negative aspects. Knox was appalled that the Japanese belles plucked out their eyebrows upon marriage.[53] Russell was shocked by the widely institutionalised practice of prostitution:

> The great national vice of Japan is incontinence. Prostitution is protected by the law, and is carried on upon a scale unexampled in any other country. Some of the brothels, contained as many as six hundred inmates.[54]

Knox was much puzzled by the information that the Japanese girls who had served in these brothels for some time could regain their liberty and marry. Perhaps obtaining this information from Thunberg or

Golownin,[55] he introduced it to his readers in the following manner:

> ... they will select a wife from a place which might have astonished a boon companion of the Regent Orleans, but they judge a violation of conjugal faith as severely as a Scotch Puritan.[56]

If Knox had read Mrs Busk's *Manners and Customs of the Japanese*, as he admitted he had done,[57] he could have emphasised that *mésalliance* in Japan was 'held to be utterly disgraceful'.[58] But Knox, as well as Russell, was eager to point out the coexistence among the Japanese of what he thought amiable characteristics and what he thought vices of an extreme kind. Knox enumerated some examples:

> They are warlike and yet averse to conquest . . . They are most cruel in their punishments, but most reluctant to inflict pain; they are gentle and courteous in their social intercourse, but more tenacious of a vindictive purpose than a Corsican mountaineer.[59]

Emphasis on these radical contradictions as well as on the immutability of the Japanese character must have been somewhat perplexing to Knox's and Russell's readers. It is, therefore, possible that both writers found it convenient to attach to Japan the general label of 'singular' or 'mysterious' in order to avoid any further inquiry.

With regard to governmental institutions in Japan, the nature of sovereignty was a matter in which these writers took particular interest. According to Russell, the Mikado was 'one of the most curious institutions of the country'.[60] Russell, following MacFarlane, committed himself to reproducing Kaempfer's theory of double sovereignty in Japan: with the Emperor and the Shogun representing the spiritual and the temporal, or the ecclesiastical and the secular. Russell quoted at length from what MacFarlane had quoted from Kaempfer's description of the features of the Japanese 'Popes by birth'.[61] They were, for instance, that 'his victuals must always be served in new dishes', and that these dishes must be destroyed after each use because it was believed that if any layman should use them they would swell and inflame his mouth and throat. Russell continued summarising Kaempfer's account of the Mikado:

> In ancient times, he was obliged to sit on the throne for some hours every morning . . . like a statue, without stirring either hands or feet, head or eyes, nor indeed any part of his body, because, by this means, it was thought that he could preserve peace and tranquillity in his empire.[62]

Still, following Kaempfer, he added to this the fact that this burdensome duty of the Mikado had been changed since then and 'the crown, alone', was 'at present placed on the throne for several hours every morning'.[63] These were the notions about the imperial person whose 'holiness' Russell could not but label 'peculiar and mysterious'.[64] Although Russell followed Kaempfer's theory of the two-emperor system of Japan, he somehow avoided explaining the role of the 'Temporal Emperor'.

Knox, on the other hand, took pains to denounce the theory of two emperors as a 'popular error'. Mainly following Mrs Busk's *Manners and Customs*,[65] Knox pointed out that real authority had departed even from the Shogun, the so-called Secular Emperor, and that it was then exercised by the President of the Council of State. He explained from a historical perspective how the power of the Mikado had become 'but as the shadow of a shadow' by the Tokugawa Shogun's usurpation of state power, and how the Shogun himself had become 'a mere cypher'[66] under the 'watchful supervision of the Council of State at Jedo [Edo]'.[67]

Knox described the Shogun as Follows:

> He is the victim of a code of ceremonies somewhat less tiresome than those which affect his brother monarch of Meaco [Kyoto]. Like him, he must admit to his lot, and remain the butt and object of never ceasing compliments and prostrations to his life's end.[68]

Up to this point, Knox's explanation was more or less detached and objective. But Knox seems to have felt that he must add 'one extraordinary constitutional custom in Japan', that is, the right of the Shogun to disapprove any resolution of the Council of State. Knox, following Mrs Busk, explained the fatal consequence of the arbitration between the Shogun and the Council:

> If they [the three princes of the Shogun's blood] arbitrate in favour of the Council, the Monarch must abdicate in favour of his next heir; if in favour of the Ziogoon [Shogun], the President of the Council is bound upon the instant to rip up his abdomen and his councillors can do little better than follow his example.[69]

Unlike Mrs Busk's paragraphs concerning this matter, Knox could not help attaching the words 'strange' and 'singular' to this custom at the end of his explanation.[70] Knox could have avoided mentioning this custom, which, according to Mrs Busk, had been rarely practised.[71] But he thought that he could 'not pass over [the matter] without a cursory notice',[72] and he wrote about it without referring to the rarity of its practice.

The third topic, which also promoted the 'singular' or 'extraordinary' tag, was the religion of Japan. Knox, in this respect, seems to have based his accounts mostly on Kaempfer's *History of Japan*. Among the various religions of the country, Knox took interest in Shintoism as 'the state religion of Japan'.[73] He first referred to the Shintoists' 'obscure notion of immortality of the soul', and second, to their indifferent attitudes towards 'a Supreme Deity'.[74] In order to emphasise this latter aspect, Knox resorted to the expression 'a happy people', a familiar leitmotif in writings about the Japanese since the time of St Francis Xavier:

> Their happiness is too transcendent to be ruffled by the sound of mortal supplication.[75]

Knox, however, admitted that the Japanese addressed prayers to inferior deities, expecting some immediate help for their daily lives. He was intrigued by Kaempfer's information about the Shintoists' mode of worship: to behold themselves in front of a plain mirror. Knox could not refrain from inserting a facetious passage:

> There is something striking in the custom, although it might lead to abuse if introduced among devout ladies of fashion at the present day.[76]

Knox's attitude towards Japanese religious practice was to regard it as one further example of the contradictory features of the people:

> ... they are not religious in sentiment, but devout worshippers in practice.[77]

His somewhat light-hearted tone in dealing with the question of Japanese religion may have reflected the secular character of the *Edinburgh Review*, which put much emphasis on political economy, social reform, science and literature.[78] Although Knox mentioned the history of Buddhism, Confucianism and Christianity in Japan, he did not deal with them in detail. His emphasis on the importance of Shintoism among the variety of Japanese religions was obviously derived from Kaempfer, but his narrow focus on the Shintoists' use of mirrors and his remarks on the custom as 'striking' were certainly his own.

Russell's tone was more serious than that of Knox so far as religious topics were concerned, but from the beginning, Russell was obliged to admit the scarcity of information about Japanese religion, in contrast to commercial and scientific information.[79] He relied on Golownin, who had also confessed that the information which he had obtained about this topic had been 'very vague and imperfect'.[80] According to Golownin, there were four religions in Japan: the one whose adherents 'adore the ancient peculiar divinities called Kami', with 'the spiritual emperor' being its 'head and the high priest'; the one derived from the Brahmins which believed in 'the transmigration of souls' between men and animals; the doctrine of Confucius which was adhered to by 'the greater part of the Japanese men of learning and philosophers'; and 'the adoration of the heavenly bodies', which had 'given origin to a sect' which worshipped fire, considering it a divinity derived from the sun.[81]

Russell tried to supplement the 'defective and unsatisfactory'[82] part of Golownin's account with MacFarlane's, and finally summarised the general character of Japanese religion in a very sweeping way:

> . . . it is plain that the popular religion of the country is but an off-shoot of the one grand system, which . . . is found, variously modified by local or natural characteristics, throughout the entire of that vast region of the East, over which, at different periods, the civilization of which ancient India was the centre, has made itself known.[83]

Russell was deeply involved in editing the *Dublin Review*, which had manifested a strong commitment to the propagation of Catholicism, inviting even the Tractarians to join it.[84] Russell had served as an apostolic vicar in Ceylon in 1842. His own experiences in 'the East' thus enabled him to perceive the affinities between religious traditions in various Asian countries. Russell, however, gave to Japanese popular religion an additional 'strangeness' on top of its 'eastern' character:

> The popular religion of Japan contains all the essential features of the Buddhism of India, though overlaid by many strange, and in some respects, irreconcilable peculiarities.[85]

In sum, both Knox and Russell, when dealing with the three topics discussed above, showed great sensitivity to whatever they found in earlier writings about Japan that differed from familiar practices in the West. It is, therefore, undeniable that some of those earlier writings were partly responsible for creating in these two writers' minds the notion of 'singularity' or 'extraordinariness' for Japan. But undoubtedly it was these two writers themselves who were responsible for putting particular stress on these notions.

They were, however, not content with repeating such words as singular, strange and extraordinary. In their effort to explain Japan's 'singularity' to their readers, they were to use some effective devices. Their method was to discover various analogies from images which were familiar to British readers. For instance, Knox described this secluded country as a tempting 'forbidden fruit'.[86] Biblical metaphors as a means of explaining Japan were to flourish in magazine and review articles even after the opening of its ports to the West. Because images of the East in the minds of many Victorians had often been formed by illustrations of the Eastern world in children's editions of the Bible, it must have been natural for writers to use tales from the Bible in order to introduce readers to the country. At a time when 'Medieval Culture' was fashionable, it is not surprising that Knox also presented a variety of analogies with Europe in the Middle Ages. The idea of the 'chivalrous Japanese' led him to use the analogy of the romantic world of knight-errantry presented by the sixteenth-century Italian poet, Ludovico Ariosto.[87] He also used the simile of the Flemish burgher of the Middle Ages to explain the strength of public opinion in Japan.[88] Marriage in Japan was explained in the following way:

> We shall find the Japanese Romeo running to the house of his lady love with the bough of a particular shrub. If the young lady dislike the suitor, the branch is suffered to wither and die; if, on the contrary, she smile complacently on his passion, the Juliet of Niphon [sic] instantly blackens her teeth, withholding the crowning favour of plucking out her eye-brows until the wedding day.[89]

In order to write these lines, Knox faithfully followed Mrs Busk's account, which had not, however, contained any allusion to Shakespearian drama.

In contrast to Knox, Russell was interested in finding 'the strange opposition' which existed between Japanese customs and the 'analogous usages of Europe'. They were, for example, that black was 'the colour of joy – white, that of mourning', and that the Japanese were 'to go abroad in their meanest dress, and to reserve for wearing in their own homes the expensive robes of ceremony'.[90] Russell pointed out:

> Many of the discrepancies in the minor details of usage are very amusing.[91]

Although this was a point which several previous travellers to Japan had mentioned as early as the seventeenth century,[92] Russell's missionary spirit might have induced him to emphasise it; any pagan nation was thought to possess very different features from those of the Europeans. However, one should note also that Russell was able to communicate smoothly with his readers by means of these comparisons with Europe.

As for Japanese governmental institutions, Knox used a colourful language such as the metaphor of the 'Mayor at the Palace' in the Merovingian Dynasty to explain the Shogun's status, or the analogy of the 'Venetian Oligarchy' to show the characteristics of the Council of State in Japan. These are expressions which those writers such as Kaempfer,[93] Golownin, or Mrs Busk, rarely tried. Knox also presented a hypothetical story about the relationship between Napoleon Bonaparte – before his seizure of the imperial crown – and Louis XVIII, making the latter 'the Mikado of France, the idol of the Faubourg, the incarnation of legitimacy'.[94]

Regarding religious customs in Japan, it seems to have been impossible for Russell to refer to them in terms of European analogies or metaphors. He described the ' "Spiritual Emperor" of Japan' as a 'brother' of the Lama of Tibet.[95] Russell might have considered that only things within the 'one grand system'[96] of the East could be used as analogies to familiarise his readers with Japanese religion. On the other hand, Knox explained Shintoism as '. . . the doctrine professed by the Established Church', suggesting an analogy with the English system.[97] He also interpreted 'Kami', chief objects of the Shintoists' devotion, in terms of 'the Deified Heroes' and then went on to suggest a similarity between the mode of Shinto worship and that of Catholicism:

> They [the deified heroes] have been beatified in swarms which would try the imagination of a Greek of the days gone by, or of a devout Roman Catholic of the present time.[98]

Although a certain affinity between ancient Roman religious architecture and Japanese Shinto shrines was suggested in Kaempfer's work,[99] such a free comparison with European usage was Knox's own invention for his *Edinburgh Review* article.

In the course of finding and using European parallels for explaining things Japanese, some writers like Knox seem to have developed a feeling of vague affinity between Japan and Britain or Europe. This fact is shown in the reinforcement of old notions about the racial origins of the Japanese and the basic difference between them and the

Chinese. Kaempfer had been chiefly responsible for the diffusion of these ideas. According to Kaempfer, the Japanese were originally from the lost stock of Babylon.[100] Although Knox did not fully commit himself to Kaempfer's view of the racial difference between the two East Asian peoples, he emphasised that the Japanese showed a difference 'of a very high degree' from the Chinese.[101] In addition, Knox revealed a strong partiality for the Japanese. He pointed out the existence of civilisation in Japan, which, he claimed, other Asian countries did not possess. For example, on India, he wrote:

> We refuse to accept the architectural monuments of India as tests of civilization. They are proofs of superstition and slavery – nothing more.[102]

He also declared that the Chinese had been held by the Japanese at arm's length through the centuries, that the latter esteemed them 'not without reason, to be an inferior race'.[103] According to Knox, the Japanese regarded the Chinese as 'Brian de Bois Gilbert would have thought and spoken of Isaac, the Money-changer, in Scott's romance'.[104] In the early 1850s, the number of Japanese intellectuals who manifested such a sweeping contempt for the Chinese as a whole was still limited, in spite of the apparent increase in patriotic sentiment.[105] The image of the Chinese as the money changer in *Ivanhoe* seems to have been shared among the British themselves rather than among the Japanese.

Knox's opinion here shows that his argument was based, consciously or unconsciously, on a sense of affinity between Europe and Japan. He also mentioned the widely established educational system of Japan in close reference to the Prussian system.[106] It might have been with such a sense of affinity in mind that Henry Morley suggested a close comparison between the educational system of Japan and that of England in order to imply his criticism of the latter:

> To boys and girls, after reading and writing, which are taught (hear, England!) to the meanest Japanese, the most necessary part of education is an elaborate training in the ceremonial rules of life.[107]

It was in the fourth chapter of Kaempfer's *History of Japan* that many of the country's geographical characteristics were portrayed as similar to those of 'the Kingdoms of Great Britain and Ireland'.[108] Among British writers who dealt with Japan in the early 1850s, this idea was reinforced and much generalised. Morley wrote: 'Nippon . . . is important enough to have been justly called the England in the Pacific

Ocean.'[109] Knox also estimated that the total population of the four main islands of Japan was 'equal to that of the British Isles',[110] and that the population of Edo was more or less the same as that of London at that time.[111] In explaining the significance of the port of Nagasaki, Knox used the expression, 'the Liverpool of Japan'.[112]

It may have been difficult for British writers to use an analogy without some sense of affinity between Britain and Japan. Russell's writing suggests this point. In his *Dublin Review* article of 1852, he never resorted to European similes in order to explain things Japanese to his readers. However, Russell's case was unique. As will be shown later, many writers from this period started revelling in their discoveries of affinity between Japan and Europe. One can easily imagine that their readers, lacking many illustrations to guide them, tended to conceive 'Japan' in terms of a mental mosaic of various images which these metaphors and analogies created in their minds. At least until the late 1850s, illustrations of things Japanese were not readily available to the public.[113] Therefore, the choice of metaphors, similes and analogies by these writers must have influenced readers' minds to a considerable extent.

This point may explain why some of these metaphors were to establish themselves so firmly as to reappear in various popular writings about Japan even in the late 1870s. Also, the creation of such durable metaphors not only reflected the way these writers smoothly accepted a strange world, but also the way in which they could place a new piece of information about the outside world within their readers' familiar world-view. Unless the readers' familiar world changed, these rhetorical elements might well affect the way future popular writers described Japan. It was an irony that their very emphasis on the 'strange' characteristics of the Japanese induced these writers to try to find proper European counterparts to those characteristics for the sake of smooth communication with their readers, and that the very effort of this kind by these writers eventually led them to feel an affinity between this 'singular' country and Europe.

On the eve of modern Anglo-Japanese relations, writers already began to think of the British as the ideal suitors of this piquant nation. There were the miserable examples of two forerunners, the Jesuits and the Dutch, and there was to be very shortly a doubtful experiment by an American squadron before a world audience. The emphasis of Japanese 'singularity' by British writers seems to have been connected with their image of Britain as a uniquely refined nation which alone could cope successfully with the 'strange' nation in the Far East. The image of the Dutch in this period was of mean merchants who had assisted the authorities in the extermination of Japanese Christians in the seventeenth century. In 1852, an anonymous article on Japan appeared in the *New Monthly Magazine and Humorist*, the editor of which was the then successful popular novelist, W.H. Ainsworth (1805–82). The contributor described the 'base conduct' of the Dutch in having given way, for the sake of commercial gain, to Japanese rulers in every instance so that they were finally confined in 1641 to Dejima, a small artificial island in the bay of Nagasaki.[114]

On the other hand, British writers were very reluctant to recommend a gun-boat policy towards Japan. This tendency was shown in their efforts to differentiate the British from the Americans. The image of the United States they drew was that of an unqualified newcomer in the business of opening Japan. Knox, for example, emphasised the long history of Anglo-Japanese relations, which dated from the early seventeenth century.[115] He elaborated on the story of the first Englishman in Japan, William Adams, who had drifted to the country in a Dutch ship in 1600. Also, Knox emphasised the date of 9 June 1613, the day Captain John Saris arrived in the country:

> We are particular in marking the date, as this was the first time an English vessel had ever approached the shores of Japan.[116]

The contributor to the *New Monthly Magazine and Humorist*, having also emphasised the long-term attempts of the British to reopen relations with Japan, analysed possible American attitudes rather anxiously:

> Our sons of the New World are neither so punctilious nor so scrupulous.[117]

As a matter of fact, British writers on the United States' expedition tended to waver between the feeling that Britain could take advantage of the Americans' possibly tough policy towards Japan and the feeling that Britain should be different from those 'light-hearted' Americans. A case in which a speculative mind was conspicuous was Russell's article: one of the important images of the Americans which Russell tried to convey regarding their relationship with Japan was that of poor righteous sufferers from the seclusion policy. Quoting extensively from Golownin's recollections, Russell introduced his readers to the case in which an American vessel repatriating Japanese castaways had been fired on by the Japanese authorities.[118] He also reported information on the current 'painful and degrading captivity' in Japan of 'a number of American whalers'.[119] Russell's idea of a suffering America was closely associated with his unmitigated approval of the American policy of sending men-of-war to Japan. After all, his main interest was the 'penetration' of the country by 'another Xavier'.[120]

An anonymous contributor to the *New Monthly Magazine and Humorist* also shared Russell's sympathy with the expedition:[121] He quoted some passages from the *New York Courier and Inquirer* in order to emphasise the inconvenience suffered by American whalers in the region. He justified the use of force on the part of the squadron as 'the means by which Americans propose to themselves to bring Japan within the pale of humanity and of international courtesy'.[122] Unlike Russell, however, this writer seems to have felt the necessity to differentiate between 'European nations' and the 'enthusiastic Yankees' who seemed to be imagining 'a war of aggression and conquest'.[123] Towards the end of his article, he added:

> If the objects of the expedition are carried out in a spirit of humanity and sound policy . . . there is no doubt that Commodore Perry will carry with him on his expedition the sympathies of all European nations.[124]

Knox's writing had a stronger tone than the above writer's in underlining the differences between the British and the Americans. First, Knox pointed out that the compulsory seclusion of the Japanese was 'a wrong not only to themselves, but to the civilised world'.[125] He claimed that the policy had been carried to excess in Japan, and that no nation had the right of exclusive use of their own territory:

> The only secure title to property, whether it be in a hovel or an empire, is that the exclusive possession of one is for the benefit of all.[126]

Knox also observed that no country had the right to remain secluded from the world. In his argument, the word 'civilisation' was conspicuously used in close association with such notions as 'that principle of development', or 'those ingenious and persevering European races'.[127] It seems that when discussing 'civilisation', Knox meant not only current material progress but also a certain state of mind which would contribute to the 'development' of a people. For example, he appreciated a mental quality which would bring about smoother relationships between people who were living in places which were remote from each other. It was by this principle that he acknowledged the 'great perfection' of Japanese roads and highways, and considered this phenomenon to be the evidence of 'a considerable degree of civilisation'.[128] Therefore, for Knox, the smooth establishment of regular communication between the West and Japan would be a grave test of the high 'civilisation' which he advocated. Great Britain, in Knox's mind, should not resort to the use of force to open the closed country. 'The affair,' claimed Knox, 'is one of far too vital importance to be treated in a light or jesting spirit',[129] which he regarded as one of the characteristics of the American mind.[130] He went on:

> Let us hope that the liberality of the English in China may be imitated by the United States' negotiators at Jedo.[131]

Knox, however, was perceptive enough to estimate correctly the shrewdness of the Japanese in their acquisition of information about the outside world.[132] The backdrop against which Knox preached the gospel of English 'liberality' as a means to 'prudent negotiation' was his confidence in the perfect Japanese awareness of 'the rapid success of the British arms in China in 1841-42'.[133] Therefore, in terms of considering the use of force as an element of British diplomacy, Knox was not so far from the apparent American attitude to Japan and it is true that by the end of the 1840s most Japanese intellectuals were overawed by the strength of the Royal Navy.[134] 'Liberality' on the part of Great Britain would be the most acceptable policy, at least to the less fanatical among Japanese leaders.

Some of these leaders had also become concerned, however vaguely, about international courtesy.[135] If Britain made her approaches in a 'civilised' manner, therefore, she would certainly be better qualified as a noble suitor for Japan. It appears that the comparative tranquillity in the Far East in the early 1850s gave British writers very relaxed feelings when they considered future dealings with Japan. In fact, they could indulge in dreams of 'civilised' and joyous encounters with the 'singular' people. There had been a long period of peace in Britain, and in 1851 she enjoyed her reputation as the leader of civilisation and progress at the Great Exhibition. It is understandable that Knox expressed his expectation that Japan would also 'enter within the walls of the next Crystal Palace'.[136]

Until the mid-1850s, British writers seem to have had ample time to nurture and reinforce their own ideas of Japan and Britain, but during the latter half of the 1850s, new information about Japan began to reach Britain. However, as will be shown later, it was not likely to change the ideas about Japan that had become so firmly imprinted in British minds. It seems that the stock of information which these writers possessed so much surpassed the amount of new information that the latter could either reinforce the former, or simply be ignored. Also, British magazines and reviews gave less attention to Japan in this period than one might expect, given the extensive coverage in the earlier half of the 1850s. This phenomenon was caused partly by great concern with a series of wars in the Near and Far East: the Crimean War between 1853–6, the 'Indian Mutiny' between 1857–9, and the *Arrow* War between 1856–8. Discussions of these wars tended to occupy all the space which ordinary magazines and reviews in Britain seemed willing to devote to Eastern affairs. Also, it seems that the British could not be enthusiastic about the treaties of 1854 between Japan and the European powers opening the harbours of Shimoda and Hakodate: they were, after all, the unexpected rewards deriving from the pioneer activities of the Americans. Admiral Stirling's treaty with Japan (1854) was, in fact, improvised on the spot without any previous approval on the part of the Foreign Office, and was indeed the result of unexpected developments owing to the poor skill of the interpreters and the preconceived ideas of the Japanese negotiators about possible British demands.[137]

Only a few short articles on Japan appeared in popular magazines and reviews in the late 1850s; these included Henry Morley's 'Far East' in *Household Words*;[138] an anonymous article, entitled 'Expedition of an American Squadron to the China Seas and Japan' in the *New Quarterly Review*;[139] and 'American Explorations: China and Japan', which was contributed to *Blackwood's Magazine* by one of the editorial staff of the magazine, William Aytoun (1813–65), poet and professor of rhetoric and *belles lettres* at the University of Edinburgh.[140] On the whole, the ideas and images of Japan which had already been established in British periodicals in the early 1850s remained firmly fixed until late 1858, when jubilation over the smooth conclusion by Lord Elgin of 'The Treaty of Peace, Friendship and Commerce, between Her Majesty and the Tycoon of Japan' echoed around Britain. This was indeed the culmination of Britain's, or rather British writers', prolonged courtship of Japan, and events were apparently following the course which Knox had advocated of employing 'civilisation' in dealing with this 'singular' country in the Far East.

2 Japan and the Edinburgh Publishers

In the late autumn of 1858, a letter and a manuscript arrived at 45 George Street, Edinburgh, the offices of William Blackwood & Sons, the publishers of the popular 'High Tory' monthly, *Blackwood's Magazine*. It came from HMS *Furious* at Shanghai, dated 20 September, and the sender was Captain Sherard Osborn (1822–75) of the Royal Navy:

> Sir, I beg to place at your disposal, on the usual terms for articles in your Magazine, the enclosed papers upon our recent visit to the Japanese Empire and the city of Yedo &c. Should they suit you please to kindly put yourself in communication with my sister Mrs Ashington, The Rectory, Anwick, Lincolnshire, or otherwise return them to me.[1]

Since 1845, this magazine had been edited by John Blackwood (1818–79), an able connoisseur of literary talent who was well known for his discovery of Margaret Oliphant and George Eliot. In the middle of the nineteenth century, this publishing house was also celebrated for its flourishing literary circle, which included such figures as Thomas de Quincey, William Makepeace Thackeray, Anthony Trollope, A.W. Kinglake, John Hanning Speke, Benjamin Disraeli and Edward Bulwer Lytton.[2] Among them was a popular young writer, Laurence Oliphant (1829–88) who was a favourite of Blackwood. It must have been at Oliphant's suggestion that Captain Osborn wrote to Blackwood, since Oliphant was also on board the *Furious*, the Flagship of Lord Elgin, as the Envoy's Private Secretary.[3]

Blackwood had been intrigued by the first account of Lord Elgin's visit to Edo which had appeared in *The Times* of 2 November but was rather sceptical about its factual accuracy. Thus, Blackwood was delighted to print Osborn's work immediately for the December issue of the magazine. This was the beginning of the anonymous series entitled 'A Cruise in Japanese Waters', which was the first lengthy popular report of Lord Elgin's Mission to Japan.[4] On 30 November of the same year, Blackwood wrote back to Osborn:

> Along with this I send you a copy of the December No. of the

Magazine which you will see opens with your delightful Cruise in the Japanese Waters. The style of this first instalment of your narrative is so pleasant & good that I look anxiously for its continuation.[5]

Since Osborn had only dealt, in his first manuscript, with his voyage from China to the port of Nagasaki, Blackwood wrote in the same letter impatiently:

It is very well done indeed & I grieved when I found that this first paper carried one no further. I expect great pleasure from your sketch of that wondrous country where I hope you landed & saw as much as time would permit.[6]

In what was an unusually generous letter, given the editor's normally severe tone of correspondence with his contributors, Blackwood seems to have made a few subtle requests by using a few words of praise. He was clearly interested in receiving an account of Japan that was 'delightful' and 'pleasant', and that would present Japan in a 'wondrous' light.

It was, however, objective sketches and not imaginative tales about the country that Blackwood was expecting. This he made clear in the same letter, criticising *The Times*' article of early November:

The first account of Jeddo [Edo] in the Times came upon one like a vision of the Arabian Nights & I am curious to hear how far if at all the clever 'Special' was assisted by his imagination.[7]

These points put by Blackwood did not directly influence Osborn. In fact, the latter's manuscripts for the series were mostly completed by the end of January 1859, that is, before the arrival of the letter from the editor.[8] As will be shown later, however, Blackwood's initial taste for accounts of Japan was to be strongly realised in the course of editing Osborn's work, owing partly to the participation of Mrs Ashington, who became responsible for revising Osborn's articles.

The criticised 'Special' of *The Times* had remarked in his article that Lord Elgin's visit to 'this singular and hitherto jealously exclusive empire' had been a 'most interesting episode in the diplomacy of Great Britain in the Far East'.[9] He emphasised various amiable features of the country without making any unfavourable observations. His sketch of the picturesque beauty of the bay of Nagasaki not only resembled but far exceeded the product of Henry Morley's imagination which had been published in *Household Words* seven years before. Their excursions and shopping in Nagasaki proved to be 'not, as in China, an offensive and disgusting operation, but a charming and agreeable amusement'. The streets were appreciated as being 'broad, clean, and free from foul odours', and the people 'civil and courteous'. The little town of Shimoda was described as 'a fairy land'. Not only the city of Edo but its suburbs were abundant in 'the extraordinary evidences of civilization which met the eye in every direction'. The 'picturesque' castle with a 'magnificent' moat, gardens 'laid out with exquisite taste', the 'personal cleanliness' of the Japanese, as well as their strong 'propensity to imitate and adopt the appliances of civilization', such as steamers and locomotives, were mentioned in a most pleasant tone.

The 'Special' was particularly attracted by Japanese tea-houses. He described them as 'a national characteristic of Japan':

> The traveller . . . need never be at a loss to find rest and refreshment: stretched upon the softest and cleanest of matting, imbibing the most delicately flavoured tea, inhaling through a short pipe the fragrant tobacco of Japan, he resigns himself to the ministrations of a bevy of fair damsels, who glide rapidly and noiselessly about, the most zealous and skilful of attendants.[10]

His 'general impression' of the country was this:

> . . . in its climate, its fertility, and its picturesque beauty, Japan is not equalled by any country on the face of the globe; while, as if to harmonize with its surpassing natural endowments, it is peopled by a race whose qualities are of the most amiable and winning description, and whose material prosperity has been so equalized as to insure happiness and contentment to all classes. We never saw two Japanese quarrel and beggars have yet to be introduced with other luxuries of Western civilization.[11]

The author, therefore, expressed his unreserved sympathy with the Japanese authorities' policy of secluding the country from the outer world; the point which Kaempfer had made one hundred and thirty years before.[12]

In contrast to Alexander Knox's or Charles Russell's comments of several years before on the coexistence of paradoxical features in Japanese society, this article utterly dropped the 'dark' side of the nation's character. A letter to the editor published in *The Times* of 20 November above the initials 'W.N.S.', pointed out the similarity of the article to what had been written about Japan by Sir Thomas Wilson

(1560?–1629), Keeper of State Papers, in his letter to King James I.[13] It was the British merchant navigator Richard Cocks who had given Sir Thomas the information about the country. Although 'W.N.S' admitted that the 'graphic pen' of the anonymous correspondent had 'not only astonished and entertained, but deeply interested the public', he could not help reproducing King James' reaction to those pieces of information from Cocks;

> The King said 'they were the loudest lies he had ever heard'.

Blackwood's critical attitude towards the extreme glorification of Japan was not a unique one. The correspondent may have been aiming at creating a sensation by presenting a colourful account, taking advantage of the supposed general ignorance about Japan among his readers.

So what kind of images of Japan *did* Osborn's serial articles convey to the readers of *Blackwood's Magazine*? Ironically enough, Blackwood, in spite of his doubts about the report of the country given in *The Times*, published a similar account. Osborn repeated the point that Japan was very different from, and much superior to, China in many dimensions such as natural scenery, climate, cleanliness of cities, and people's character, taste and intellectual capacity. Everything in Japan was described in most favourable terms. If one tries to find any difference between Osborn's style and that of the article in *The Times*, Osborn frequently referred to things in the European world in order to explain Japan. Here is one example:

> The scenery [of the Bay of Edo] was neither Indian nor Chinese . . . Take the fairest portion of the coast of Devonshire, and all the shores of the Isle of Wight, form with their combined beauty a gulf forty-five miles long . . . In every nook and valley, as well as along every sandy bay, place pretty towns and villages, cut out all brick and plaster villas with Corinthian porticoes, and introduce the neatest *chalêts* Switzerland ever produced . . . strew the bright sea with quaint vessels and picturesque boats, and you will have the foreground of the picture. For background, scatter . . . the finest scenery our Highlands of Scotland can afford . . . Far back . . . rear a magnificent cone, the beautiful Fusi-hama [Fujiyama], the 'Matchless Mountain' of Japan.[14]

Osborn also pointed out that the Japanese climate and that of England 'were much alike'.[15]

As regards the racial origin of the Japanese, Osborn first noted their apparent resemblance to the Kanaka races of the South-Sea Islands,[16] but gradually became convinced of Kaempfer's theory about their Semitic origin.[17] Encouraged by this belief in the original affinity between the Europeans and the Japanese, Osborn also compared the Japanese with the people of 'Morea [Peloponnesus]', and pointed out:

> Japan shows signs of a high order of civilisation, energy, industry and wealth, which modern Greece decidedly does not exhibit, whatever it did in olden days.[18]

Japanese women were prominent among the things which attracted Osborn. He generalised the image of women he saw in Nagasaki:

> The grown-up women were modestly attired in dark-coloured garments, their beautiful hair neatly dressed, and but that nails were dyed, there was a general appearance of beauty about them, combined with much grace in the figures of younger ones.[19]

In his reports, quite a few impressive Japanese women appeared. For example, Lord Elgin and his suite went out of Edo for an excursion and took refreshment in a peach-garden. They were attended by 'a remarkably good-looking, lady-like woman'. According to Osborn, 'nothing could have been more graceful than her manner; and the posture of kneeling, accompanied by a low bow to signify prostration at one's feet'.[20] Osborn was impressed by 'a high social position' held by the Japanese women, and made the following comparison:

> She is not cooped up in pestiferous apartment to delight some fattened-up Chinese mandarin, or greasy Brahmin, but . . . she has succeeded in asserting her right to be treated like a rational being, quite as well able to take care of herself as the sterner sex.[21]

The Victorian naval officer was astonished at the sight of Japanese women taking baths in the open air, though he appreciated their 'highly commendable liking for scrupulous cleanliness', and called them 'the fair Eves' of Japan.[22]

Next came Japanese officials. They were also described in a favourable tone. Their intelligence and shrewdness were matters of wonder. Commenting on the Royal Yacht, Her Majesty's present to the Shogun, Osborn wrote:

> When one saw how full of intelligence all the higher classes in Japan were – how capable of appreciating the skill and mechanism employed in any of the marvels of scientific labour Great Britain

contains – it was a subject of regret that a screw-schooner . . . should have been the only specimen sent of our mechanical or manufacturing skill.[23]

According to Osborn, the Japanese officers' 'acquaintance with the theory of their profession was highly creditable'.[24] Among several Japanese senior officers who were highly estimated by Osborn, 'Fghono-Kami' [Lord Higo, Iwase Tadanari], the third senior Commissioner, was described as being 'most industrious and curious as to all that related to England or America'. With his notebook always in hand, Iwase showed his great power of scrutiny and observation. Osborn also appreciated Iwase's sense of humour which had rescued all parties from embarrassment whenever the conference for the treaty met with a hitch, by dissolving them all in hearty laughter. Osborn concluded this way:

> . . . from the specimen the Commissioners afforded of the diplomatic skill of the servants of the Taikoon, there was no doubt that many would be found qualified to represent Japan at our own court, or elsewhere in Europe.[25]

The Japanese people, in general, were appreciated for their politeness, civility, frugal living and happiness. Their quiet taste in clothing was impressive to the visitors. Osborn observed:

> If squalor and poverty were not to be found in Yedo, neither was their ostentatious magnificence or extravagance among the higher and wealthier classes.

According to him, 'the Japanese men may be said to be the Quakers of the East'.[26] Certainly Osborn was aware that his account was more or less similar to that of William Adams, who, in the early seventeenth century, regarded the Japanese as 'good of nature, courteous above measure, and valiant in war'. Among the lines Osborn quoted from Adams' writing, the following one is remarkable:

> I think no land better governed in the world by civil policy.[27]

Osborn also noted some words about 'the Japanese in general' which were expressed by a Russian naval officer he met in Nagasaki:

> Lieutenant L — declared them to be the finest race on the earth; and as he lived amongst them . . . he was in a very good position to form an opinion on the subject.[28]

Japan and the Edinburgh Publishers 27

In presenting such rosy images of Japan in *Blackwood's Magazine*, Osborn received the co-operation of the editor, John Blackwood, and Osborn's sister, Mrs Ashington. The above-mentioned letter of 30 November 1858 from Blackwood to Osborn reached the *Furious* in Canton about 10 February 1859. However, Osborn had already got from Mrs Ashington the information about the publication of his manuscript, and had written to Blackwood on 23 January with 'nearly all' of his manuscript for the series, and promised to send thirty more pages for the conclusion. This letter contained three interesting points in terms of offering information about Japan to the readers of the magazine. First, Osborn was none too confident of the degree of curiosity about Japan on the part of his readers. He wrote:

> I fear I have drawn it out too much, but in truth, the subject is so interesting even to us to me [sic] on the spot that I have taken it for granted you at home care as much about it.[29]

Secondly, Osborn revealed that he intended to avoid in his manuscripts comments on the complicated diplomatic disputes in the Far East. This fitted in with the vague hint Blackwood had given in his letter of 30 November 1858 to Osborn, that accounts of Japan should be 'pleasant'. Osborn requested the editor's assistance:

> If you see anything in my M.S.S. which appears to you to reflect upon individuals, or bear harshly and unjustly upon Americans or Dutchmen, pray erase or modify. I write warmly, but I do not want to give pain in articles upon which I have amused myself, rather than spent any great amount of thought.[30]

Lord Elgin had in fact experienced many diplomatic difficulties particularly in China owing in some measure to the lack of smooth co-operation by the Royal Navy.[31] Also, Admiral James Stirling's previous convention with Japan had precluded future alterations to agreements by any 'high officer'. In view of these, it is notable that Osborn and Blackwood were so determined to present a harmless account so far as the political aspects of Japan were concerned. In addition to those two points in Osborn's letter, which might well encourage Blackwood's editorial revisions, Osborn gave, in the same letter, a considerable amount of freedom to Mrs Ashington to revise his manuscript:

> I have got into such a bad habit of writing very carelessly, and correcting only in the proofs, that I fear you will be put to much

inconvenience where I cannot be on the spot to do it myself. But if you will let Mrs Ashington have the proofs to correct she will I am sure do quite as well as I could, or better.[32]

In reply to Blackwood's letter of 30 November 1858, Osborn wrote back on 14 February 1859 that the final chapter of the 'Cruise' would be sent to Mrs Ashington by the same mail and that since he did not 'despair of returning again to Japan' that year, he would be able 'to produce a better account of the present state of the country'. It seems that Osborn was not too happy with the series. He added these lines:

> Of Japan in the past day, there is no lack of information. But I have in my articles purposely abstained from more than a mere sketch of its history illustrative of European intercourse. Because I feel sure what must interest you all is Japan in 1858–9 – not of 1700.[33]

Blackwood took no note of Osborn's comments in the reply he drafted in April 1859. Instead he confessed that he 'uncommonly' liked Osborn's work:

> What a delightful expedition it must have been. Indeed your description admirably conveys the sense of how it was enjoyed.[34]

In his correspondence to Mrs Ashington, Blackwood praised 'the workmanlike' style of Osborn's writing,[35] his 'descriptive powers',[36] and their 'very graphic & good' result.[37] However, the readability of Osborn's 'Cruise' seems to owe much to Mrs Ashington's revision, if one reads her letters to Blackwood despatched during the time from December 1858 to April 1859. Occasionally she provided not only readability but also a certain 'pleasant' quality. In her letter of 19 March 1859 to Blackwood, she explained that she had shortened some sheets of Osborn's manuscripts on her 'own responsibility' as 'Sherard's [i.e., Osborn's] Censor of the Press', by saying:

> There was no Japanese news in what I retained but a great deal against the Americans and also against the British System in China.[38]

She was in fact 'bold and certain' in correcting her brother's writings, as she herself admitted.[39]

In any case, the publishers, W. Blackwood & Sons, were becoming a centre for the introduction into Britain of new information about Japan. Osborn had informed them that their friend Oliphant had written 'a great mass of valuable M.S.S.' about Lord Elgin's Mission to

China and Japan.[40] Blackwood, at the beginning of 1858, had already been anxious to receive Oliphant's manuscripts from the Far East. In a letter to Oliphant in January 1858, Blackwood discouraged Oliphant's proposal to create a volume from his South American articles which had previously been published in *Blackwood's Magazine,* and wrote that he felt 'very confident' that the work on the Chinese Expedition would be 'a successful one'. The reason Blackwood gave for his suggestion was that 'public interest' was 'fixed so exclusively upon the East' at the time.[41]

If one looks at the publication ledgers of the firm for the period from the middle of the 1850s to the 1870s[42] the number of copies of *Blackwood's Magazine* which were printed shows the following fluctuations. In the mid-1850s, about 7500 copies were printed, with occasional rises to 8000. However, from early 1858 the number consistently reached about 8000, and from April 1859 it reached 8100. During the one year from February 1860, it became even higher, and sometimes reached 8400. This period saw the peak of the magazine's publication, and the number of copies began declining to 7350 in the mid-1860s, and to 6000 in the 1870s. It was at the time when the magazine was nearing its peak circulation that Osborn's 'Cruise' appeared. Although it has been difficult to prove that Osborn's series of articles actually stimulated the sale of the magazine, it seems likely that the firm decided to print more than the previous average number because of the series. It was against such a background that Blackwood offered 'a good thing' to Osborn in April 1859 to 'reprint the Series in a little volume' with the author's name on it after its completion in the magazine.[43]

In May 1859, Osborn's series in the magazine was completed. The following month, Major William Blackwood, John Blackwood's nephew who, after retiring from the Indian Army, had been assisting the editor in the management of the firm for ten years, began his preparation for the reprint of the series. On 1 June, William Blackwood wrote to Mrs Ashington, explaining the firm's idea about the matter: '. . . if the Cruise is republished, it ought to be so immediately'. The reason he gave for this point was that Oliphant was planning to publish from the same firm his work on China and Japan in the coming winter, and the two books 'had better not be published' at the same time as their sales were likely to damage each other. He briefly discussed the form Osborn's book might take and the scale of its first printing, but added carefully the following lines:

We ought to mention that we are not so sanguine of the work having a great sale now as we were when the first portions reached us, the attention of the public is so much directed to the war in Europe.⁴⁴

The publishers were confessing their belief that the market for books on Japan had not been firmly established. At Blackwood's request, Mrs Ashington wrote back immediately saying that she had 'no hesitation' in saying that their plan for 'immediate republication' was the one she believed Osborn 'would agree to'. She even proposed that she would be willing to make suggestions for a few corrections in each original magazine article.⁴⁵ Although both the Blackwoods and Mrs Ashington knew that Osborn had expressed his desire to touch up and improve the articles in case of reprinting, they decided after about ten days' correspondence to republish the 'Cruise' without waiting for any further word from Osborn himself. In his letter to Osborn dated 9 June, William Blackwood apologetically explained that it had been Mrs Ashington's opinion that had led them to make the decision⁴⁶ and on 17 June, 'a complete set of sheets of the Cruise' as it had appeared in the magazine was sent from Blackwood to Mrs Ashington for her 'corrections'.⁴⁷ Early the next month, the proof print was ready.⁴⁸

Apparently, everything was going well for publishing the little book by Captain Sherard Osborn, amended by Mrs Ashington, but then, trouble developed. Osborn returned to England much earlier than expected, leaving China before receiving any correspondence concerning the re-publication of his magazine articles.⁴⁹ On 28 July, Osborn despatched a curt letter to Blackwood having heard on his arrival in London of the publisher's advertisement of the reprint of his 'Cruise'. He scrawled briefly that he was rushing to Blackwood's London office near St Paul's Cathedral:

> Will it be too late for me to see and correct the proofs? I think [some] of it will bear mending. I direct to Pater Noster Row instead of Edinburgh for expedition['s] sake.⁵⁰

However, Osborn seems to have been pacified and by early August when the book-binding was completed, he himself wrote to Blackwood thanking him for his 'kindness and liberality'.

> You only do me justice in supposing that I should be unwilling to do anything to interfere with the perfect success of my friend Oliphant's Book.⁵¹

The same point he made in his letter to his old friend John Murray, the

London publisher, 'It must come out before Oliphant's work'. Osborn expected a high demand for Oliphant's book on the Far East comparing it with that of Henry Williams, the missionary to the islands of the Maoris:

> China will interest the public a great deal more than Henry Williams' Land, or I'm much mistaken.[52]

Certainly, the public interest in China and Japan was strong at the time. Blackwood printed 1575 copies of *A Cruise in Japanese Waters* at the price of five shillings per copy.[53] Within a few months, all the copies in stock were cleared.[54] Blackwood's estimate in the previous June of the potential sale proved to have been too cautious, and the publishers saw no reason not to proceed swiftly to the second edition of the *Cruise*. Even though he had been unable to subdue his complaint about the first edition, this was also Osborn's desire. In the reprint, Mrs Ashington's alterations had been confined to only a few stylistic points since she had probably done enough in the magazine articles, and also had very little time, and this failed to meet Osborn's main complaint, which was about the 'rather disjointed' nature of the chapters, as he had produced them one by one on board the *Furious* without comparing them.[55] However, a more delicate question was emerging in the Admiralty concerning Osborn's passage dealing with Admiral Stirling's convention in the *Cruise*. Already in his letter to Blackwood dated 5 August, Osborn confessed:

> Had circumstances allowed of it, I would have erased or modified my strictness upon Admiral Stirling's Treaty.[56]

Osborn was, however, encouraged by *The Times*' leader-writer, the historian, George Wingrove Cooke (1814–65), who had been stationed in Shanghai as the paper's correspondent at the time of Lord Elgin's expedition to China. In the same letter, Osborn explained:

> . . . as Wingrove Cooke observes, if you can get up 'a jolly row' over a new book, it will [be] sure to sell well.[57]

Blackwood did not like this type of sensationalism, and Osborn was also embarrassed at the row his writing had stirred up in the Admirality.

Thus, a second edition was planned, and already in his letter to Blackwood of 6 September 1859, Osborn wrote that he was 'correcting a copy of the "Cruise" ' and would complete the work in a few days.

However, he was becoming busy again with the preparation for his return to China, and his changes were bound to be fewer than he had expected:

> There are few if any errors and I will only expunge my strictness upon poor old Stirling as I hear that the admirals who did not take Cronstad or Revel or Sveaborg want to make him the scape-goat of all Naval shortcomings.[58]

Osborn was, however, a writer who tended to become feverish whenever he took up his pen.[59] Contrary to his original intention, the passage which he changed became extremely adverse to Stirling. Was it the idea that a book would survive longer than magazine articles that made Osborn's mind rather stiff and made him record the facts as he saw them? Or, was he under the influence of the agitator Cooke, as at this time they were becoming closer to each other?[60] The astonished William Blackwood wrote to Osborn on 19 September:

> Are you right do you think in stating so boldly as you do in the corrected passage p. 91 about Admiral Stirling's Treaty, that it was disregarded? That it was an impediment which deserved to be committed to the waves, as it was.[61]

In the first edition, Osborn had observed that the Crimean War had made the Japanese islands an area 'for a game of hide-and-seek played by the Russian and Allied squadrons', and then he added these lines:

> Then everybody wanted treaties with the Japanese; and in apparently a waggish humour, they gave a British admiral one in 1854.[62]

Blackwood emphasised in the same letter that the original passage had had 'a pleasant ambiguity'. However, he found even that unsatisfactory, as it implied criticism of the admiral's achievement, and he suggested that the part might be 'omitted altogether'.[63] The publishers insisted on the idea of 'pleasantness' for a book on Japan. Osborn, who was then leading a hectic life in London, was to yield. On 21 September, he wrote to Blackwood:

> I dare say you are perfectly right, as to the addition in p. 91. Being unnecessary, pray let the passage terminate as in the first edition, merely erasing Stirling's name if it was there.[64]

Ultimately, Blackwood attained a compromise on the issue. The original passage was retained. Besides, the most offensive line: 'they gave a British admiral one' was changed into a more ambiguous statement: 'they gave us one'.[65]

Blackwood was given another chance to maintain the book's 'pleasantness'. In another letter of late October, Osborn wanted to alter a section in the first page in which he had added, for the second edition, a new passage about the lack of military support to Lord Elgin on the part of the 'Admiral and Generals' in his diplomatic operation *vis-à-vis* the Peking Court during 1857 and 1858. Osborn wrote:

> A judicious friend of mine who read the proofs has called to beg me to modify the terms . . . He says that that assertion must rest upon other information than that contained in the Blue Book [produced mainly by Lord Elgin].[66]

Blackwood, at this request, restored the page to its original form, and was thus able to avoid stirring up a fresh row among the book's readers. According to the publication ledger of the firm, 1050 copies were printed for the second edition in November 1859, and they sold steadily. By April 1861, the number of copies remaining was 56.[67]

The first two points made by Blackwood in his initial letter to Osborn of late November 1858 – that an account of Japan must be 'pleasant' and delightful, and must be 'wondrous' – proved to have been adhered to throughout the course of publishing the magazine articles and the two book editions of Osborn's work. It was, however, difficult for anyone in Britain at the time to judge whether the third point Blackwood made – that an account of Japan must not be imaginative – had been observed by the writer or not. It may have been a matter of the writer's preference whether or not to devote his writings entirely to what he had observed in Japan. Also, in one's eagerness to emphasise the first two points, one was likely to neglect the third. This was, in fact, to happen, as will be shown later.

So far, it is clear that a magazine article on Japan or its reprint edition could well have been a product of much group effort in the sense that it is difficult to attribute the contents of such publications in the main to the pen of the author who actually experienced the country. The notion about 'the public' was fairly important to all who were concerned with the work; the direction of the reading public's interest was often discussed and certainly Japan was regarded as a risky topic in the publishing business. Also, if one reads their correspondence carefully concerning the editions of Osborn's work, it becomes clear that the opinions expressed among *The Times*' staff,[68] in the Admiralty, or within Blackwood's circle of friends,[69] mattered. Another undeniable factor in publishing Osborn's work was the time-lag of about two months which was inevitable for the correspondence between Britain and the Far East. This gap had the effect of introducing Mrs Ashington, who knew little about Japan, to the task of 'censoring' the original manuscripts. Our study of the next venture, the publication by Blackwood of Oliphant's report on Lord Elgin's mission to the Far East, will provide us with more information to enable us to evaluate the significance of these observations in the history of British popular images of Japan.

As was mentioned before, Blackwood had developed high hopes for the commercial success of Oliphant's account of the Far East less than a year after the latter's departure for China with Lord Elgin in the spring of 1857. The publisher's anticipation was not without reason. Since the mid-1850s, an ever-increasing proportion of the overseas news which reached England was from the East. Also, it was Oliphant's reputation that made the publisher anxious to receive his manuscripts. Although barely thirty years of age, Oliphant was then already a well-known writer who had published several books on his travels in Nepal, the Middle East and North America. In the early 1850s, he had been Secretary to Lord Elgin's Mission for a commercial treaty between Canada and the United States of America, companion to Lord Stratford de Redcliffe on the latter's visit to the Crimea, and *The Times*' correspondent in Circassia. The name Laurence Oliphant seemed to appear whenever imperial and overseas affairs became hot news.

Therefore, in the spring of 1859, when Osborn's letters from China alerted Blackwoods to Oliphant's manuscript,[70] John Blackwood was already prepared to express his confidence in the future success of its publication:

> He [Oliphant] is a man who never throws away an opportunity and I feel sure his work will be very valuable.[71]

Blackwood was certainly conscious that the firm would again be able to become, after the publication of Osborn's articles, the sole provider of authentic and detailed information about Japan. In his letter to Oliphant, Blackwood could not help showing his excitement:

> ... from what he [Osborn] says I suppose it embraces the whole Chinese expedition as well as Japan.[72]

Oliphant and Blackwood met each other in London in late May 1859 for the first time in two years, and they lost no time in starting the preparation for the two-volume book: *Narrative of the Earl of Elgin's*

Japan and the Edinburgh Publishers   35

Mission to China and Japan in the Years 1857, '58, '59.[73] Even so, the preparation, including printing, proof-reading and binding, took six months, and the book was not published until the very end of the year. During this period, numerous letters were exchanged between the author, the firm and other people who were concerned with the book. Much of this correspondence reveals the considerable extent to which a number of people, besides the author himself, were involved in the course of publishing this work. It will be useful to examine the contents of these letters in terms of the following considerations which are relevant to preparing any manuscript for publication: the book's content; writing style; book design; and number of copies to be printed.

First, with regard to the content of Oliphant's manuscript, Blackwood's participation was not so conspicuous as was the case when he published Osborn's *Cruise*. It seems that Blackwood suggested only once that Oliphant should alter a part of his manuscript. They thought that Oliphant should elaborate on the state of the traditional Chinese prison which had been found by Lord Elgin in Canton.[74] Oliphant insisted on his original version, which had referred only briefly to Wingrove Cooke's description of the state of the prisoners there. Oliphant, in his letter to Blackwood, explained that he had not been present at the time of discovery, and 'in fact' had been 'astounded when [he] saw Cooke's highly emblished [*sic*] account some months afterwards'.[75] In this letter, Oliphant expressed his own high standard of only reporting what he himself had observed at first hand, by subtly criticising *The Times* correspondent's article published on 30 March 1858. This attitude of Oliphant towards his writing seems to have satisfied the publishers in the earlier stages of preparing the book, and they later said very little about the content of the book, in spite of the fact that Oliphant was still writing up later chapters and, therefore, might have listened to suggestions from the publishers.

In influencing the book's contents, the role played by Lord Elgin was important. Since the summer of 1859, political and diplomatic circles in Britain had been engaged in a dispute as to the real value of the Elgin Mission's achievements in China. A fresh military confrontation had been brewing between the Chinese and the Western powers concerning the ratification of the Tientsin Treaty, which was meant to secure an expansion of British trade with China. The controversy in Britain became even hotter towards the end of 1859, and Lord Elgin wanted another means of defending himself from political attacks besides his official reports published in the Blue Book. Thus there was ample reason for him to want to participate in the shaping of

Oliphant's *Narrative,* and the author was well aware of it. At Oliphant's suggestion, Blackwood decided to send a set of the proofs to Lord Elgin, and to be an intermediary between the author and Elgin in case either side desired any substantial change.[76] About ten letters from Oliphant to the firm show directly or indirectly the intervention of Lord Elgin in the course of proof-reading. Although many of the latter's comments were not of a 'material' kind,[77] sometimes the author himself seems to have revised his proof, expecting that a considerable alteration would be suggested by Lord Elgin.[78] Of course, Lord Elgin did not miss checking the crucial parts for himself. One example is shown in Oliphant's letter of late November to Blackwood:

> Lord Elgin is very anxious to change three or four words in 274th page of the 1st vol. He would substitute others to fill up the place. Please let me know whether it is feasible, and if so what would be the expense and what the delay as he is rather anxious about it.[79]

In the published *Narrative,* this particular page explains how the lack of the Royal Navy's smooth co-operation increased Lord Elgin's diplomatic difficulties with the Peking Court at the time when he was heading on to Tientsin. This was, in fact, the very point that political and military circles in Britain were disputing at the time. In reply, William Blackwood informed Oliphant of the firm's readiness to 'cancel' the entire page and to accept Lord Elgin's alteration.[80]

Thus the contents of *Narrative* were affected by the sequence of various events both in China and in Britain during 1859. The author himself confessed that his pen was under the influence of these occurrences. In a letter from Aberdeen, Oliphant wrote to Blackwood:

> This abominable China news will oblige me to alter a good deal of the line of my attack.[81]

Oliphant, however, tried at the same time to attain apparently impartial descriptions by way of quoting official reports in the Blue Book or those by Thomas Wade, Chinese Secretary to the Mission. At the time, Oliphant regarded himself as a 'doing historian'. Unlike Osborn, he took plenty of time in touching up his writings and sometimes insisted on putting in as many documentary sources as possible about British diplomacy in China at the risk of making the China chapters unbalanced in length and content compared with those on Japan.[82]

Oliphant's ambition for the factual accuracy of his writings did, however, have limits. Judging from his correspondence with the publishers at the time, it seems that his interest was predominantly in Britain's problems with the Far East but not always in Far Eastern societies or civilisation. As regards the latter topic, Oliphant was one of the few contemporary authorities in Britain and there was little room for anyone to argue with him. Still, Oliphant could have paid more attention to accuracy regarding these topics. A line in one of his letters to Blackwood suggests the point:

> . . . it is impossible to carry Chinese spelling in one[']s head. Discrepancies do not very much matter however.[83]

Had he been writing on any European country, would he have uttered such words?

Among the total forty-one chapters, more than twenty-five dealt with China, but most of them were on wars and diplomacy, and the parts in which Oliphant mentioned the manners and customs of the Chinese were very limited in length. Except on the occasions of excursions to the interior or of military operations, Oliphant had been on board ship most of the time. There had been few chances for him to have close contact with ordinary inhabitants of the country. In contrast, the twelve chapters on Japan only dealt with diplomacy to a small extent. They were mainly accounts of the beauty of the scenery, pleasant experiences of meeting people of various classes, or observations on their manners and customs.

The second consideration was writing style. In his letter attached to the first batch of proofs, William Blackwood congratulated Oliphant on the smooth readability of these sheets: 'One slips over the pages very pleasantly'. He requested Oliphant, however, to 'break up' his 'rather long' paragraphs for the sake of printers' convenience.[84] Both of these stylistic points might be attributed to the fact that a considerable portion of *Narrative* was written at the same time as Oliphant was giving public lectures on the Far East, particularly on Japan, to country societies and academic meetings which were held in various places such as Edinburgh, Dunfermline, Aberdeen, Stirling, Greenock and Glasgow. Oliphant intended at the time to stand for Parliament, either for Glasgow or for Stirling and he had to undertake numerous social engagements to win votes.

Many parts of the book seem to have been written with a clear idea of the sort of people to whom he was to tell his story. In this sense, Oliphant's manuscripts were far more a product of social interaction than those of Osborn's *Cruise*. Osborn, while writing in the Far East, was unable to see the immediate response to his writings on the part of his would-be readers, but Oliphant tried to make his descriptions of his experiences in China and Japan as acceptable as possible. He often wrote to Blackwood that his lectures would 'help the book', however much time their preparations might require.[85] On the other hand, it is likely that the lengthy paragraphs resulted from his fluency in his public lectures. For example, the way he wrote to his mother about his lecture on Japan at Greenock seems to suggest a certain relationship between his lectures and his smooth, sustained writing style:

> I looked over my red pulpit cushion and saw the old minister giggling immensely. Altogether I think it was the most successful lecture I have given. I despise even notes now, and find practice is improving my delivery. Nor did I feel the least fatigued.[86]

At that time, Oliphant was certainly a popular figure among British, and especially Scottish, country societies, as a passage from another of his letters to his mother shows:

> . . . just now here I am scarcely able to turn, for a press both of business and pleasure. Half-a-dozen lectures to prepare, proofs constantly to correct, and book not yet finished. Charming women at hand when I am inclined for a cosy chair in the drawing-room and a touch of the aesthetic. Any amount of game merely for the trouble of strolling through a few turnip-fields . . . any number of horses to ride.[87]

The third consideration was book design. As a whole, Oliphant paid great attention to the quality of the illustrations, maps and tables, which he had access to through the co-operation of Lord Elgin, one of the attachés to the mission and some of the Royal Navy officers.[88] It is remarkable that the book should have contained as many as twenty coloured lithographs and fifty black and white engravings on wood. Among them were about forty pictures of things Japanese, and, unlike the case of illustrations of China and her neighbouring countries, half of the forty were reproduced from native woodcuts done by popular artists such as Hiroshige, Hokusai and Kunisada. Oliphant was interested in showing specimens of Japanese art because of its own merit but there was a risk of conveying to his readers certain Japanese images which were drawn in traditional patterns. It was indeed left to the readers to decide whether these pictures, which had a considerable amount of distortion, as was particularly so in the case of Hokusai's work, were more or less accurate representations of the country and people, or specimens of its native art, or both. It is difficult to know how far Oliphant and his publishers were aware that they were about to risk spreading in Britain a set of fairly unrealistic images of Japan. On one occasion, Blackwood apparently did not understand Oliphant's wish to put in the book a native map of Japan, chiefly on artistic grounds. Oliphant made his point as follows:

> I return the map with the references which occur to me. I think when colored [sic] that as a specimen of Japanese Art it will be highly interesting. More on that ground than on account of references.[89]

The map did not appear in the book.

Also, there is one example in the book's structure to show the delicacy of the author and the publishers. The topic of prostitution in Japan could have been treated within one of the book's chapters which dealt with manners and customs of the people. However, both Oliphant and Blackwood decided without much hesitation to put this 'never an agreeable subject' into the final part of the book as one of the appendices.[90]

Lastly, as the fourth consideration that sheds light on the role of external factors in publishing *Narrative,* let us see briefly how the size of the print-run was decided. To put the conclusion first, the firm printed and published a total of 5267 copies, the first edition being 3150 and the second being 2117.[91] This unusually large number of copies was due partly to the fact that a number of influential reviewers had requested proof copies well in advance and the firm was encouraged to expect a good sale. Also, the initial swiftness of the sale of the first edition was impressive enough to let them venture a very large second edition.

Osborn was the first person to request a set of proofs. As early as the beginning of November 1859, he was asked by his friend John Murray to write a review of the book for the latter's periodical, the *Quarterly Review,* the editor of which was Whitwell Elwin. Blackwood was astonished at this hurried request and was rather embarrassed that the proofs for the second volume, which contained the Japanese section, were not yet ready.[92] Osborn intended to participate in the controversy about the mission by expressing his own opinion in the form of a review of Oliphant's work. Henry Reeve (1813–95), perhaps one of the most well known men of letters in Europe at the time, also requested the proofs for a review in the *Edinburgh Review.* Reeve had started his forty-year-long editorship of the review in 1855. In addition, Delane of *The Times*, the *Examiner*, and 'a man who corresponds extensively for country papers', requested the proofs in early December.[93] Such early interest caused Oliphant joy but also embarrassment as he and Blackwood knew the number of proofs was limited:

> I don't know what the etiquette in these matters is, but I have had various applications in the same direction.[94]

The publishers, much encouraged by such information, eagerly tried to publish an American edition in addition, through their agent in the United States. However, this project came to nothing, and William Blackwood wrote to Oliphant: 'I cannot help thinking the Yankee publishers are wrong.'[95]

Blackwood's confidence was not without reason. The publication ledger of *Narrative* shows that all the copies of the first edition left the publishing house within the short period from December 1859 to May 1860.[96] Judging from the correspondence between Blackwood and Oliphant, the first edition went on sale, at the latest, about Christmas 1859,[97] and by early February 1860, 2800 copies had been sold.[98] Later that month, Blackwood wrote to Oliphant: 'The first edition of your work is now about exhausted.'[99] The speed of sale was viewed as remarkable by the firm. As early as 4 January 1860, the excited William Blackwood informed the author of the firm's plan for the second edition:

> Things look so well for the immediate disposal of this first edition of your book that we are going to set the presses to work immediately with another.[100]

In the same letter, he proposed to pay Oliphant the first instalment of five hundred pounds in cash half a year earlier than its due date, and also informed him of the probability of a change to earlier dates for the remaining one thousand pounds.

So far, it has become clear that a number of factors were involved in the making of *Narrative*. This very fact also meant that, before it was published, the book was bound to be fairly readable as well as widely publicised because the author accepted or rejected numerous suggestions expressed by those concerned with its publication.

Things, however, did not remain so hopeful. In early February, Blackwood noted an ominous slow-down in the sale of the first edition. He expressed his anxiety to Oliphant: '. . . we begin to think we have been too prompt in printing the second edition'.[101] Blackwood knew that the total 1575 copies of the first edition of Osborn's *Cruise* had sold in three months in the previous year. But its second edition of about 1050 copies was not selling nearly as rapidly as had been the case earlier. In early 1860, they still had some stock in hand and it was not until July 1863 that Blackwood eventually cleared the stock.[102] The price of five shillings per copy was attractive, so one could not apply these criteria to the case of Oliphant's more voluminous *Narrative*.

In addition, it seems that Blackwoods strongly wished to make the young Oliphant one of their few highly popular authors whose regular contributions would be published solely by them. This desire was often expressed in their letters to Oliphant or to his mother.[103] The publishers' payment to Oliphant was, therefore, unusually generous, at least by their standard. This was not only in the case of *Narrative*, but also in the case of his contributions to *Blackwood's Magazine*. On one occasion, for instance, Blackwood suggested that Oliphant should send 'some very interesting papers' from Paris covering the ambitious intrigues of Napoleon III towards Italy in early 1860. One of the old principles of editing the magazine was that the editor should not make any commitment to any author before he received the latter's manuscript. Blackwood modified this principle, writing to Oliphant this way:

> . . . these [papers] I should look upon as different from your ordinary contributions and acknowledge at the rate of say £25 per sheet.[104]

This figure was extraordinary. Twenty-five pounds was then about the average payment for the majority of the contributors to the magazine for articles of twenty-odd pages. In fact, the size of the second edition of *Narrative* showed the publishers' confidence mixed with their expectation that Oliphant's work would sell 'uncommonly well'. However, this printing soon proved so hazardous a venture that Blackwood was obliged to take some desperate measures to encourage sales.

It is ironic that Blackwood should have committed himself to the kind of sensationalism which he had once despised when Cooke had encouraged Osborn to raise 'a jolly row' in the Admiralty with *Cruise*. On 23 February 1860, Blackwood urged Oliphant to write 'immediately' 'an effective preface for the second [edition]', encouraging Oliphant to put himself 'in a capital position' in his disputes about the Tientsin Treaty with Sir Michael Seymour, the Admiral of the Royal Navy at the time of Lord Elgin's expedition.[105] However, Oliphant did not respond promptly to Blackwood's idea. The Foreign Office had been considering the appointment of Oliphant to a resident secretary's post in China. Being in a dilemma between the attractions of permanent employment by the Foreign Office and the unpleasant notion of returning to China – the country where he had felt so unhappy last time, Oliphant had 'imposed high conditions' on the Foreign Office as the 'price of his services'.[106] Probably concerned with this question of Oliphant's appointment, the Foreign Secretary Lord John Russell had criticised Oliphant's lack of discretion in having revealed in his book the 'differences' that might have existed among the officers with whom he had been serving.[107] Oliphant, therefore, wished to use the chance of writing a new preface to criticise Lord Russell rather than Admiral Seymour. But Oliphant postponed for some time sending the preface to the firm. He explained:

> I am only holding back the preface because it contains reflections on that little beast Johnny, which I must omit if he appoints me permanently into the Service.[108]

It was as late as 5 March that the preface was finally despatched to Blackwood with Oliphant's note:

> I am happy to say that I am not going to China. The alternative of staying at home is by no means disagreeable.[109]

Although Admiral Seymour was not attacked in the preface, as Blackwood had wished, a more important figure, Lord Russell, was introduced to the controversy, and Blackwood's intention of creating a sensation over the book was thus realised.

In order to encourage sales of the book, Blackwood also compromised his proud refusal to publish imaginative accounts – which he had once expressed to Osborn when criticising *The Times'* correspondent's account of Japan as being 'like a vision of the Arabian Nights'. Blackwood first intended to have Osborn write a favourable review of *Narrative* in his magazine, whose circulation had steadily increased, reaching 8100 copies in April 1859.[110] But Osborn had already decided to write a review for the *Quarterly Review*. He was then very critical of the Admiralty as well as of Lord Elgin and used the chance to express his own opinion concerning British policy towards China. He even omitted mentioning the second volume. Blackwood was much depressed by reading Osborn's anonymous review which appeared in the *Quarterly Review* in January 1860. Blackwood sent to

Osborn a letter criticising *him* as well as the editor, Elwin:

> From the look of your paper in the Quarterly I guessed that you had either been writing to some degree in fetters or that your M.S. had been interfered with. The paper wants the life and spirit natural to anything you write. I suspect Mr Elwyn [*sic*] is rather a mild specimen of the human intellect.[111]

In the same letter, Blackwood mentioned that the book had been 'very handsomely reviewed' in other periodicals as it 'really deserve[d]'.[112] Among those reviews, there was a lengthy article published in *The Times* on 3 January 1860, which was by Cooke himself.[113]

Having failed to use Osborn effectively to popularise the *Narrative*, Blackwood went so far as to approach James White (1803–62), formerly the vicar of Loxley and the author of romantic stories in Scottish history, who lived a monastic life on the Isle of Wight and had little concern with the Far East. White was embarrassed at Blackwood's request. Although he agreed to send in a short time 'a notice of Oliphant's admirable book', he could not help wondering if Blackwood could make 'any other hand' work for the task.[114] Taking up his pen, however, White's 'notice' grew into a lengthy article, and he sent it to the firm on 18 January 1860. White, in his letter accompanying the article, explained that he had written a less complimentary review than the book deserved, 'considering the modesty of Maga to a contributor'.[115] Obviously, White was not aware how desperate Blackwood had been in choosing him for the task.

The letter John Blackwood sent back to White on 25 January contained some remarkable lines, which not only denied 'the modesty of Maga' but also cast away whatever preference the editor had shown for factual accuracy concerning accounts of Japan. First, Blackwood complained that White's review had come 'so late' and was 'so long' that he could not use it for the February issue of the magazine. He also suggested some general techniques for writing a 'telling' review, and added these lines:

> I should like too to have a page or two from you on the Japanese of whom I am sure you could do a capital sketch. There is a blushing & delighted first Lieutenant being helped to Coffee by one of the nymphs in the Tea Gardens which might make a good point.[116]

This was the very image of Japan that the anonymous correspondent had presented as a 'national characteristic of Japan' in *The Times* in the autumn of 1858. Blackwood, as the editor, had become so anxious for the book's success as to be easily irritated by White's 'modesty' principle:

> My friend Larry [Laurence Oliphant] will not object to any amount of butter & he deserves a good deal.[117]

White obeyed this thunderous letter and rewrote the review which was printed in the March issue of the magazine. This review is of particular importance in studying the history of British popular ideas about Japan. The point is that this article was so designed as to enforce and strengthen those popular ideas about China and Japan which were then more or less entertained by the British reading public. The designers, Blackwood and White, were conscious of the fact that they were presenting to their readers something unreal. The major characteristic of these popular images was that the Chinese and the Japanese were sharply distinguished, and that the former were described as a people in hell whereas the latter were treated like those in heaven. This characteristic had been the traditional one which had been reinforced in the early 1850s.

But White, under Blackwood's instruction, exaggerated the distinction of the two peoples to a romantic extent. For example, he described the Chinese, using references to *Gulliver's Travels*:

> But the sight of that ideal Chinaman, low-browed, broad-mouthed, twinkling-eyed, cunning, sneaking and altogether fantastical in his divergence from the ordinary workmanship even of nature's journeyman, separates him from our sympathies, and we look on him as if he were a native of Lilliput or Brobdignag.[118]

In contrast, the Japanese were highly praised for their pleasant looks and cleanliness. Oliphant's passage about a Japanese daimyo's life was mentioned as something which had 'slipt, by some chance, out of the *Arabian Nights*'.[119] On the departure of Lord Elgin's mission from Japan, White remarked: 'The fairy tale closes with the last look we get on Nagasaki'.[120]

Had John Blackwood read such accounts during the previous year, he would certainly have criticised them as 'imaginative'. But now he was the very propagator of the imaginative, rosy view of Japan and appreciated the article as 'an excellent paper'.[121] Perhaps as a result, he increased the circulation of the magazine from 8100 to 8300.[122] Blackwood wrote to Lord Elgin, emphasising the practically harmless nature of the review:

> In the following No. of our Magazine, we have a lively readable paper on the Mission which without pretending to any political character, does we hope justice to your labours.[123]

About the same time, Blackwood also wrote to Oliphant:

> It [the March issue of the magazine] contains a review of your book about as pleasant & readable a paper as one could wish to see. It made me laugh uncommonly & should do good as it is peculiarly adapted to make the reader to [sic] turn to your book with the expectation of a treat in which he will not be disappointed.[124]

It seems that in his desperate endeavour, Blackwood discovered his own way to sell *Narrative* well, that is, to stir up on the one hand a sensational argument among those who were concerned with the mission, and on the other to meet the would-be readers' desire to experience a 'treat' in a fairy-land Japan.

So the publishers retreated from their initial standard of factual accuracy for writing about Japan in the face of commercial considerations, and several reviews of *Narrative* published at the time presented more or less similar images of the Far East, with a particularly rosy view of Japan. This phenomenon needs explanation. The responsibility partly lies with *Narrative* itself. Although Oliphant intended to maintain his standard of objective writing as was noted before, he himself was conscious of his drawing a 'coloured' picture of Japan. In *Narrative*, he wrote:

> I find it difficult, in attempting to convey our first impressions of Japan, to avoid presenting a too highly coloured picture to the mind of readers. The contrast with China was so striking, the evidences of a high state of civilisation so unexpected, the circumstances of our visit were so full of novelty and interest, that we abandoned ourselves to the excitement and enthusiasm they produced. There exists not a single disagreeable association to cloud our reminiscences of that delightful country.[125]

However, it was also possible for a reviewer to pick out from *Narrative* various pieces of information which were not altogether favourable to Japan and the Japanese. But this was not the case for most of the review writers. Why? The next chapter will analyse the characteristics of the ideas of Japan presented in the reviews of the *Narrative*, and compare them with the ideas of Japan presented in other articles dealing with the country at the time, as well as before the publication of *Narrative*.

3 Britain, the Happy Suitor of a Fairyland

One of the most conspicuous ideas about Japan which dominated the reviews of Laurence Oliphant's *Narrative* was the simple one that the amiable nature of the Japanese had not changed for centuries. Henry Reeve, in his review published in the *Edinburgh Review*,[1] quoted extensively the accounts in *Narrative* which seemed to emphasise this point:

> Universal testimony assures us that in their domestic relations the men are gentle and forbearing, the women obedient and virtuous . . .[2] Upon no single occasion . . . did I ever see a child struck or otherwise maltreated . . . Kaempfer, Charlevoix and Titsingh, agree in saying that the love, obedience, and reverence manifested by children towards their parents is unbounded; while the confidence placed by parents in their children is represented to be without limit.[3]

Narrative itself, however, had provided his readers with a few reservations on this point, mentioning 'sundry weaknesses' of the Japanese such as vindictiveness, superstition or cruelty in protecting their honour.[4] But most of its reviewers were eager to emphasise as much as possible the favourable aspects of the Japanese character. Charles Russell, the then President of Maynooth College, was also intrigued by Oliphant's report about the immutably good characteristics of the people and wrote enthusiastically in his *Dublin Review* about the country, a topic with which he had not dealt for eight years. Russell was moved by Oliphant's suggestion that St Francis Xavier's description of Japanese characteristics was still valid,[5] and he quoted the saint's words: 'So far as I have been able to judge, they surpass in virtue and in probity all other nations hitherto discovered'.[6] Russell also quoted more or less the same part of *Narrative* as Reeve did:

> We left Japan thoroughly agreeing with old Kaempfer who, after a residence of many years there, thus sums up his estimate of the character of the people: 'United and peaceable, taught to give due worship to the gods, due obedience to the laws, due submission to their superiors, due love and regard to their neighbours, civil, obliging, virtuous; in art and industry excelling all other nations'.[7]

These notions of the good nature of the Japanese and of their unchangeableness had, however, as fragmented pieces of information, already been prevalent among the articles on Japan published in periodicals in the early 1850s. In the latter half of the 1850s, it seems that these points, together with various pieces of information about the manners and customs of the Japanese, had become quite commonplace components in stereotyped images of Japan. Some writers had even avoided repeating clichés about various features of the Japanese by simply mentioning relevant publications as the references.[8] However, after the publication of the extensive reports from members of Lord Elgin's Mission, particularly Oliphant's, these somewhat antique ideas were revived so freshly and strongly in the notion of 'immutable amiability' that they began to dominate almost all arguments about Japan in magazine and review articles. As already mentioned, the popular ideas in Britain of the Japanese before Perry's Expedition were often a set of contradictory features such as 'amiable but incontinent', or 'courteous but cruel'. Towards the end of the 1850s, however, within the framework of the traditional ideas about the Japanese, the attention given to the favourable features of the people expanded at the expense of the space given to the unfavourable features. For instance, Reeve, in his review of Oliphant's *Narrative* mentioned only briefly, in several lines out of a total of twenty-three pages, the previous extirpation of Christians in Japan, confining himself to such remarks as: 'We know enough of the darker side of the Japanese character'.[9]

In the early 1850s, the dominant Japanese topics in most of the articles in periodicals were the people, governmental institutions and religions of the country. However, by the end of 1860, topics such as the natural and manufactured products of Japan became the serious concern of British writers, and the space in their articles devoted to the government and religions of Japan was later contracted. Japanese products were, as will be discussed later, described in a highly favourable manner in connection with the authors' hopes for the development of Anglo-Japanese trade. Alongside the agreeable topics, there was another fresh one, for whose prevalence Sherard Osborn was particularly responsible – the beauty of Japanese scenery.

On 24 August 1858, an excursion was arranged for a dozen members of Lord Elgin's Mission. The account of the event by Osborn had a delightful tone. On a hilly suburb of Shinagawa, they passed a nobleman's grounds. Osborn felt that these gardens did 'credit for their neatness and good keeping to any park in Britain'.[10] There were also tea-houses, and Osborn had this to say about the waitresses:

> . . . we were waited upon, not by nasty fusty waiters redolent of bad cigars and bear's grease, but by brisk damsels, as modestly and quietly dressed and neat-handed as any English Susan Nipper.[11]

Oliphant appreciated the beauty of the roadside no less than Osborn:

> These charming little cottages, raising their thatched roofs amid the fruit trees and creepers which threatened to smother them in their embraces, were surrounded by flower-beds tastefully laid out, resplendent with brilliant hues, and approached by walks between carefully clipped hedges.[12]

In a small article entitled 'Far East' published in *Household Words* in 1856, Henry Morley quoted from a newly published book by an officer of the Royal Engineers, Captain Bernard Whittingham, some passages on a 'country ramble' in the neighbourhood of Hakodate:

> The ditches on each side, the flowery banks, the willows growing in the hedgerows, all reminded us of home scenery, and the thatched cottages gleaming here and there at intervals were Englishlike.[13]

Morley also noted that the scenery had reminded Whittingham of a Quebec village:

> The straight, level roads, the divisions of property, the separate yet contiguous cottages, the mild politeness of the peasantry, and their sombre grey robes, reminded me of the happy domestic scenery of Lower Canada.[14]

Thus, when John Blackwood required James White to draw a paradise-like picture of Japan in his review of Oliphant's *Narrative*, this was basically in accord with a general trend in popular ideas about Japan. White was not excessive when he called the passage in *Narrative* which had described the residence of a Japanese nobleman as something which might have 'slipt, by some chance out of *The Arabian Nights*'.[15] Obviously, the editor was right in assuming that many contemporary readers were looking for some 'uncommonly pleasant' account of an Eastern country, or even wishing to superimpose something which they wished to discover in Japan. In fact, there was already the beginning of a vague anxiety among British intellectuals that all English encounters with the East might turn out unhappily. For example, the journalist Francis Maurice Drummond-Davies (1839–1921) pointed out in the radical utilitarian *Westminster Review* in April

1860 that 'the fate of India' had 'already caused distrust of England in the East' and could not help emphasising the importance of 'uprightness and liberality' on the part of the British in their relations with Eastern countries.[16] Thus, the vision of a happy British experience in a tasteful tea-garden with 'brisk damsels' quietly dressed and neat-handed was very welcome, and it could be observed that Japan was increasingly discussed as if the country itself had been such a charming damsel.

Parallel to the reinforcement of the attractive features of Japan, the sense of Japan's affinity with Britain, or with Europe, grew among many writers. This is shown in the fact that the language used to describe Japan, such as metaphors and similes drawing on Europe or on the Bible, became more popular than in the early 1850s. For example, this is how Osborn described the children in summertime Nagasaki: 'Many of the children might have just escaped from Eden, so innocent were they of any clothing.'[17] In Nagasaki and Edo, the members of Lord Elgin's Mission were bound to witness naked citizens' evening ablutions in the open air. The Victorian Naval Officer Osborn expressed his astonishment in a reserved way:

> The manner in which the fair Eves stepped out of their baths, and ran to stare at us, holding a steaming hot and squalling babe, was a little startling.[18]

It was not only in the case of Osborn that the image of the Biblical paradise was used. Surgeon John M. Tronson's group of the Royal Navy, on their arrival at Hakodate in 1854, first of all directed their steps 'towards the Bath House', since they had heard much of that 'strange establishment'. Tronson witnessed a very primitive type of bath for families taken by men and women simultaneously. He thought it striking that 'the exhibition' was not looked upon by the Japanese as being at all 'indelicate', and his conclusion was this: 'It may be from Adam and Eve like simplicity on their part'.[19] In 1859, an anonymous contributor to the *North British Review*, the politically liberal and Christian-toned magazine which had been started in 1844, one year after the establishment of the Free Church of Scotland,[20] quoted this account by Tronson extensively in his article on 'Japan and the Japanese'.[21] Logically speaking, these Biblical descriptions might suggest that they were employed in order to emphasise the remoteness of Japanese society from that of the contemporary West, but in reality, as will be discussed further, this language was closely connected with the writers' belief that the Japanese race was of the same origin as Europeans. Street scenes in Edo made Osborn confess that much he saw in Japan carried his thoughts back to 'the feudal days' in England.[22] The quiet taste of the clothes worn by the Japanese attracted members of Lord Elgin's Mission. The climate of Japan was thought similar to that of England.[23] Russell confessed: 'The public amusements of the Japanese present some curious analogies to our own'.[24] This writer, who eight years before had never used any European metaphors to explain things Japanese, had begun to admit the existence of European counterparts such as 'Aunt Sally' and 'Mrs Jarley' for some Japanese street entertainments.[25]

What factors encouraged this growing belief in the affinity between Britain and Japan? First, the historical timing of the conclusion of the Anglo-Japanese treaty of 'Peace, Friendship and Commerce'; it was immediately after the long, irritable and violent dealings with the 'haughty' mandarins and the 'treacherous' people in China in concluding the Tientsin Treaty in 1858. Thus, when Lord Elgin's mission arrived at Nagasaki, they were just like the crew of the *Phantom Ship* in Henry Morley's *Household Words* article of 1851, who had uttered the cry: 'Surely we shall like Japan'. James White, in his review of *Narrative,* described the mission's voyage from China to Nagasaki in these words:

> Over four hundred and fifty miles of smooth sea, full of expectation, and rejoicing at their escape from Shanghai, like noisy children just let loose from school.[26]

It is striking how the descriptions of China suffered in comparison with those of Japan in most British magazines of this period, although it was commonly recognised that China was far more important for British trade than Japan.[27] A particularly cruel example was the image of an 'ideal Chinaman' presented by White, as we saw in the last chapter. He also rationalised what Britain had done in China in this way: 'We looked on China as a shop which we had the right to enter, and resented any insolence shown us'.[28]

It is true that several passages in *Narrative* presented some people in China in a favourable tone, particularly those who were living in the Su Chou district. But the favourable mood in the mission towards Japan in general was almost too strong, of which at least Oliphant and Osborn themselves were aware. Osborn recollected the time they had approached Nagasaki:

> Oh! It was a goodly sight; but we were all in the mood to be pleased;

and had the sky been less clear, the air less bracing and the climate as bad as that of China, we should assuredly still have admired it.[29]

As regards magazine writers, most of them seem to have readily been in a mood to be pleased when the news of Lord Elgin's success in Japan reached Britain. There is one example which makes an enormous contrast with White's dealings with China: as early as December 1858, a short article on Japan appeared in *Fraser's Magazine,* a literary miscellany with an emphasis on politics, religion and social conditions.[30] The article was published above the initials of Mark Prager Lindo (1819–77), an English humorist who lived in Holland. In his article, Lindo mainly intended to inform British traders of Japan's potential as a new market, and seriously proposed four requisites which were remarkable if compared with contemporary European attitudes towards Asia in general: first, to appear before the Japanese with some military rank, wielding a sword, since the Japanese would respect military men but not merchants; second, to possess an intimate knowledge of the Dutch language in order to communicate freely with the Japanese intellectuals, many of whom, Lindo mistakenly thought, knew Dutch; third, to show 'the greatest urbanity and courteousness'; and last, to furnish themselves with 'a good stock of general knowledge on all subjects'.[31]

Certainly, interconnected with this historical timing, was another factor which encouraged the British belief in their affinity with the Japanese. That is the reinforcement of Kaempfer's theory about the origin of the Japanese race. As was already mentioned, Kaempfer had written that the Japanese were descended originally from the lost people of Babylon. Towards the late 1850s, this idea of the Semitic origin of the Japanese became much in vogue especially among popular magazines.[32] In June 1857, William Aytoun contributed to *Blackwood's Magazine* an article based on a report by Lieutenant A. W. Habersham[33] of Perry's Expedition. Aytoun was much impressed by the fact that 'the notions of the Japanese with regard to money matters and traffic were singularly acute', and confessed:

> Surely Japan must have been originally peopled from the lost tribes of Israel, for no other race could have devised a scheme so eminently subtle and successful.[34]

The information that the Japanese behaved like Jewish people enabled Aytoun to connect them with the Judaic-Christian background of European civilisation. Osborn also was much impressed by the

Japanese authorities' elaborate device for taxing the foreign currency exchange at Nagasaki. On a broader observation than Aytoun's, Osborn confessed:

> It was impossible not to recognise in their colour, features, dress and customs, the Semitic stock whence they must have sprung.[35]

For the anonymous contributor to the above-mentioned article of the *North British Review,* the belief that the Japanese and the British had originated from a common source was a matter of serious concern. It meant for him that he could cherish the great hope that Christianity would one day be smoothly reintroduced into Japan.[36]

Encouraged by such a belief, British writers' attacks upon China and the Chinese were to become distinctly emotional. Aytoun described the Chinese, in contrast to the friendly Japanese, as 'dogmatic' people who had an 'obstinate antipathy to strangers'.[37] Osborn used such expressions as 'foul and fusty China', 'the piratical Cantonese'[38] or 'strong-smelling China and its unpoetical inhabitants'.[39] White summed up the image of the Commissioner Yeh as 'the incarnation of Chinese insolence and stubborn pride' or as a 'barbarian' who was 'brutally ignorant and blindly obstinate'.[40] The anonymous contributor to the *North British Review,* in his review of the works by Tronson, Osborn, and Oliphant, used such adjectives for the Chinese as 'stolid' and 'cunning and carnal', in contrast to the Japanese ready susceptibility to European ideas and development.[41] Reeve used such general adjectives as 'crafty and sagacious' for the Chinese.[42] On balance, White's description of an 'ideal Chinaman' was not even a strong expression of the generally bad image of the Chinese in contemporary British periodicals.

Many of the favourable conclusions which British diplomats and naval officers drew about Japan were, however, based on misreadings of the phenomena they saw. For example, the prevalence of subdued colours in Japanese clothing was less the result of refined characteristics than of the elaborate sumptuary laws and decrees repeatedly issued by the authorities for almost two centuries. Dark blue and brown were almost the only colours allowed to peasants for everyday clothing, while the only pattern they could use was a fine stripe. The samurai was also discouraged from wearing any large-patterned, brightly-coloured clothes except on ceremonial occasions. From the mid-eighteenth century, sumptuary decrees became more detailed as a reaction to the tendency of increased consumption by the merchant class and rich farmers. Besides the regulations of colour, pattern, shape and quality of the clothes, these decrees governed even sashes, linings and underwear. Food habits were similarly regulated; there were edicts prescribing the number of courses and the number of bottles of sake to be consumed, as well as the admissible qualities of tableware on a given occasion. As far as housing was concerned, not only the appropriate building materials, but also the question of who was to be permitted a gate and a porch, sliding doors, warehouses, even roof-tiles – all this was subject to official decree.[43] Particularly, in the early 1840s the Tokugawa government issued a series of the most restrictive and effective sumptuary decrees to cope with the financial crisis of most of the daimyo-domains after the famine of the 1830s: the so-called 'Tempô Kaikaku' (Tempô-Reforms). To use things highly ornamented with gold and silver had become almost taboo, particularly in the daily life of the inhabitants in Edo before the country was opened to Western powers. The quiet but refined taste of many Japanese people's lives, shown in the streets and in villages and which attracted the eye of the visitors was, therefore, the result of the interactions between the people's desire for luxury and the authorities' admonitions which had been repeated for generations.[44]

Thus, this feature of Japanese life, which British writers appreciated as close to their own taste, might have been a testimony to the Shogun's successful rule, but could not be attributed to the nature of the Japanese. In fact, in the mid-Tokugawa period, numerous records had been written about the gaudy clothes of city inhabitants. For example, a Korean scholar Shin Yoo Han, who accompanied the Korean Mission to Japan as the literary attaché in 1719, noted the glittering attire and ornaments of well-to-do citizens in Osaka, Kyoto, Nagoya, Edo, and even in small castle-towns. Because people were certainly better clad than usual on this festive occasion, eager to look at the foreigners' procession, Shin was mistaken in describing the Japanese as luxury-loving and sensual.[45] Osborn knew, however, probably through the reports of Perry's Expedition, of the existence of the sumptuary laws, and even mentioned them briefly in his *Cruise*. But it is natural that he was not able to judge how strict the regulations were and to what extent the colours worn by people were the expression of their own taste. 'The women,' concluded Osborn, 'very properly are allowed, and of course avail themselves of the privilege, to wear brighter dresses. Yet their taste was so good that loud and noisy colours were generally eschewed.'[46] For most reviewers of *Cruise*, only the point that the Japanese had good taste in clothing seems to have been important and the existence of sumptuary laws was not mentioned in their articles.

Similarly, the fact that British visitors saw very few beggars in the streets was the result of the common regulations of the Tokugawa era that applied whenever daimyo and important officials such as the Tokugawa Inspectors, Junkenshi, proceeded on tour. Usually a few days beforehand, all beggars were ordered to hide, and women and children were required not to go out to the streets on the days when these processions passed. Villagers in the area were ordered to clean the road.[47] On the occasion of Lord Elgin's landing at Edo, however, the decree issued by the city authorities, Machi Bugyô, contained the words *'Kitto Naku* (not so rigidly)'. Therefore, the regulations then were not so strict as had been the case when Commodore Perry had visited. Citizens were allowed to walk out as usual so long as they did not cause any traffic problems. Merchants were allowed to open their shops and sell their goods as usual.[48] But to enjoy looking at the Mission from any highly elevated spot or stage was prohibited. The people living alongside the street where the Mission was to pass were not ordered to repair their houses but just to clean the street so that it would not look *migurushi* (unseemly). To 'clean the street', of course, meant that any beggar was not allowed to wander about. With an additional order to take 'special' care not to cause any fire, the decree was conveyed to all the inhabitants in the commoners' area of Edo, ranging from landlords, house tenants and shop tenants to servants living in back streets.

According to Oliphant, on the day of the Mission's landing, the wooden gates set about every two hundred yards in the principal street were shut behind the procession after it passed to stop the crowds following, and this measure was very effective,[49] although it had not been ordered by the decree mentioned above. In the case of the mission's excursions to the countryside and Asakusa, the East End of Edo, the special decrees issued beforehand were stricter than the general one. In particular, some blocks near Asakusa were specifically ordered to close the street gates if necessary, in order to prevent people from rushing to see the excursion party.[50] Therefore, the British Mission of 1858 observed only one face of Japan. Osborn was well deceived. He concluded that he had seen during an excursion of twenty-two miles 'at least 80,000 Japanese, the majority of them men' and that 'only two beggars' had been seen in that ride. He dismissed his original suspicion: 'we can hardly believe that the paupers were put out of sight during the stay of the English'.[51]

In contrast to the revival of Xavier, Adams and Kaempfer, an increasingly cynical, sophisticated criticism of newly-published travel books developed towards the end of the 1850s. In fact, the discovery of Japan by the British expeditions unexpectedly revealed not a *terra incognita,* but the same 'unchanged' country which had been reported to Europe centuries before. The anonymous author in the *North British Review* frankly complained about the small contribution to his knowledge made by those recent reports:

> Neither Mr Osborn's able and dashing sketches, nor Mr Tronson's fact-full work, admits us to much with which we were not already acquainted in the pages of Engelbert Koempfer [sic].[52]

The writer emphasised the contemporary popularity of old travel books:

> How seldom do the lovers of travel-talk return to recent books for amusement and information! How often such pages as those of Koempfer [sic] have been lovingly perused by the same eyes, and lingered over with an affection like that which we cherish for dear old friends![53]

This comment reveals two concerns of the writer: on the one hand he wanted new knowledge from recent travel books on Japan; on the other, he desired a pleasant amusement from Japanese accounts. Judging from his tone, the latter mattered to him no less than the former.

It appears that another element of mistrust and distaste for recent travel books also became prevalent in the late 1850s. Aytoun, being a professor of rhetoric and *belles lettres,* in 1857 generally criticised the lack of charm among recent travel books. He attributed this phenomenon to the invasion of science in the field of the travelogue:

> Modern books of voyage . . . want picturesqueness, they want poetry, and they are intolerably scientific.[54]

In these books, plants and animals were not sketched as they appeared to the outward eye, but were 'catalogued in preposterous Latin'. He also attacked all the scientific measurements 'which possibly might interest a small minority of the members of a Royal Society'. There had been, in fact, an increasing zeal for this type of precision among British intellectuals since the mid-nineteenth century. For Aytoun, it was indeed lamentable that numerous 'ologies' should be rapidly 'annihilating' the descriptive power of the English language.[55] However, he was also mistrustful about the descriptive parts of the report by Lieutenant Habersham:

> In fact, we make it a regular rule never to believe more than one-fourth of the narrative of any individual who recounts feats which he has performed beyond the ken of credible witnesses.[56]

Behind these critical remarks, we might see the influence of the development of steam navigation upon travel literature around the middle of the nineteenth century. Certainly, the steam engine had been gradually making ocean travel a common affair, and long journeys away from Europe were becoming private undertakings rather than pioneering ventures backed by the support and expectation of the general public. As travel books became commonplace it is not surprising that some of the reading public tended to show little enthusiasm about new information from recent travellers. The cultural milieu in which those writers tried to cherish the unchanged images of Japan was in this sense favourable for them.

After all, Oliphant, Osborn and others, in their short stays in Japan, saw and described what they knew already from their reading, with much assistance from the Japanese authorities eager to show the country to best advantage. The reviewers of their accounts, on the other hand, were bound to be much impressed when already familiar ideas about Japan were repeated in these recent reports, and they were therefore inclined to exaggerate these points for their readers, using the familiar stock labels. Thus, the image of 'an immutable, amiable nation', owing its establishment to historical factors, seems to have started acting as a barrier, preventing the circulation of unfamiliar information, seemingly inconsistent with the accepted features of Japan. The gradual decline of the initial interest in factual accuracy about Japan on the part of the publishing house, W. Blackwood and Sons, which was noted in the previous chapter, could thus be interpreted as part of a growing tendency in the Victorian attitude towards Japan.

One psychological effect of the establishment of such rosy images of Japan was that the British magazine writers became inclined to confine their interest to uncovering the more attractive aspects of Japan, and subsequently developed a more elaborate categorisation of these aspects. They began to spend much space in their writings, elaborating the characteristics of particularly refined aspects of Japanese culture. Thus, images of a fairly sophisticated country were bound to emerge. A most conspicuous example was their dealings with Japanese women. So far as British visitors' reports from this period are concerned, they contained quite a few unfavourable comments on Japanese married women's faces, thickly coated with powder, their eyebrows plucked and their teeth artificially blackened.[57] However, writers in British periodicals not only discussed eagerly the original facial beauty of Japanese women, but showed great interest in conveying a sense of their elegance and grace.

The anonymous author of the article in the *North British Review* quoted extensively from Tronson's description[58] of two young Japanese ladies met with at a tea-party in 'a pretty summer house' in Hakodate:

> ... their skins clear and white as that of a Circassian, with a healthy blush on their cheeks ... finely arched brows, over bright black eyes, which grew brighter when the owners became animated, and were shadowed by long curling eyelashes.[59]

He went on quoting from Tronson's remarks on their small and well-shaped noses and lips, 'even rows of teeth of pearly lustre', and 'jet black hair' fastened 'in a knot on the top of the head, by a fillet of pale pink silk'. Tronson had been particularly impressed by the 'gracefulness' in every movement of the elder of the two. The contributor to the *North British Review* also reproduced Tronson's minute description of the taste in clothes of the women. For instance:

> ... the married ladies were attired in robes of a fabric resembling cashmere, and of a sombre lavender colour.

It is interesting that at this meeting both Englishmen and Japanese seem to have been trying to find out as many details as possible about each other's tastes. The Japanese in the party joyfully 'examined minutely' the uniforms worn by Tronson's party.[60] Certainly, Tronson had been able to share the Japanese pleasure party's concerns, and the author in the *North British Review*, besides his business of discussing the possibility of introducing Christianity to Japan, also shared Tronson's enjoyment.

Writers for British periodicals seem to have developed a strong sensitivity to anything refined which visitors encountered in Japan. Japanese 'delicate' and 'highly finished' handicrafts,[61] as well as small gardens of 'good-taste' and 'just proportion'[62] were much appreciated. Even F.M. Drummond-Davies, a most sober writer about Japan, could not help admitting in his article in the *Westminster Review* that the Japanese had 'few equals' in 'individual ingenuity – for instance, in carving of ivory and the working of wood', although he was eager to emphasise the European superiority to Japan in 'extensive and useful branches of industry'.[63] Probably Osborn's case illustrates the dominant trend towards appreciating the arts and crafts of Japan at that time. He was not satisfied with describing what he had seen himself, and allowed his imagination to dwell upon more sophisticated Japanese gardens, judging that the good one he had seen must have been still only 'a very inferior specimen of the art of the Japanese gardener'.⁶⁴

By praising, for example, such qualities as 'ingenuity' or 'good taste', these British writers revealed the principles which dictated their choice and definition of the qualities in question. The words, 'grace' and 'gentleness' were used conspicuously not only to describe Japanese ladies, but even the peasants. Morley quoted from Whittingham's account of Hakodate long passages about the 'rosy-cheeked, fat and civil' peasants, one of whom Whittingham had called 'a disciple of the gentle art'.⁶⁵ 'Delicate', 'elaborate', 'perfect', 'consummate' were the terms favoured by those writers whenever they mentioned the sophistication of Japanese craftsmanship, particularly in their metalwork and lacquering. Even subtler definitions were used in judging the personal qualities of high Japanese officials with whom the British visitors had close encounters. Reeve remarked that 'the ministers of Japan, acting under the most singular political constitution that exists in the world . . . showed themselves to be men of a high sense of personal dignity'. Reeve cited the reasons for this judgement:

> . . . they resorted to none of those puerile equivocations and artifices which are common to most of the Asiatics, and preeminent among the Chinese; their administration is singularly free from corruption; their great ingenuity and acuteness are not applied, as in China, to surround themselves with an imaginary halo of unapproachable superiority, but on the contrary, to penetrate with singular rapidity the intentions and habits of the foreigners with whom they were thus suddenly brought into contact.⁶⁶

Morley extensively quoted Whittingham's high praise of the Governor of Hakodate, who had made 'most pertinent inquiries concerning every object' that had struck him at the time of his inspection of the British man-of-war:

> There was a calm dignity and good-breeding in his method of eliciting information which was really admirable.⁶⁷

Morley called this person 'an enlightened governor' and, following Whittingham, emphasized that he was 'said to be the blood of the Ziogoon [Shogun]'.⁶⁸

The three Commissioners who negotiated the treaty with Lord Elgin were, according to Osborn, 'men of very superior ability and attainment'. In particular, the Third Commissioner Iwase was most remarkable to the British officers. Oliphant recalled Iwase in his *Narrative* as 'the most agreeable and intelligent person' he had met in Japan.[69] The lines from *Narrative,* which Reeve quoted, pointed out a variety of Japanese traits in the Commissioners; their 'great acumen in the discussion of points in detail' and 'the perpetual laughter' in which they had indulged. Thus, according to Reeve, the Japanese had a motto of *seria ludo,* that is, to 'laugh over serious things, instead of making laughable things very serious'.[70] He reproduced Oliphant's account of the negotiations in detail, observing that the proceedings were 'amusing' and increased his 'liking for this people'. Reeve interpreted the Japanese Commissioners' 'courtesy', 'self command' and 'good temper' not merely as their 'consummate address', which was shown just on that occasion, but as their 'good breeding'.[71]

These categorisations, expressed mostly in the form of adjectives when appreciating the cultured Japanese, were, in fact, relative notions and were, therefore, necessarily balanced by things that would fulfil their logical counterparts. This symmetrical arrangement of categories, as a whole, constituted a hierarchical system of meaning by which anything coming from the newly-opened country was pigeonholed. Morley, for example, classified the 'restrictive' officials of Nagasaki as belonging to the Japan of 'incivility and ill blood' in order to set a standard to appreciate the 'liberal' Hakodate officials.[72] However, as has been shown already, the logical counterbalance was very often provided from their stock of various unfavourable ideas about China and the Chinese, leaving Japan unblotted. It may appear that there was an arbitrarily wide range in the variety of British writers' standards for distinguishing and classifying certain things Japanese as 'good'. However, about the late 1850s and the early 1860s, the range was in fact not so great. The terms used for appreciating the Japanese were in fact those household words used among the upper classes in Britain in perceiving each other. Parallel to this phenomenon, the word 'singular' which had been so conspicuously used in the early 1850s as the adjective which was applied to the Japanese in general, became less common in such a sweeping context. It seems that the word 'singular' narrowly survived this period, occupying only marginal positions in some writings about the country, such as Reeve's usages quoted above: 'their administration is *singularly* free from corruption', or '. . . to penetrate with *singular* rapidity the intentions and habits of the foreigners'.[73]

Strong feelings of the Japanese affinity with British upper-class society encouraged the emergence of key terms which provided authors with a standard of judgement. Perhaps, the word 'civilisation' was one of the most fundamental concepts. Since the success of Lord Elgin's Mission, the word 'civilisation' was frequently used in connection with Japan, often with a strong overtone to suggest the 'civility' of the inhabitants.

Of course, at the time, a new notion of 'civilisation' was prevalent, particularly among the liberal or progressive thinkers in Britain. They tended to see various forms of civilisation as following a unilinear course of evolution of human history with an emphasis on material wealth, individual liberty, and rational organisation of the society. We have seen an example of this trend in Alexander Knox's argument about Japanese 'civilisation' in the *Edinburgh Review* of October 1852. So far as the early 1860s is concerned, a similar but increasingly elaborate type of argument on civilisation was presented concerning Japanese 'progress'. Drummond-Davies was the writer who then tried an ambitious general description of Japanese civilisation. Depending partly on the old sources, Kaempfer, Charlevoix and Thomas Rundall's compilation of the sixteenth- and seventeenth-century British navigators' reports,[74] and partly on new reports by Francis Lister Hawks,[75] Tronson, and Oliphant, he forecast 'a bright future for the Empire of Japan'.[76] For this judgement, he thought it important 'to take into consideration those various external agents of soil, climate, and the general aspects of nature', 'together with the peculiarity of Race'.[77] For him, it was important for any civilisation that its members had rational intelligence enough to overcome any superstition, and that its society had enough flexibility to improve the position of women and the condition of slaves.[78] These points constituted Drummond-Davies' argument about the 'progressive' Japanese civilisation, in addition to the more current topics such as government, agriculture, industry and art.[79]

However, apart from this kind of sophisticated argument about civilisation, most of the British writers who dealt with Japan used the word 'civilisation' in less theoretical ways. For example, when Osborn and his party were approaching the landing place in Edo, many well-to-do citizens came out in boats to see the foreigners. Among them, Osborn saw a lady sitting 'in the most matronly manner' and pointing out to her daughter what she deemed 'most worthy of notice' among Osborn's crew. Her expression of curiosity without any tinge of fear towards 'the genus Man', observed Osborn, was never 'unladylike'. He considered that her gentle air 'betokens even a better state of civilisation than we had been led to expect by what we witnessed at Nangasaki [*sic*]'.[80] The 'civil' aspect of the inhabitants seems to have been the most essential point whenever Osborn considered the quality of Japanese civilisation, and this view was commonly shared by Oliphant and most of the contemporary British writers who were interested in Japan.

The discovery of a sophisticated 'civilisation' in Japan seems to have had a certain impact on the minds of British visitors to the country as well as on the reviewers of their reports. Their repeated descriptions of a 'civilised' Japan, based on their own idea of 'civilisation', were bound to make them more conscious of their own country, Great Britain. They could possibly criticise Britain and the British, making certain notions of Japan their standard of judgement, but it seems the happy suitors of Japan could not be sufficiently cynical to do that at the time. In fact, many writers started emphasising the better features of Britain itself, as if to make it a more suitable counterpart for the 'Japan' of their perceptions. For instance, the contributors to British popular periodicals on the topic of Japan were nonetheless preoccupied by notions such as 'dignity', 'civility' and 'politeness' when they described the attitudes of the English negotiators faced with Japanese officials.[81] It is even possible to note that, among British writers, there was a feeling of competition with the Japanese in manners. This may have been a natural phenomenon since, with their belief in the affinity between the two nations, they wished to find out and emphasise the favourable aspects of both the Japanese and the British. Thus, one might say that, consciously or not, British writers were facing and competing with a mirror image which was an idealised self-image.

It seems that British writers' creation of such romantic images of Britain and Japan was furthered by their knowledge that the Japanese were extremely sensitive to British attitudes to Japan. Oliphant touched on this point in his lecture before the British Association for the Advancement of Science held in Aberdeen in September 1859: '. . . of all nations in the East the Japanese are most susceptible to civilizing influences'.[82] His argument was based on his observation of many sensitive and shrewd responses shown by the Japanese to whatever they had thought better than their own. Oliphant noted in his *Narrative* that their thirst for knowledge was backed by their anxiety lest they be criticised by foreigners: 'They are extremely sensitive at being supposed incapable of acquiring any branch of knowledge which is possessed by others'.[83] This mentality was, in fact, their traditional attitude to strangers which was interconnected with the sense of pride and shame commonly shared by the samurai and most well-to-do commoners in the country.[84] According to Osborn, 'two facts' should be remembered in Christendom. One was that the Japanese knew what foreigners had said about them, and the other was that they were 'very sensitive under criticism'.[85] Thus, British writers thought that due respect and good manners shown to the Japanese by the British would be well reciprocated. It is not surprising, therefore, that some writers like Mark Lindo should have urged on British visitors to Japan the importance of the 'greatest urbanity' for maintaining the initial happy encounter with Japan.

Besides this sort of sensitivity, most of the Japanese in those days, including the commoners, shared with one another an extreme class-consciousness. This had become particularly so since the early 1840s, when the Tempô Reforms, the last large-scale effort to reinforce the moralistic régime of the Shogunate, were inaugurated. In 1841, the Chief Councillor Mizuno Tadakuni began issuing a series of orders to restore strict segregation among social classes. Because of the traditional idea of ranking Kabuki actors at the bottom of society, theatres in Edo were ordered to move to the segregated theatre district in Asakusa. In 1842, the population which had flowed into Edo since the late eighteenth century to constitute an unstable lower class of *mushuku* (literally, people without sleeping places) was forced to return to the countryside. Increasing social mobility made both the rulers and the common people fairly class-conscious. Since the early eighteenth century, it had been in vogue among the well-to-do commoners to adopt certain aspects of samurai culture and behaviour. Claiming samurai descent was also popular among them. Mizuno tried to prevent mingling between social strata and, to cite an example, banned commoners from attending fencing schools.[86]

Osborn was astonished at a set of detailed questions put to Lord Elgin's Mission by Japanese officers when the mission arrived at Nagasaki. They wanted to know as precisely as possible the ranks, titles, and offices of 'everybody' on board. Osborn wrote:

> Indeed, a Russian customhouse agent, or a British census paper, could not have put more astounding questions, whether in number or nature, than did these Nagasaki reporters.[87]

According to Reeve, 'one of the causes of Lord Elgin's success among them, was that they acknowledged in him a rank equal to their own'.[88]

When asked in Japan, Lord Elgin was led to explain his rank, according to the Japanese notion of hierarchy, as a hereditary prince, that is, a daimyo. Reeve therefore argued how proper it was that Rutherford Alcock should have been promoted by the Foreign Secretary, Lord John Russell, from a Consul-General to the rank of Minister Plenipotentiary, since the Japanese had been shrewd enough to regard Consul Alcock as a mere trading agent.[89]

However, the image of the class-conscious Japanese may have been, to a large extent, a mirror image conceived and enhanced by British writers who shared these attitudes. Without knowing how the classes worked in Japan, writers tended to emphasise this particular idea about the Japanese, and they reiterated it, basing their views on their own experience of a class society. This point, besides the fact that the Japanese were in their own way very class-conscious in those days, may explain, for instance, Lindo's advice to future British visitors to Japan to assume some military rank.

However, sudden contacts between different nations at the time also tended to make them conscious of their own traditional ideas of classes. Japanese and British, meeting each other, looked for correspondences between the social hierarchies of both countries, and the personal relationship between an Englishman and a Japanese was based on estimates, on each side, of the other's social importance at home. In 1849, about a decade before Lord Elgin's arrival in Japan, HMS *Mariner* approached the town of Uraga at the entrance to the Bay of Edo. Some subordinates of the Governor of Uraga visited the ship in order to persuade the British to leave Japanese waters. Commander Charles Mitchell Mathison, having learned that the officers were only minor figures, treated them with disdain. After this experience, Egawa Tarozaemon, the Governor of Nirayama, visited the commander when the ship started surveying the Shimoda Bay which was within Egawa's jurisdiction. He introduced himself to the commander as the ruler of 150,000 people. For his visit, the governor changed his usual costume drastically, and wore gilt robes and bore swords decorated with gold. A remarkable change occurred in the commander's attitude. According to Katsu Kaishû's *Rikugun rekishi* (History of the Japanese Army), 'his [Mathison's] courtesy in receiving the guest and in bidding him farewell was very great, and his civility was so true as to offer the best seat for the visitor'.[90] Mathison, in his report to Captain Edward Norwich Troubridge of HMS *Amazon* about his survey of the bay, explained: 'the mandarins [the subordinates of the Magistrate of Uraga] appear of an inferior class'. As to Egawa, Mathison wrote: 'He was evidently a man of rank, from the respect shown to him by his followers'.[91] For the commander, the ranks of Japanese officers mattered greatly, and the Japanese availed themselves of information about the commander's concern. As in this case, meetings between the two nations often stimulated traditional attitudes of deference to the higher on both sides, and this phenomenon led each party to assume unusually haughty attitudes. Therefore, mutual images which were formed by British visitors and the Japanese, particularly those concerning the other's class-consciousness, were based on subjective considerations and tended to distort actual social conditions. But it was an undeniable fact that British visitors as well as writers at home were highly conscious of the Japanese sensitivity to class differences.

There were some other concepts of Japanese sensitivity that also complicated the British attitudes towards the Japanese. One was the image of a nation of taste, a nation so sensitive as to notice and appreciate whatever was most refined. Many Western travellers to Japan from this period onward reported having their clothing examined minutely for quality by many common people; these reports do not appear to have been exaggerated, because a good many diaries by Japanese common people from that period have survived in which one can find their opinions about Western visitors' taste. One of the earliest examples is a diary by Kojima Matajirô, merchant of Hakodate, who held the office of head of one of the city's blocks. In 1854, when Commodore Perry's crew landed there, Kojima estimated the quality of clothes worn by various American officers, discussed whether their buttons and epaulettes were genuine gold, examined their manners in the street, and judged each individual's taste in souvenirs. Evaluating them by the standards that applied to Japanese samurai, Kojima concluded disdainfully that some of the American naval officers were of inferior calibre.[92] The idea that the Japanese were, as a whole, connoisseurs, certainly made British visitors and writers conscious of their own tastes, manners, and customs. British writers even came to describe themselves from an imagined Japanese point of view, such as the Englishmen and officers in 'gayest' attire,[93] or the 'wild' English custom of drinking toasts.[94]

Another image of Japanese sensitivity concerned their speed in imitating whatever they considered to be superior. Lord Elgin's staff were amazed by the Japanese Comissioners' readiness to use Western cutlery at table.⁹⁵ White commented that 'they entered into our habits with utmost felicity, and behaved with a politeness worthy of Mayfair'.⁹⁶ Reeve expressed his feeling of astonishment at the 'extreme aptitude in applying all they have learned of European arts from the Dutch factory' and he enumerated many modern examples of native manufacture, including 'a very neat steamer'.⁹⁷

British intellectuals were facing a most troublesome problem – how to deal with the apparent hypersensitivity of the Japanese. Suppose British visitors assumed refined airs of superiority in front of the Japanese; immediately the latter would copy and reflect the former, which would then, in turn, encourage the British to be more and more 'civilised'. On the contrary, suppose British visitors behaved badly, then what would happen in Japan? Some of the British writers seem to have shared a certain anxiety: the anxiety of facing a distorting mirror in which either a better or worse self-image would appear in an exaggerated form. Lindo's rather unusual recommendations of delicate attitudes to be adopted when in Japan might have been the product of this sort of anxiety. In the end, this anxiety proved correct. Charles Russell, in an article based on a report on Japan presented by the Foreign Office to the Houses of Parliament as early as 1860,⁹⁸ pointed out with anger what was going on in Japan:

> Conflicts of a highly irritating character have taken place, provoked . . . by . . . the avarice, profligacy, arrogance and licentiousness of the European settlers!⁹⁹

Since the autumn of 1859, *The Times* had been publishing disturbing news about clashes in Yokohama between adventurous European merchants and Japanese samurai.¹⁰⁰ In the early 1860s, the conflicts became more frequent and serious.

It was in 1861 that Oliphant returned to Japan. His *Narrative* had brought him an official appointment as First Secretary of the British Legation at Edo in January 1861.¹⁰¹ Lord John Russell, who had once been hated by Oliphant, wrote the Queen a letter of recommendation for Oliphant, mentioning that his 'account of Japan, when serving with Lord Elgin, [was] given with much ability'.¹⁰² John Blackwood congratulated Oliphant on his appointment and wrote to him with much expectation:

> It puts your foot on the ladder and Japan may prove a great field. Certainly you will find materials for writing and I hope to see you

turn out a valuable work on that extraordinary country.[103]

Oliphant arrived in Edo towards the end of June 1861, but hardly a week passed before the sensational Tôzenji Incident occurred. During the night a band of *rônin* (masterless samurai), most of whom had belonged to Mito-*han* (Lord of Mito's domain), attacked the British Legation. Oliphant was seriously wounded in the hand, and was moved to a British man-of-war. He was eventually given a special mission to Tsushima and Korea, and returned to Britain within the year. Ten years of courting the Eastern fairyland on the part of the British were about to close with disillusionment and agony on both sides.

There was also a small problem for the publisher Blackwood. The second edition of Oliphant's *Narrative* was not selling as briskly as had been hoped. It was in May 1860 that the firm published the 2117 copies of the second edition. In April 1861, they still had 1800 copies on their hands.[104] In a letter of early 1861, Blackwood complained about the sale:

> The first edition went off at once and knowing as we did that the book was a good one and would be well received, we were justified in printing a large second edition, but as the devil would have it, the sale stuck after hardly breaking bulk upon it.[105]

The slowdown of sales of the first edition which Blackwood had noted as early as February 1860 proved to be a really bad omen,[106] yet in July 1860, William Blackwood had expected that the work would be 'a standard book about China and Japan for a long time' and that it would always 'be selling a few'.[107] However, the observations about Japan in *Narrative* gradually proved to have been too romantic. A new 'standard book' was about to appear which would be published within a few years by Sir Rutherford Alcock and a new stage in the history of British perceptions of Japan was about to open.

4 Britain, the Suitor Disillusioned

Early in 1861, Sir Rutherford Alcock (1809–97), who had been in the British consular service in China for about fifteen years, and from 1859 Her Majesty's Representative in Japan, called for the need for a new type of realism in writing about Japan:

> Some such true impressions of photographic accuracy are becoming more than ever needful in the plethora of new compilations, and the dearth of new authentic matter to fill them with.[1]

'Photographic accuracy' was the notion which preoccupied Alcock whenever he tried to describe Japan and her inhabitants. His emphasis on the importance of such realism was indicative of a definite change in the approach to Japan inspired by recent developments in photography. The essence of photography could be said to be fidelity and precision, although one should also take into account the arbitrariness of the photographer in choosing his subjects and the photochemical bias in the sensitivity of the wet-plate.[2] Photography was neutral, in the sense that any image which might be focused on the plate was reproduced faithfully regardless of its cultural connotations. During the 1850s, photography had been growing past the experimental stage. Particularly in the late 1850s and 1860s, stereoscopic photography became so popular as to bring photography into almost every drawing-room. Various photographic subjects, foreign views in particular, opened up a new world to the Victorians.[3] It seems that Alcock, in his effort to present to his readers 'new points of view' towards Japan was strongly impressed by this new technology. He aimed for:

> ... something of a stereoscopic view, in which some of the leading features of people and landscape may pass in rapid review, showing how the former dress and work, live and trade, fight and revel, being very much given to both the last, it seems; how their streets and houses change their character with the quarter, and Yeddo puts on a new physiognomy twenty times a day, according to the hour and the direction in which the traveller wanders.[4]

Within three or four years of the opening of the treaty ports of Kanagawa (Yokohama), Nagasaki and Hakodate in May 1859, it was said that there was a British community numbering some three hundred persons in these ports of Japan.[5] Certainly, British visitors to Japan and the publications of their accounts of the country increased. In April 1862, Laurence Oliphant wrote in *Blackwood's Magazine*: 'Since Lord Elgin's visit to Yeddo, we have had a fair sprinkling of works on Japan,' which were, according to Oliphant, 'monotonous' and 'almost identical' reproductions of the earlier visitors' accounts of those already familiar subjects such as the two emperors, pretty countryside, attractive teahouses, advanced art and sciences, or the custom among married women of blackening their teeth and plucking their eyebrows.[6] It was natural that people who had experienced a long stay in Japan tended to be irritated by these publications. On the other hand, the word 'resident' seems to have given a magical tinge of authenticity whenever it was used to qualify the reporter. In February 1863, Alcock used the title *The Capital of the Tycoon: A Narrative of a Three Years' Residence in Japan*;[7] in 1861, Christopher Pemberton Hodgson, British Consul for Nagasaki and Hakodate, had published a narrative entitled in a similar fashion: *A Residence at Nagasaki and Hakodate in 1859–1860*. Another example emphasising the author's long-term experience in the area is the work by Major Edward Barrington de Fonblanque of the British Army: *Niphon and Pe-che-li; or, Two Years in Japan and Northern China*, which was published in 1862. On the other hand, short-term visitors were well aware of the possible inaccuracies of their observations of Japan and fairly defensive against criticisms by resident writers. For example, George Smith, Bishop of Victoria, Hong Kong, published a book of his visit to Japan under the humble title of *Ten Weeks in Japan*.

As for Oliphant himself, in spite of John Blackwood's expectation that Oliphant would soon become one of the leading resident writers on Japan,[8] the attack on the Edo Legation made the dream impossible, and subsequently led this talented young man to enter an eccentric life of mysticism. The early 1860s marked the climax of the anti-foreign movements led by samurai and commoners who were under the influence of the chauvinistic interpretation of Japanese history known as Mitogaku, a variety of Confucian learning which had developed in the Mito domain. Acts such as assassinating foreigners, firing on foreign vessels, or setting fire to foreigners' houses eventually led to the bombardment of Kagoshima by the Royal Navy in 1863, and of Shimonoseki by a squadron of ships from Britain, the United States, France, and Holland in 1864. These two towns were, together with Kyoto, the chief nests of the fanatic loyalists of the time. The price of goods in Japan was disturbed by foreign trade, and this became an issue of intense concern, particularly among the people of Edo and surrounding provinces.[9] Along with this development, popular disturbances in the cities and in the countryside became endemic.

Many transient visitors to Japan were, however, still entertaining happy illusions of a meeting between the East and the West. Alcock, in his article in the *Edinburgh Review* in 1861, expressed his irritation with those writers who, 'on the strength of a very superficial observation or a flying visit to Nagasaki', had led 'the credulous public in Europe and America to believe that the triumph of European civilisation in Japan' was 'already secure'.[10] As a matter of fact, Japanese society was then undergoing a profound change. It was difficult, however, even for long-term British residents to obtain an overall view of events in Japan, as they were confined, with other foreign inhabitants, to small communities in the treaty ports. Contact between foreigners and the indigenous population was gradually increasing, despite the regulations imposed in various ways by the Japanese authorities, but the lack of a common language was always the problem on both sides. However, Student Interpreters at the British Legation in Edo had been learning Japanese since 1859,[11] and their master, Alcock, ventured, just eighteen months after his arrival in Japan, to publish his booklet on elementary Japanese,[12] although he had to admit, in its preface, the imperfections of the work. He himself contributed an anonymous review of this work to the *Edinburgh Review* in 1861.[13]

Certainly, during the first half of the 1860s, Alcock was the leading British authority on Japan. Since the summer of 1859, he had been despatching detailed reports from Japan to the Foreign Office, first as Consul-General and then, from December 1859, as Minister. It was in the spring of 1860 that his correspondence with the Foreign Office was first presented to Parliament, and the publication of this seems to have drawn considerable attention from the reading public in Britain.[14]

Alcock's correspondence was just a prelude to the publication of his major work, *The Capital of the Tycoon*. In this two-volume work, Alcock presented a chronological account of his experiences in Japan. About ten chapters out of the total of thirty-nine contained minute records of the assassination of foreigners and of prolonged protests by diplomats against the Japanese government. Accounts of bloodshed caused by the clashes between Japanese political factions and of fires and earthquakes were also abundant. Another characteristic of this work was that it introduced readers to living conditions in the interior of Japan. Alcock, using his diplomatic privileges, made a largely overland journey from Nagasaki to Edo, the then restricted route of the Dutch traders' former annual visits to the Shogun. In addition to these major topics, the book contained several chapters on language, arts and crafts, political institutions, social classes, religion, manners, and customs.

Alcock's publishers (Longman, Green, Longman, Roberts & Green) printed two thousand copies of *The Capital of the Tycoon*,[15] and during the first year of its publication, several influential periodicals reviewed it.[16] Oliphant, in his review in *Blackwood's Magazine*, pointed out that Alcock's description of the moral and social state of Japan was 'most detailed and graphic'.[17] Henry Reeve also thought that the work was 'remarkably graphic and amusing', and regarded it as 'the most accurate and comprehensive account yet published of the people of Japan'.[18] Behind Alcock's call for a 'photographic accuracy', there was his strong confidence that he had already surpassed Kaempfer in his acquaintance with Japanese society. Even by 1861 he had started expressing this feeling. For instance, in his account of the sensational assassination of *Tairô* Ii Naosuke, the 'Great Principal' Minister of the Council of State, which had taken place near a gate of the Shogun's castle in 1860, Alcock mentioned some 'remarkable features' of the deed which would distinguish the samurai attackers from 'common assassins'. Apart from their boldness and deliberateness, their readiness to sacrifice their lives on the spot impressed Alcock deeply. He explained his observation this way:

> Certainly this picture is very unlike any we have heretofore been presented with, either by painstaking Koempfer [sic] or Thunberg in past generations or hasty visitors since.[19]

Also, in the preface to *The Capital of the Tycoon*, Alcock set out his own qualifications as a writer on Japan:

> I have had better opportunities of observation than anyone, perhaps, since the Portuguese and Spaniards wandered at large through the Empire, . . . and travelled and seen more with my own eyes.[20]

Thus, Alcock and reviewers of his reports started out fighting against the old ideas of Japan, then prevalent. 'Error' was the word which was much used among them for the purpose. For example, Alcock pointed out that 'the old Dutch writers, Koempfer [sic] and Thunberg, and others' had made 'a grave error' in describing all the female attendants at the tea-houses as courtesans.[21] Many of Alcock's reports seemed to imply a criticism of Oliphant's *Narrative,* too, and Alcock was conscious of it:

> The narrative I have given would have a certain interest, I conceive, if all other were wanting, as a contrast to the pleasant and amusing account furnished by Mr Oliphant of Lord Elgin's mission.[22]

In Alcock's writings, readers learned that members of the British Legation at Edo often encountered drunken and hostile samurai carrying swords in a menacing way.[23] The general character of the agricultural areas was reported as 'poverty-stricken'.[24] Numbers of beggars were met on the streets.

The Japanese governmental system became a particularly important topic in British periodical articles on Japan at that time. It was in this field that a new realism was particularly desired. For example, the journalist John Henry Tremenheere (1807–80), who contributed numerous articles on countries all over the world to the *Quarterly Review,* was one of the persons who was not satisfied with Western writers' easy resort to European analogies to explain things Japanese. In October 1863, he published in the *Quarterly Review* an extensive review of those various books on Japan by Alcock, Oliphant, Osborn, Hodgson, Smith, de Fonblanque, Robert Fortune, the botanist, and Hermann Maron, a German doctor. Tremenheere wrote:

> It is an error common to most of the writers on Japan to describe the political state of that country as being an exact counterpart of the feudalism of the Middle Ages.[25]

The writer's serious concern with Japanese governmental institutions was not unwarranted. Within a month after the conclusion of the Commercial Treaty between 'Her Majesty of Great Britain and the Tycoon of Japan', the Emperor at the Court of Kyoto officially protested to the Shogun's, that is, the 'Tycoon's' government for neglecting to request imperial permission for their negotiations with the foreigners.[26] This protest was one of the early events in the antagonism between the Tokugawa regime and the anti-Shogunate factions in Japan. At this time, the main stream of the latter was strongly opposed to the opening of the ports to the West. Serious anxiety that the Tycoon's authority might be vulnerable and that Britain might not have concluded the treaty with the sovereign of Japan was shared by writers and politicians alike in Britain. The theory of the two emperors in Japan was repeatedly criticised. Even the title of Tycoon for the Shogun was reported by Alcock as a recent invention by 'a preceptor' of the Shogun for the negotiations with Commodore Perry and as 'hardly known by the Japanese'.[27] Events since the late 1850s had gradually led Alcock and other foreign residents in Japan to understand that the Tycoon had no attributes of sovereignty.[28] Reeve, in his review of Alcock's work, admitted that the 'ignorance' of the British had been 'unavoidably so great' as to deal with 'the Tycoon as the sovereign of the country'. Reeve boldly explained that the personage with whose ministers the British had been negotiating had been 'in fact at the moment a corpse'.[29] Tremenheere was more careful than Reeve in characterising the Tycoon. According to him, the holder of this title was in charge of 'the government of the army, the control of finances', and of 'the regulation of the external relations of the empire'.[30] He also explained that the Shogun was 'only the Lord Lieutenant or Vicegerent of the kingdom and hereditary Commander-in-Chief'.[31]

However, in spite of the theoretically inferior position of the Shogun in the Japanese government, it was certain that the Shogunate was exercising actual power at this time, and the political role of the Mikado in Kyoto was still vague. Thus, it may have been quite right for the lawyer, James Fitzjames Stephen (1829–94), an active contributor of essays to the *Saturday Review* and other periodicals since the mid-1850s, to point out in *Fraser's Magazine* that Japan had no sovereign who could ratify the treaty.[32] The argument naturally extended to the question of the institutional character of the Mikado. Reeve extensively quoted Alcock's explanation of the relationship between the Mikado and the Tycoon.[33] According to Alcock, the first Tycoon, Yoritomo, started his rule of Japan by 'usurping the quasi sovereignty of the [emperor]', and the later 'Tycoons' gradually became 'the virtual and *de facto* Sovereigns'. But Alcock pointed out that the 'only acknowledged Suzerain of all' was the Mikado, and explained the celebrated unbroken family line of the Mikado which traced itself back even to divine figures in a mythical age. Thus, he admitted that it was theoretically essential for the Tycoon to receive the Mikado's ratification of any treaty with a foreign nation.[34] However, Alcock, in view of the actual weakness of the suzerain's political power, described its character this way:

> They [The Mikados] continued inheritors by right divine of their phantom sceptre, preserving still some remnants of their former unlimited and absolute power.

In contrast to Alcock and Reeve, Tremenheere's explanation of the position of the emperor maintained some of the characteristics of Kaempfer's theory of two emperors in Japan, although he also admitted that the Japanese acknowledged but one emperor:

Britain, the Suitor Disillusioned

The Spiritual Emperor remained the supreme head of the Church, the fountain of honour, the high priest of the nation, the defender of the faith.[35]

However, he tried seriously to examine 'many extravagant stories' about the Mikado's 'peculiar establishment and mode of life' which had been propagated by Kaempfer and writers such as Charles Russell and Henry Morley in the 1850s. The realistic compiler Tremenheere emphasised the ignorance of the native people on the matter.[36] He observed that the reluctance of the Shogun to open other ports at Niigata and Hyôgo to foreigners must have been caused mainly by strong pressure from the Court in Kyoto, and thus concluded that the life of the Mikado was 'much more sublunary than spiritual'.[37] A new image of a secular emperor gradually became clear in British periodicals in the closing days of the Tokugawa regime. By 1867, Oliphant became confident that the Mikado was no more spiritual than was the Queen of Great Britain. The popular image of the Mikado surrounded by women and passing his time in a state of ecstatic contemplation was, according to Oliphant, 'an entire misapprehension'.[38]

In addition to these arguments, another new idea concerning the Japanese political structure was introduced by Alcock's revelation of the extreme wealth of some daimyo, lords of Japanese principalities, and the comparatively modest incomes of the office-holders in the Shogunate. Based on a translation of a *Bukan*, or Japanese Red Book, he produced in his book detailed lists of all the daimyo and important officials. According to these lists, the richest daimyo, the Prince of Kaga, had an annual revenue equivalent to £769,728. Reeve was amazed by the figures for the revenues of daimyo:

> If they were true, those nobles would be the richest aristocracy in the world, far exceeding in wealth the highest classes in the British Empire.[39]

By contrast, the annual revenue of Kuse Yamato no Kami, the highest member of the *rôjû*, the Council of State, was only 5.5 per cent of that of the Prince of Kaga. British writers naïvely overlooked the question of each daimyo's massive expenditure for maintaining his domain and retainers. Therefore, the office-holders of the Shogunate were imagined by British writers, who assumed a direct correspondence between wealth and power, to be puppets of the rich daimyo.[40]

It would appear that the early 1860s was a period when more detailed images of the Japanese government and society were created in Britain. Certainly, writers in Britain were able to discuss confidently the complex system of Japanese government and the social environment in which it functioned. However, increasingly accurate knowledge of various particular aspects of the society did not erase the old general image of Japan in Britain. In April 1862, Oliphant tried hard to organise numerous pieces of information about Japan within a consistent theory. He compared in vain diverse theories put forward by old and new visitors to the country: 'The more we compare and endeavour to reason out theories they propound, the more mystified do we become'.[41] He confessed that the attempt to reach, for instance, 'any trustworthy account of the state of politics in Japan' was a 'heartbreaking' one.[42] It is interesting that the publication of *The Capital of the Tycoon* did not alter Oliphant's feeling. In his article published in *Blackwood's Magazine* in April 1863, he sympathised with the difficulties which the diplomats in Japan were facing in their effort to realise each article of the treaties, particularly the opening of two more ports, Hyôgo (Kobe) and Niigata, and the cities of Edo and Osaka to foreigners. Oliphant enumerated obvious factors which were hampering British diplomacy in Japan such as 'the excessive reticence of the Japanese in all their communications with foreigners', and 'their habitual mendacity'. However, his point about the real difficulty for the British Envoy was this:

> The longer the diplomatist resides in the country, and the more he studies its institutions and the character of the people with whom he has to deal, the more is he puzzled in deciding upon the best course to adopt.[43]

Since the early 1860s, there were sometimes readable accounts of Japanese society published in Yokohama English newspapers, and cuttings from them often reached Britain in various ways, including the diplomatic channel. But 'intellectual' periodical writers in Britain were merely irritated by them. For instance, Oliphant wrote:

> The only persons who feel no difficulty on this score are the merchants' clerks who have just arrived, and who love to propound their views in the local newspapers.[44]

The feeling that the true Japan was difficult to grasp seems to have continued up to the latter half of the 1860s. Already in January 1864, about a year after the publication of *The Capital of the Tycoon*, Stephen frankly expressed his dismay at the work: 'Sir Rutherford Alcock's book is not a satisfactory one. It is diffuse and lengthy'.[45]

In their effort to acquire accurate knowledge, British writers seem to have introduced, more or less unconsciously, new elements into their mode of dealing with information from Japan. One was the fragmentation of the images of Japan. In 1861, Alcock emphasised that a study of the religion, literature, and political institutions of Japan was insufficient if it was not 'coupled with' an examination of the manners and customs 'in all different classes' of the nation.[46] Alcock's book, in fact, fragmented the image of Japanese nobles, breaking it into many categories. Reports of his journey through various daimyo-domains in the interior conveyed diverse pictures of local towns and villages, their inhabitants and botanical specimens. Specialised books also began to appear. Alcock's book on Japanese grammar was one of the earliest examples. In 1863, Robert Fortune (1813–80), an occasional traveller in China since 1842, and Honorary Member of the Agri-Horticultural Society of India, published through John Murray *Yedo and Peking, a Narrative of a Journey to the Capitals of Japan and China*. This book gave British readers a fair amount of knowledge about Japanese natural products, agriculture and horticulture.

The actual introduction of goods and people from Japan to Europe was increasing. Of course, some Japanese luxuries like porcelain and lacquerware had already been imported to Europe via the Dutch trade, but their number was limited. The first exhibition in Britain of things Japanese was the 1854 exhibition of Japanese applied art held at the Old Water Colour Society's premises in Pall Mall East.[47] Japanese prints had been highly prized among connoisseurs of art in Europe since the latter half of the 1850s. In 1856, the printmaker Felix Bracquemond discovered by accident in Paris Katsushika Hokusai's *Manga*, or leisurely sketches, and started copying from them.[48] In 1858, Daniel Lee of Manchester produced cotton prints with Japanese woodblock patterns.[49] By the early 1860s, a few shops had already been opened in Paris where Japanese goods were available and enthusiasts in both France and Britain frequented those places.[50] However, it was the London International Exhibition of 1862 which first provided the British public with an opportunity to inspect Japanese works of art and industry on a large scale. Among the more than six hundred Japanese articles exhibited, there was Alcock's collection of paintings, silk, paper, porcelain, lacquer work and bronzes.[51] It was in this year that the young Arthur Liberty (1843–1917), the future founder of Liberty's and one of the great promoters of Japanese taste in Britain, was employed by Farmer & Rogers Co., the Regent Street merchants. The shop bought some Japanese goods from the exhibition and began selling them.[52] Near the end of 1862, Messrs Christie, Manson and Woods held a four-day sale of Chinese and Japanese works of art from the Exhibition. *The Times* noted that the sale 'attracted unusual interest and was well attended throughout'.[53]

The first Envoys of the Shogun arrived in London on 29 April 1862, just one day before the opening of the Great Exhibition. Besides requesting the British Government to agree to postpone the opening of the two cities and two ports to foreigners, the Ambassadors and their suite frequented the exhibition and made zealous study tours to Woolwich, Portsmouth, Aldershot, Newcastle, Liverpool and Birmingham. *The Times*, as well as popular newspapers such as *The Illustrated London News*, described the public sensation which the appearance of the Japanese in Europe aroused.[54] In May 1863, the Supernumerary Assistant at the British Legation in Japan, John MacDonald, who had been in attendance upon the Japanese Ambassadors from Edo to London in the previous year, published anonymously an article describing the impressions of the Japanese Ambassadors upon encountering an utterly new world.[55] This article was published in the *Cornhill Magazine*, perhaps the most popular magazine of its day, ranging in content from general reviews to serialised novels at the unheard of price of a shilling per copy.[56] This magazine was founded in January 1860 by George Smith, one of the most commercially able Victorian publishers, and helped by the fame of its editor, William Makepeace Thackeray. The first issue is said to have sold an unprecedented total – for this genre – of 120,000 copies.[57]

Five years later, the International Exposition in Paris contributed further to the introduction of Japanese material culture to Europe. In the latter half of the 1860s, increasing numbers of young samurai were despatched to Europe to study Western civilisation.[58] This change of attitude among the Japanese authorities towards the West became evident after the bombardment of the territories of the Lords of Satsuma and Chôshû. These demonstrations of the modern military technology of the West, including new rifled Armstrong guns, were impressive enough to change the ideas of those powerful daimyo who had been the champions of the anti-foreign movement.[59] In 1867, Oliphant mentioned a new phenomenon in Europe: 'There is scarcely a capital in Europe now which has not been visited by young Japanese students making the "grand tour" '.[60] Obviously, information about Japan started flooding into Europe. Tremenheere expressed his heartfelt welcome for 'a number of new flowering plants' from Japan, which would 'greatly enrich' shrubberies and gardens in Britain.[61] Each product and visitor from Japan might well have produced one fragment of the image of Japan in observers' minds.

Interconnected with such fragmentation of the image of Japan, there developed among some writers a very strong disinclination to generalise about 'Orientals', or 'Asiatics'. Although it was common in the 1850s to mention the difference between China and Japan, most of the writers did not discuss the question of their mode of understanding the Eastern world. In 1863, Oliphant strongly criticised those who would 'profess to understand how to deal with "Orientals" on the basis of their experience of a stay, for instance, in Bombay'.[62] This type of attack had, on the other hand, the radical implication that one was logically ready to admit varieties of new facts as 'exceptions' to the 'general rule', or to accept facts as facts with little reference to any theory. Such a flexible attitude was also shared by Alcock when he completed his book without 'express[ing] any opinion' as to what might be best for British policy *vis-à-vis* Japan.[63] Already in 1861, Alcock had written: 'As regards Japan, a great experiment is in progress, and with what result time alone perhaps can determine with any certainty'.[64] It can be observed that those who preferred facts to theories developed another characteristic style of writing about Japan: to follow minutely the sequence of events occurring in the country. Many writers consciously rejected general statements about Japan, but emphasised its changeable and unstable character. Stephen examined the Anglo-Japanese Treaty in terms of 'international law', and concluded that it was of doubtful validity because no sovereign power had existed in Japan to ratify it. He proposed an approach similar to that of Alcock towards changes in Japan:

> The only sensible, and indeed the only possible course . . . is to fall back upon a direct consideration of the probable consequences of the course which we propose to take – the consequences to ourselves and the consequences to the Japanese – and to guide our conduct accordingly.[65]

It is highly likely that Alcock's call for a photographic realism was closely connected with his awareness of the difficulty of creating a clear, comprehensive idea of Japan.

What then *was* produced by authors of articles on Japan who never visited the country? Most of them showed, perhaps unconsciously, a certain common pattern of arranging things Japanese, and subsequently reproduced some general views on the country which were not entirely new to British readers. Two characteristics became conspicuous in their arrangement of the increased information about Japan. One was to emphasise the coexistence of contradictory features, and the other was to stress the extreme character of each of these noticeable features.

Certainly, information about the dark aspects of Japanese society was abundant in Britain in the 1860s. Many cases of the daring deeds of the anti-foreign samurai were reported to Britain. In *Blackwood's Magazine*, Oliphant was even obliged, for the sake of his readers, when quoting Alcock, to delete words from the 'graphic' description in *The Capital of the Tycoon* of the ghastly cuts inflicted upon a Russian officer and his companions.[66] Foreigners were not the only victims; the story of violence seemed endless. The fire in the Shogun's castle, earthquakes, and murders and suicides of Japanese high officials also caused sensations in the British press. In Henry Reeve's words, this 'multitude of frightful crimes and atrocities,'[67] seems to have made British writers more conscious of the 'cruel' and 'uncivilised' aspects of the Japanese military classes. The old idea from Thunberg's time or even before, that in Japan crimes were always punished with a Draconian type of severity, was repeatedly mentioned. Tremenheere wrote:

> There is scarcely any graduated scale of punishment; almost all crimes are punished alike. There is but one recognised offence – that against the law – and the penalty is death.[68]

Not only the 'cruelty' but also the 'mendacity' and 'insincerity' or 'irresponsibility' of the government of Japan were emphasised whenever there was a mention of the evasive attitudes of Japanese officials towards the obligation of the treaties.[69] The disastrous experiences of many foreign residents in Japan had the effect of blackening the image of the entire country in the British mind. The 'licentiousness' and 'intemperance' of the nation were freshly and gravely mentioned. Reeve criticised Oliphant's *Narrative* for saying that Lord Elgin's party had never encountered a drunken man.[70] Stephen pointed out that some of the plays and literature of Japan were 'grossly indecent', that the Japanese appeared 'to have settled down into a sort of contented and narrowly limited formalism' in terms of religious life, and that the moral condition of this nation was, after all, 'very wicked' by British standards. He judged that the Japanese were 'inveterate liars'. Stephen also criticised the 'common' custom of Japanese women to 'pass their early years in professional prostitution, after which they marry without loss of character or standing'.[71] As to the popular idea of the cleanliness of the population of Japan, Reeve observed that if the Japanese often wash their bodies, they neglect washing their clothes.[72]

It is not likely, however, that the whole list of Japanese 'national vices' was accepted without demur by British writers in periodicals or by their readers. The established image of the amiable nation was persistent enough to survive in almost all the magazine and review articles dealing with Japan. For instance, in 1861, Andrew Wilson (1831–81) a seasoned traveller in India and, at that time, editor of the *China Mail,* contributed an article to *Blackwood's Magazine* about the Inland Sea of Japan. The chief impression conveyed by this short-term visitor to Japan was the quiet, beauty, and peacefulness of the area.[73] Wilson's impression was good enough to urge him to conclude that there were 'many indications of the existence of a large, industrious, comfortable, and almost wealthy population'.[74] Such a tendency was not confined to temporary visitors. Oliphant mentioned, reviewing Alcock's work, that in spite of the hardships from which Alcock suffered, 'Sir Rutherford, after all' had given 'quite as favourable a picture of Japan as any of the "hasty visitors" '.[75] Alcock's appreciation was not confined to the natural beauty of the country, but included its 'happy and contented population', in spite of 'the despotic sway of these feudal lords'.[76] Even the Japanese mode of rule was, for him, worthy of consideration. Oliphant agreed with Alcock's point that the institutions in Japan 'must have some merit' since they were able to 'so satisfactorily secure the material prosperity of a population'.[77] Stephen emphasised the old idea about the frugality of life in Japan even among the aristocracy:

> There is little wealth and no misery in Japan; and if equality is an object, they appear to possess its advantages in an unusual degree.[78]

Stephen's knowledge about the prevalence of prostitution in Japan seems to have been no obstacle to this statement. The new information about poverty-stricken villages in Japan was often interpreted in the light of ideas about Japanese frugality. Tremenheere was enthusiastic in mentioning the independent growth of the 'high degree of material civilization' in Japan:

> Their swords and cutlery are of finer temper than any which Birmingham or Sheffield produce, their silk manufactures are admirable, their landscape gardening is distinguished for its taste, and they are no mean proficients in the arts of design.[79]

Oliphant also repeatedly emphasised the point made by Alcock about the ability of the Japanese to adopt the appliances and inventions of the West.[80]

Obviously the darker and brighter aspects of this newly opened country were producing sharp contrasts. The first impression on readers might well have been one of paradox and disorder. However, generally speaking, these magazine articles had a simple framework in which to place their ideas about the country. This framework seems to have had three characteristics. One was the clear-cut classification of contradictory features: for instance, the good temper of the commoners and the ill-temper of the samurai; the high material development and the low moral level. Other sets of notions to facilitate this black-or-white type of explanation were institution-and-people, society-and-nature, or adults-and-children. The second characteristic was a tendency to accept paradox. For example, Tremenheere enumerated the 'graces' of the Japanese character, such as quickness, shrewdness, tact, intelligence and good manners, which arose either from 'a natural courtesy' of the peasants or from 'a studied dignity of refinement' of the middle and higher classes. But his aim was to underline the contrast between these 'graces' and the 'serious licentiousness', 'universal deception', 'indifference' to death, and 'abominable immorality' with which religious rites were combined.[81] The third characteristic was a tendency to push each paradoxical feature of Japanese society to its extreme. With this tendency, the scale of balance between these concepts was to become larger and clearer. Generally speaking, the style of those who had not seen Japan with their own eyes, was less restrained than that of, for instance, Alcock. Reeve is a good example. According to him, the Japanese were 'a very humorous people', but in their commercial dealings, they showed their 'extreme mendacity'. He also mentioned the 'extremely' low morality of the Japanese, and their 'incredibly degraded' notion of religion.[82]

Two things help to explain this tendency; first, the persistence of amiable images of Japan had been much reinforced in the beginning of the 1860s; second, British writers in the 1860s were more or less ready to accept any kind of information about Japan however contradictory it might appear to be. In other words, the entire image of Japan in this period was fragmented, with many pairs of coexisting opposites; apparently there was no dominant or representative picture.

What, then, *was* the dominant idea in this wide range of contradictions? Was there no central idea of Japan at all that would provide the balance? In such a vacuum, the word 'singular' and synonyms such as 'extraordinary', 'bizarre' and 'anomalous' were dominant – the words resorted to by periodical writers. In March 1863, an anonymous article appeared in *Fraser's Magazine,* caricaturing the Vatican's canonisation in 1862 of the Japanese Christian Martyrs who had been crucified in Japan during the sixteenth and seventeenth centuries. The author, hinting that the Vatican's crafty manoeuvring to win favour in Japanese minds would fail, labelled the Japanese as 'that singular race of humanity', and emphasised their basic difference from Europeans.[83] Phrases such as 'this strange people', 'this extraordinary country', 'this singular people', and 'that singular region' were conspicuously used.[84]

These words might sound too vague and too detached from particular features of Japanese manners and customs. There were, however, some notable practices which justified these descriptions. The best example was the Japanese custom which Victorians called 'happy despatch', namely *seppuku,* or self-disembowelment. Although the origin of the Victorian term is unclear, it could possibly have arisen from a literal translation of a samurai's will written in accordance with formalities before this kind of ceremony. This mode of dying was indeed a 'privilege', which was granted to samurai only on certain occasions to allow them to fulfil their obligations and responsibilities, and to save face. In most of the magazine and review articles on Japan in the 1860s, the topic of 'happy despatch' was indispensable. For British writers, this custom, which seemed to them to combine merriment and sorrow, was nothing but 'singular'. After the publication of Alcock's work, the idea that everything is reversed in Japan became more popular among British writers than in the early 1850s. Alcock had written:

> Japan is essentially a country of paradoxes and anomalies, where all – even familiar things – put on new faces, and are curiously reversed. Except that they do not walk on their heads instead of their feet, there are few things in which they do not seem, by some occult law, to have been impelled in a perfectly opposite direction and a reversed order.[85]

Reeve quoted extensively the passage in which Alcock enumerated many examples of this point.[86] For example, the Japanese wrote 'from top to bottom, from right to left' in perpendicular lines; their books began where Western books ended; a Japanese carpenter used his plane by drawing it *towards* himself; a tailor stitched *away from* himself, and so on. Alcock wrote: 'This principle of antagonism crops out in the most unexpected and *bizarre* way in all their moral being, customs and habits'.[87]

Also, the notion that Japan was a singular country was in accordance with the feelings of early enthusiasts for Japanese arts and crafts, who were impressed by the uniqueness of Japanese design – particularly in the deformed features of men, women and animals in prints or in the minute carvings of netsuke. Alcock noted that the Japanese loved the humorous and the grotesque in their works of art.[88]

The phase under study began in the early 1860s with Alcock's call for a new realism which sought to crush the old images created by Kaempfer and other early travellers. However, it is ironic that the very effort to criticise Kaempfer and other old writers should have reproduced a pattern of images not greatly dissimilar from theirs. In the early 1850s, several writers produced the concept of the 'singular' Japanese with many contrasts between the nation's virtues and vices. Although richer in the variety of information and stronger in the emphasis on 'extremity', the pattern of the image seems to have changed little. So far as the field of magazine and review articles was concerned, the more the British knew of Japan, the more its 'singularity' was reinforced.

There was, however, some change in the general tone with which Japan was described. Throughout the 1850s, there had been an increasing tendency to emphasise the 'affinity' between Britain and Japan. Now, entering the 1860s, the sense of remoteness from Japan seems to have become dominant. This inclination is shown in a general reluctance among British periodical writers to describe things Japanese by using European counterparts. For example, we have already seen Tremenheere's caution with the Japanese political state, avoiding the easy analogies with the European Middle Ages. Stephen was aware of the practical danger of such a mode of perception. He even pointed out the necessity of discovering 'some other way of regulating' Anglo-Japanese relations than the attempt to impose analogies derived from the usual relationship between Western countries based on their international law.[89] It should be noted that the inclination of many writers to see Japan as alien from Europe was based on the report by Alcock, who, on the contrary, did not take the trouble to avoid European metaphors to describe Japan. For instance, he suggested in 1861 that his readers put 'a magic tube' to their eyes in order to shut out the preconceptions of a later period and thus go 'back to the twelfth century in Europe'. 'For there alone,' wrote Alcock, 'we shall find the counterpart of "Japan as it is" '.[90] He also wrote in 1865: 'The Mikado occupies a position not very different from that of the sovereign in a constitutional monarchy with a representative government'.[91] However, compared with Oliphant in the late 1850s, it is clear that Alcock did not regard Japan as a country having a close kinship with the West. He did not show any reluctance in confessing his notion about the basic 'Oriental' character of the Japanese:

> The Japanese, notwithstanding their advanced state and unquestionable superiority in many respects over every other Oriental nation, still remain true to the original type, to the traditions and the instincts of their race.[92]

He also wrote: 'Here we have a far distant family of the Oriental race to deal with.'[93] In 1863, Oliphant supported Alcock's publication, defending it against possible criticisms concerning the revelation of diplomatic procedures by an actual minister. Oliphant made the remoteness of Japan from Europe an excuse for Alcock's revelations.[94] It is not difficult to assume that the reinforcement of the idea of 'singularity' about Japan in the 1860s was interconnected with the growth of such a sense of distance from Japan, and the growth of this sense was much more evident among writers who did not visit Japan themselves.

However, British writers' sense of geographical and cultural distance from Japan did not always mean that Japan became insignificant in their minds. On the contrary, they were conscious of some British responsibility for the sensational events and tragic social changes that were occurring in Japan. What was the result of this British recognition of their grave responsibility for the helpless tragedy of a 'remote' people whom they once courted? A kind of self-directed satire, using Japanese images against Britain itself, was growing in the middle of the 1860s.

In April 1867, about a year before the Restoration and the subsequent civil war in Japan, Oliphant expressed his deep sense of British responsibility for the disorder in Japan which had been increasing since the opening of the ports: 'Infinite misery throughout the country . . .'. He enumerated the facts such as rice-riots, the partial ruin of Edo, the bombardment of two cities, the 'utter demoralisation' of the native populations of Nagasaki and Yokohama, the menaces of civil war and the disappearance either by assassination or by self-immolation of many important figures of the country.[95] Since his return from Japan in 1862, Oliphant, although active in his literary as well as political circles, became year by year so cynical about Western civilisation as to resign his seat in the House of Commons in June 1867 and to depart for America to become a devoted follower of the mystic, Thomas Lake

Harris.⁹⁶ If Oliphant's case was special, Tremenheere, Reeve and others were also expressing their grave concern at the drastic social changes which were taking place in Japan.⁹⁷ In particular, the report from Lieutenant-Colonel Edward St John Neale, the *Chargé d'Affaires* at Edo during Alcock's leave, concerning the bombardment of the city of Kagoshima, caused Stephen to reflect seriously on British activities abroad. According to Stephen, the course which the British had followed until they had set fire to 'a town upwards of 100,000 inhabitants, in the process of punishing the government for the murder of one of our subjects',⁹⁸ was an indictment of Western morality. Alternative policies for better Anglo-Japanese relations were discussed in both political and journalistic circles in Britain. Anxiety about Japanese affairs might have been graver among the people who were engaged in those discussions if they had known that the Japanese authorities were more or less aware that there were disagreements among British leaders as to policy towards Japan. For instance, details about the parliamentary debate on Japan between Earl Grey and the Foreign Secretary Earl Russell in July 1864 were printed in the *Japan Commercial News* published in Yokohama on 7 and 14 September 1864, and these articles were soon translated into Japanese by a Tokugawa official, Mitsukuri Teiichirô, Professor at the Kaiseisho (The Centre for Western Learning), for circulation among high-ranking figures in the Tokugawa government.⁹⁹ However, it is clear that British anxiety was grave enough, if one notes the common reaction to this situation, the assumption of what may be called a 'holier-than-thou' attitude. For the British, the question of self-image seems to have gained greater importance. Immediately after mentioning the 'serious moral responsibilities' involved in Western relations with Japan, Tremenheere wrote: '. . . we are glad that England was not the first to undertake [the responsibilties]'.¹⁰⁰ Oliphant also maintained that careful readers of Alcock's work would 'learn' how it had 'happened that a treaty' had been 'as much forced upon us by circumstances as upon the Japanese'.¹⁰¹

Although motivated by such serious feelings, writers' arguments for 'better' British policies towards Japan were not altogether constructive. There were a few issues which they regarded as important. So far as the outcome of trade with Japan was concerned, the figures reported to Parliament by the Foreign Office were not at all encouraging.¹⁰² Reeve wrote:

> It is certain that at present, and probably for a long time to come, our mercantile relations with Japan are scarcely worth the anxiety and bloodshed they have occasioned.¹⁰³

However, such a statement hardly implied the possibility of Britain's withdrawal from Japan, and all the writers, for the sake of British 'dignity' and diplomatic 'prestige' in the East, were against withdrawal.[104] Another issue was whether or not to use force in order to compel Japan to observe the treaty in opening the two cities and two ports to foreigners. After his recall by Lord John Russell, in 1864, Alcock became a strong advocate of a tough approach to the Japanese government, perhaps partly as a result of his need to rationalise the British bombardment of Shimoneseki, which he had ordered against the wishes of the Foreign Office.[105] However, it is paradoxical that almost all the magazine and review writers who were disciples of Alcock should have already been expressing contrary opinions from the one Alcock began advocating at the time. In Alcock's mind, there was anxiety caused by perpetual Russian expansion southward in the Far East.[106] But it seems to have worried other writers that this problem could be used to rationalise British force against Japan. Already in 1863, Reeve anxiously remarked of Alcock's hint in *The Capital of the Tycoon* that a forceful policy would be necessary, that it 'would have the effect of adding a European quarrel to an Asiatic difficulty'.[107] However, Alcock himself seems to have been aware that his 'theory' of using force against the Japanese government was not always applicable to practical policy.[108] One reason was the technical difficulty of any military operation in densely populated Japan.[109] Another was the growing insecurity of the Shogun's government. According to him, the decentralisation of power in Japan was 'the worst danger'. Without a central authority in Japan which was capable of binding the nation by its treaties, it would be no use for Britain to maintain superior power to impose a treaty upon Japan.

However, 'the worst danger' was becoming only a matter of time in the mid-1860s and a feeling of helplessness seems to have become widely shared by British writers. Even Alcock, who firmly believed that 'Christianity and commerce combined' were 'destined' to modify the whole social structure of Asian countries, was obliged to admit that the 'aversion and repugnance' of their rulers to the West was a 'natural' and 'inevitable' stage in the process of the modification.[110] Until the beginning of the 1860s, there had been various proposals in British periodicals of ways to deal politely with the Japanese government and people, and many strong criticisms of the misconduct of European adventurers in Japan. However, after late 1863, such proposals became rare. In the eyes of the British observers, changes in Japanese society appeared too rapid and the bombardment of Kagoshima by a British squadron was the symbolic end to their 'politeness'. At the same time, detached speculation about the future of Japan, rather than discussions of the principles of British attitudes towards her, became prevalent. In October 1863, Tremenheere pessimistically anticipated that 'grave complications' would arise in the year 1868 when the cities of Edo and Osaka and the ports of Hyôgo and Niigata would be opened to foreigners.[111] In 1867, Oliphant observed the irresistible trend towards the destruction of the traditional life of the Japanese and could not help crying: 'Alas, alas! how long will they remain such?'[112]

'Why did Britain start this unrewarding business? What on earth do we want? What kind of people are we who are involved in such troubles in the Far East?' It would have been possible for any British writer to have asked such questions when considering Japanese affairs. At least many of them were led to perceive themselves in a new light, different from the one to which they had been accustomed – different in the sense that their new impressions of themselves were less self-confident, less forward-looking, and increasingly cynical. Various reflections on Britain arising from the intercourse with Japan gave birth to peculiar satires of Britain, or of Europe as a whole, expressed in the camouflaged settings of an imaginary Japan which prevailed among reviewers of Alcock's reports. For example, Reeve was 'amazed at the touches of satire which the experience of Japanese society suggest to an accomplished English observer':

> They have a priesthood as ceremonious and a people as superstitious as in the worst ages of Roman Catholic bigotry; they have statesmen as crafty as Machiavelli and as faithless as Borgia.[113]

Oliphant, on the contrary, idealised Japan in order to criticise Western civilisation. He wrote:

> When the ladies of Japan know a little more of their Parisian sisters, they will learn to show more of their shoulders they now so carefully conceal, and consider more lightly the virtue of chastity . . . The Prince of Satsuma, when he understands political economy, will never again be so absurd as to have the whole infant population of his principality vaccinated at his own private expense, as he did the other day.[114]

These writers were freely using new pieces of information about Japan which Alcock's 'photographic' realism provided. But it is obvious that in such passages their interest was more directed to Britain than to Japan itself, and if they indulged in such rhetoric, as they often did in those days, their realistic interest in Japan as a whole was to become of secondary importance. For them, if Japan was in any way unusually different from Britain, it was enough. Stephen's case, too, was not an exception. His style was based on his radical relativism and his cool laughter at ideas like 'civilisation'. He proposed a drastic alteration of certain legal notions, which were frequently used concerning treaty-questions between Britain and Japan, into more realistic terms:

> What we called agreement to a treaty of commerce was in reality submission to superior force, and what we call breaches of the treaty were in substance partial, fretful, and ignorant attempts to shake off what the Japanese regarded and could not but regard as a foreign yoke forcibly laid on their necks.[115]

He considered that the British interest in maintaining some intercourse with Japan was mainly based on their 'curiosity', and gave a piece of advice to his readers – a poignant one to Alcock and his naïve followers: 'Let us say as little as may be about civilization and Christianity'.[116] However, Stephen's argument was based on a logical analysis of the treaty-making process between Britain and Japan, and compared with Alcock, he was less concerned with knowledge about Japanese society. In addition, the then editor of *Fraser's Magazine*, the historian James Anthony Froude (1818–94), printed an anonymous poem beneath Stephen's article. The motif of the poem was drawn from *Isaiah*, xxxiii, 17: 'The Land that is very far off'. The poem was entitled 'Far Away'. One wonders what kind of impression the readers of Stephen's article had regarding 'complications' in the country called Japan.

The Japan represented in popular periodicals around the mid-1860s seems to have begun taking on a peculiar character. Japan became a country which, because of its remoteness, authors felt free to use for any kind of argument. However, it seems that the general image of Japan in the 1860s had too large an element of tragedy to be made fun of, and therefore could not easily be rendered as a comic version of British society. A kind of satire on Britain using a 'happy', and 'joyous' image of the Japanese, as in the case of Gilbert and Sullivan's *Mikado* of 1885, would not be produced until Japan achieved a certain social order in the course of 'Westernising' herself during the ten years or so after the restoration of Imperial Rule. Before then, there would be a period of serious study of the 'Old Japan' which was in the process of disintegration. A confession of infinite affection for the withering society of 'Old Japan' would be made by Algernon Bertram Mitford, a young diplomat, the focus of the next chapter.

5 In Quest of the Inner Life of the Japanese

The year 1869 marked an important event in the history of ideas about Japan in British periodicals. This was due to the publication of three short articles on Japan in the *Cornhill Magazine*. The author of these articles was Algernon Bertram Mitford (1837–1916), the future Baron Redesdale, who now can be identified in England as the father of the eccentric 'Uncle Matthew' who appears in the novels of Nancy Mitford. After Eton and Christ Church, Oxford, Mitford entered the Foreign Office in 1858 at the age of twenty-one, and within a few years was sent to China. It was in the autumn of 1866 that he first went to Japan as Acting Third Secretary.[1] He stayed in Japan until the end of 1869, and during that time the country underwent a period of drastic political and social change – the restoration of imperial rule in 1868, and the subsequent civil war.

Mitford's three articles were entitled: 'A Japanese Sermon', 'Another Japanese Sermon' and 'The Execution by Hara-Kiri'.[2] The first two were his literal translations of *Kyûô Dôwa* (Kyûô's Moral Tales), a collection of lectures made by Shibata Kyûô (1783–1839), the most popular wandering preacher of the Shingaku school, the mission of which was to spread among the common people, including less literate women and children, the combined essence of the morals of Confucianism, Buddhism, Taoism and Shintoism. Mitford's third article was a description in minute detail of the ceremony of self-disembowelment by a samurai who had been accused of having given an order to his troops to fire on the foreigners at Hyôgo on 4 February 1868. The incident is known as the Kobe Incident, and it had taken place only about a month after the opening of the port to foreigners.

The case bore a tragic tinge from the beginning. The accused samurai, Taki Zenzaburô belonged to Bizen Province, and was the commander of one of the province's infantry corps, which had been directed by the imperial government to maintain order in Nishinomiya, near the newly opened port, at the beginning of the civil war. It is commonly said that the clash was started by a foreigner's neglect of 'due respect' to the procession of the Bizen force. It soon developed into exchanges of fire between Bizen samurai and British, French and American marines. However, owing to the Bizen troops' inexperience

Pl. 14 Seppuku, or Hara-Kiri (from a Japanese drawing). Reproduced from Silver, *Sketches of Japanese Manners and Customs*, facing p. 26. Mitford was impressed by the solemnity and punctiliousness of a similar 'ceremony'.
See p. 40.
See p. t.40.

Pl. 15 Japanese Sermon (by a Japanese artist commissioned by Mitford). Reproduced from Mitford's *Tales of Old Japan* (London, 1871), vol. ii, p. 124. 'Jokes, stories, and pointed application to members of the congregation are common in these sermons as dry, rigid formality is with us'. (Mitford's *Cornhill* article of August 1869). See p. 101.

Pl. 16 Nihonbashi, or Japan Bridge, Edo. Reproduced from Saitō's *Edo meisho zue* (Edo, 1834–36), vol. i. According to Mitford, this place was 'the Hyde Park corner of Yedo'. See p. 100.

Pl. 17 Public Bath-House in Edo (from a Japanese drawing). Reproduced from Humbert's *Le Japon illustré* (Paris, 1870) vol. ii, p. 117. A familiar motif in western books on Japan from the mid-1850s. See pp. 49, 103.

Pl. 18 The Japanese Women in the Paris International Exposition. Reproduced from *The Illustrated London News* (16 November 1867). Three geisha from Yangibashi, Edo, represented by Japanese tender sex. See p. 76.

Pl. 19 Fashionable Costumes of Modern Japanese Officers. Reproduced from *ibid.* (7 April 1886). See the astonished face of a samurai of the old school (extreme right). See pp. 107, 137.

Pl. 20 Occupations of Ministers to Japan. Reproduced from the *Japan Punch* (Yokohama, January 1867). The British Minister Sir Harry Parkes (right), and the French Minister M. Léon Roches (left). See p. 107.

Pl. 21 Opening of the First Railway in Japan: Arrival of the Mikado at Yokohama Station. Reproduced from *The Illustrated London News* (21 December 1872).

Pl. 22 Worcester 'Japanese' Porcelain at the Vienna Exhibition. Reproduced from *ibid.* (1 November 1873).

Plates 21 & 22 'A game of cross-purposes': An event in Japanese westernisation (Pl. 21), and specimens of English *Japonisme* (Pl. 22). See pp. 111, 115, 136, 162.

Pl. 23 *Daibutsu*, or the Great Image of Buddha, at Kamakura. Reproduced from R.W. Leyland's *Round the World in 124 Days* (Liverpool, 1880), frontispiece. A 'must' for Victorian tourists visiting Japan. See p. 129.

Pl. 24 Globe-trotters in Rickshaws. Reproduced from the Marchioness of Stafford's *How I Spent My Twentieth Year* (Edinburgh & London, 1889), frontispiece. A favourite photographic motif for fashionable western travellers in Japan.   See p. 155.

Pl. 25 *Miyako Odori*, or the Kyoto Dance, at the Minamiza Theatre. Reproduced from *The Illustrated London News* (15 February 1873). Cyprian Bridge wrote: 'Such pantomimic dancing might have been performed in days of old by bands of modest Dorian youths and maidens . . .' (*Fraser*, January 1878).   See pp. 161, 206n 51.

in using guns, they fled, and no one was killed on either side.

At the time this incident occurred, the new imperial government had not yet publicly announced its already determined policy of friendly diplomacy towards the Western powers, and of observing the existing treaties. However, since most of the leaders of the new government had formerly been radical advocates of anti-foreignism, the Bizen samurai had naturally expected that the new regime would be severe with foreign countries. On the other hand, in the eyes of Westerners, the Kyoto Court had already ratified the treaties which had been concluded between the Shogun and foreign powers in 1865. For them, therefore, the firing by Bizen troops was nothing less than a grave violation of the treaties. After severe protests and pressure from the powerful Western countries, the new government could do nothing but express their 'apology' by executing the person who had been directly responsible for the firing. At the government's request, the Bizen authorities reluctantly presented a 32-year-old samurai, Taki Zenzaburô, as the man responsible.[3] On 2 March 1868, the self-execution took place at a Buddhist temple in Hyôgo. Seven Japanese officers and seven representatives of the Western powers were chosen as witnesses of the event. Mitford and the Japanese Secretary of the British Legation, Ernest Satow, were present.

Now, let us see – in detail – how Mitford informed the British public, through the *Cornhill Magazine,* of what he had witnessed twenty months before. He first translated hara-kiri into 'self-immolation by disembowelling', avoiding carefully the use of the word 'suicide' which would inevitably carry a negative nuance in English-speaking countries. Mitford then set out to explain why he had decided to write the article:

> As the *Hara-Kiri* is one of the Japanese customs which has excited the greatest curiosity in Europe, although, owing to the fact that it had never hitherto been witnessed by foreigners, it has seemed little better than a fable, I will relate what occurred.[4]

As was shown in Chapter 4, the dominant British idea about Japan in the 1860s was that of a 'singular' and 'strange' country, and this remarkable custom, the Japanese samurai's privilege, was termed by the Victorians the 'happy despatch'. Certainly, Mitford knew what needed to be said in his article to destroy such a facetious perception of Japan. He took his readers to the imposing scene of the execution, the main hall of the temple, which was dimly lit by tall candles. When Taki walked into the hall in his ceremonial dress, Mitford was struck by his 'noble air'.[5] Taki was accompanied by a swordsman, the *kaishaku*, whose office was to assist the despatch and was, according to Mitford, 'that of a gentleman'. He rejected using the English word 'executioner' as it was 'no equivalent term'. In fact, the *kaishaku* was often chosen from the kinsmen or friends of the condemned samurai.[6]

Mitford followed the beginning of the proceedings of the ceremony, noting all Taki's movements, which were 'slow, and with great dignity'.[7] After those formalities, Taki admitted 'with no sign of fear either in his face or manner' that he alone had given the order to fire on the foreigners, and begged the people present to do him the honour of witnessing his act. When Taki was naked to the waist, he tucked the sleeves of his upper garment under his knees. Mitford explained that this was to prevent oneself from falling backward and that 'a noble Japanese gentleman should die falling forwards'. Then Mitford presented a highly detailed description of the deliberate movement of Taki's dirk:

> . . . stabbing himself deeply below the waist on the left-hand side, he drew it slowly across to the rightside, and turning the dirk in the wound, gave a slight cut upwards.[8]

Mitford drew the attention of his readers to the following fact: 'During this sickeningly painful operation he never moved a muscle of his face'.[9] Then Taki leaned forward and stretched out his neck, and the head was severed by one single blow of the *kaishaku*'s sword:

> A dead silence followed, broken only by the hideous noise of the blood gushing out of the inert heap before us, which but a moment before had been a brave and chivalrous man.[10]

Mitford then made a few points. One was that the ceremony 'was characterized throughout by extreme dignity and punctilliousness', and that those characteristics were 'the distinctive marks of the proceedings of Japanese gentlemen of rank'. Another point was that for him 'it was impossible not to be filled with admiration for the firm and manly bearing of the sufferer'. In Mitford's eyes, such composure was a demonstration of 'the force of education', and he explained how a 'gentleman of the military class' in Japan was instructed from his childhood concerning the ceremony of honourable expiation of crime or the blotting-out of disgrace.[11]

In addition, Mitford, being critical of the view which advocated mercy to the victim, asserted that the offence would have developed into 'a universal massacre', had the Bizen army been skilled, and that, therefore, 'death was undoubtedly deserved'. Mitford extended his point: 'The form chosen for the execution was in Japanese eyes merciful and yet judicial.'[12] The article continued for a few more pages, in which Mitford explained the three different types of hara-kiri ceremony performed by a retainer of the Shogun, a daimyo's retainer, and by a daimyo. He also mentioned two recent episodes of self-disembowelment, one of which he considered to be 'a marvellous instance of determination'.[13]

This article by Mitford contained the following four notable attitudes towards things Japanese. First, he was careful in considering whether something Japanese had an equivalent in Europe. So he refused to translate certain Japanese nouns such as *hara-kiri* and *kaishaku* into English and used them in italic letters. Secondly, he allowed himself considerable freedom in using certain English notions of whose correspondence with those in Japan he felt sure. A good example was his usage of the word 'gentleman'. His serious argument about successful education in Japanese samurais' houses shows his firm belief in the correspondence of the two classes. If one reads Mitford's later autobiography, he mentions chivalrous actions of his Anglo-Saxon knightly ancestors, and also hints at the very strict education he experienced at Eton, including a punishment called 'execution'.[14] He was also much devoted to boxing games while he was at Oxford. Therefore, one could argue that Mitford was particularly qualified to have great sympathy with a samurai like Taki, whom Mitford called 'a noble gentleman'. The usage of these words was different from the popular conception in Britain of the Japanese military class. In the middle of the 1860s, the popular idea was that the samurai were an uncivilised, savage race. Inspired by Alcock's work, many writers used the words 'swashbucklers' or 'ruffians' not only for *rônin,* but often more broadly for the samurai class.

Thirdly, Mitford made good use of his fluency in Japanese, which, according to Satow, he had been able to acquire very rapidly within a year of his arrival in Japan.[15] Towards the end of his first stay in Japan, therefore, he became increasingly able to obtain reliable information from Japanese intellectuals. He was careful to ask any informant whether the story he was telling was based on his personal experience. If he found the informant trustworthy, Mitford often asked him to write the story on paper, which Mitford translated literally. An example of this method was clearly shown in the latter part of his article on Taki's execution.

Lastly, he fixed his standard for judging Japanese customs firmly on 'the Japanese point of view'. As regards the background for such an open-minded attitude towards a non-Christian world, one could point to the prevalence of secularism among British intellectuals who had been under the influence of Charles Darwin and Thomas Huxley since the early 1860s. However, in Mitford's case, there was the more direct influence on him from his student days at Oxford of Professor Max Müller's comparative and objective approach to the Eastern religions and languages, as Mitford confided later in his memoirs.[16]

His article on Taki's execution was published more than a year and a half after Mitford had witnessed the ceremony. Naturally, one would assume that the 'Japan' in Mitford's mind might have changed owing to the lapse of time; or the very idea that he was to write on a Japanese theme for the general public which was supposed to be little acquainted with the country, might have influenced Mitford's writing style. The Foreign Office Papers contain a copy of Mitford's manuscript report of Taki's execution, which Mitford wrote the morning after the ceremony in accordance with the order of Minister Sir Harry Parkes. This report[17] was attached to the Minister's despatch of 11 March 1868 to Lord Stanley.[18] It seems worthwhile trying to examine the difference between Mitford's manuscript report and the *Cornhill* article.

At first glance, it is obvious that Mitford used his former diplomatic report as the basis for writing the *Cornhill* article, as the main parts of the two documents do not differ from one another. However, if one examines them carefully, it becomes clear that the magazine article contains some subtle alterations of the former report, and that, owing to these changes, the basic tone of the article sounds different from that of the report. There are several such alterations: first, concerning the public feeling about the case, Mitford had mentioned in his report the critical attitudes of the crowd near the temple towards foreigners:

> A crowd which lined the approach to the temple showed that the execution although conducted in private was a matter of public notoriety.[19]

But in the magazine, the word 'notoriety' disappeared and instead he wrote as follows: '. . . it was a matter of no little interest to the public'. Mitford and Satow had been strong advocates of the execution, considering it to be a question of 'justice', but it is true that there had been many criticisms of the execution even among foreigners in Japan. As early as May 1868, *The Times* had published a small article on this execution under the title of 'Harikari [sic]'.[20] Although this was based on an indirect source,[21] its tone was strongly hostile to the Western diplomatic line and, after mentioning that no one had been killed in the incident, stated:

> Great illfeeling is likely to arise out of this bloodthirsty policy of a life for limb, or even less, and it certainly seems unjustifiable, and decidedly impolitic.

Satow in his later memoirs wrote that Charles Rickerby, the then owner and editor of the *Japan Times* of Yokohama had been responsible for the attempts to 'mislead public opinion'. Rickerby had criticised the foreign witnesses' 'disgracefulness' in the light of Christianity. Satow wrote:

> It was no disgusting exhibition, but a most decent and decorous ceremony, and far more respectable than what our own countrymen were in the habit of producing for the entertainment of the public in the front of Newgate prison.[22]

Mitford, of course, shared Satow's opinion and was also much concerned about such criticisms.[23] In the *Cornhill* article he also added a point that 'one of the ablest Japanese Ministers, Gotô Shôjirô', was 'quite' of Mitford's opinion.[24]

The second point is about the interpretation of the fact that the voice of Taki Zenzaburô sounded broken. In the diplomatic report, Mitford had written:

> . . . the condemned man in a voice of some emotion and with just so much hesitation as would be natural in a man about to make a disagreeable confession . . . spoke as follows.[25]

On the other hand, in the magazine article the word 'disagreeable' was changed into 'painful'.[26] By these two apparently trifling changes mentioned above, the *Cornhill* article presented to its readers the clear idea that noble gentlemen of the West and Japan commonly shared justice in the solemn ceremony, denying deliberately the then more popular idea in Britain that the execution was the 'disgusting' revenge of the Western diplomats against the savage samurai.

In addition to these two points, another remarkable alteration of the original report was made for the magazine article, namely the less frequent usage of the word 'samurai' in the magazine than in the report. For instance, about Taki's tucking his sleeves under his knees, the report explained: '. . . that he might die as a Samurai should falling forward'.[27] However, in the magazine the passage reads as follows:

'... for a noble Japanese gentleman should die falling forwards'.[28] By this change, Taki became less abstract a figure whose culture could easily be compared with that of English gentlemen. In other words, the exotic feelings which inevitably encircle the word samurai were cut out. Otherwise, the readers would have regarded the incident as an unimportant episode which took place in a remote country.

Perhaps interconnected with this tendency, the *Cornhill* article added one paragraph in which the old-fashioned system of family education in Japan was commented on in an admiring tone. Samurai culture was treated not as strange but as equivalent to aristocratic culture in the West. The readers of the magazine could well have been led to reflect upon their own education at home. A notable fact in Mitford's writings on Japan is that it is difficult to find such words as 'singular', 'strange', 'queer' or 'quaint'. So far as explaining manners and customs of the Japanese was concerned, it seems that he was consciously avoiding these words. However, in the magazine article one can find two exceptional cases, although the adjectives were used only for describing a building and a garment. Let us see one example. In the original report Mitford wrote: 'The Courtyard was filled with infantry and lighted by large fires and lanterns'.[29] In the magazine, this part was expanded to:

> The courtyard of the temple presented a most picturesque sight; it was crowded with soldiers standing about in knots round large fires, which threw a dim flickering light over the heavy eaves and quaint gable-ends of the sacred buildings.[30]

It is most likely that this adjective 'quaint' induced many readers of the magazine to imagine the long, upwards curving gable-ends as they had sometimes seen in the drawings of Eastern pavilions on the blue and white willow-pattern china plates sold in Britain. Although the word could have conveyed different images, the readers' stock of images about Japan was not yet rich at that time, and the imprecise nature of such adjectives must have given much freedom to the readers' minds to resort to familiar ideas about the East.

In addition, one can notice that in a few parts of the *Cornhill* article the tone of the description of the execution was more romantic if compared with the same part of the original report. For example, the expression in Taki's face just before stabbing the dirk into himself had been described in the original report as follows:

Deliberately with a steady hand he took the dirk that lay before him. For a few seconds he seemed to collect his thoughts.[31]

But in the magazine, another sentence was inserted between these two sentences: 'he looked at it [the dirk] wistfully, almost affectionately'.[32]

To summarise, the magazine article showed a strong tendency to identify the samurai with the British gentry, which would have helped to increase interest in the story on the readers' part. At the same time, a very slight tinge of exoticism was added to some of the material things of Japan, together with a certain emotional tone suitable for tragic romance. It is an interesting question whether these changes can be attributed to the power of the editorship of the magazine. Particularly in this case, as the author was still in Japan, it is not likely that he could have had any chance to discuss stylistic alterations with the editor. But on the other hand, Mitford had much to say to the British public, which, he thought, had had misguided ideas about Taki's execution. Since the documents relating to the editorial correspondence of the *Cornhill Magazine* have been scattered, it seems impossible to give a solid answer to this question.[33] However, one could argue that this case at least demonstrates the possibility that a magazine article could be made substantially different from the original source by various outside influences, and judging from other later writings by Mitford, the adjective 'quaint' in the article about Taki was more than likely introduced by one of the then co-editors, Edward Dutton Cook, George Henry Lewes or George Smith, who would not have understood this young diplomat's personal concern with understanding things Japanese.

Mitford returned to England in 1870 and wrote three articles for the *Fortnightly Review*. This periodical was started by George Eliot and George Henry Lewes in 1865, aiming at 'a national forum for responsible expression of a wide variety of opinion'.[34] The journalist John Morley (1838–1923), a close friend of John Stuart Mill, succeeded to the editorship of the *Fortnightly* in 1867 and, when Mitford contributed his articles to this review, it had a more liberal colour than before, although it was always a responsible, respectable and costly periodical with a small circulation of about 2500 copies. One of Mitford's articles was entitled 'Tales of Old Japan, No. I – The Forty-seven Ronins'.[35] This was the famous vendetta story of *Chûshingura*, which had been popular among the Japanese for more than two centuries. It seems that Mitford became even more sympathetic to the culture of the Japanese military class after writing about Taki's execution for the *Cornhill Magazine* and in this *Fortnightly* article he explained confidently that the story was 'truly characteristic of Japanese ideas of honour'.[36] Mitford again used the notion of 'gentleman' to explain the word *rônin*:

> It is used to designate persons of gentle blood, entitled to bear arms, who, having become separated from their feudal lords by their own act, or by dismissal, or by fate, wander about the country in the capacity of somewhat disreputable knight-errant, without ostensible means of living.[37]

This was a radical change in the idea of *rônin* in Britain if compared with that in the early 1860s. The story contained many scenes of bloodshed and self-disembowelment, but Mitford concluded it this way: 'A terrible picture of fierce heroism which it is impossible not to admire'.[38] At the end of the article, he added a remarkable footnote, in which he apologised for his use of the word *hara-kiri* instead of 'the more elegant expression *Seppuku*': 'I retain the more vulgar form as being better known, and therefore more convenient.'[39] It is clear that Mitford stood apart from his contemporaries, who were still amused to call this Japanese custom the 'happy despatch'.

Mitford's sympathetic attitude to Japan was not confined to the military class. In the beginning of this article, he emphasised the importance of knowing Japanese religion, superstitions, their way of thought, literature and history; that is, in his words, of knowing 'the inner life of the Japanese', or 'the hidden springs by which they move'.[40] One month before this article appeared, he had contributed to the *Fortnightly Review* another article, 'A Ride through Yedo [Edo]'.[41] In this article he had made clear what he thought to be important in order to know the city of Edo. According to him, there had been many pleasant accounts of the city by foreign travellers, but nothing had been written about it for the English public 'from a Japanese point of view'.[42] The questions to be asked were: why were the Japanese paying visits to certain places, and what significance did those places have for them?

He found two ways of reaching 'the inner life of the Japanese'; one was through reading popular native story books which had become accessible to him through his increasing knowledge of the language, and the other was through excursions beyond the boundaries of the treaty ports into the interior of the country. As for the latter, Mitford was concerned not only with geographical scrutiny but with the discovery of history and legends which were attached to certain areas and were cherished by the inhabitants there. For 'A Ride through Yedo', he adopted a remarkable method in order to introduce the city to British readers. He followed two popular guidebooks for Japanese visitors to Edo: one was the Saitô family's *Edo meisho zue,* (Pictorial Guide to the Famous Spots of Edo),[43] and the other was Terakado Seiken's amusing tales of the city, *Edo hanjô ki,* (The Record of Flourishing Edo).[44] In 1872, Mitford also published two articles in a series, 'Wanderings in Japan – I, II', in the *Cornhill Magazine.* These were his travelogues from his trip to the Kamakura, Izu and Hakone districts. For this journey he had 'persuaded a native scholar' in his employ to accompany him in order to make his trip 'a means of collecting some of the old legends', which Mitford had expected to be abundant en route.[45] He had also decided to be guided around Kamakura by the mayor of the village, who, according to the native scholar, was 'a perfect storehouse of old world lore, knowing and loving every nook and stone within his jurisdiction'.[46]

Mitford's 'Ride through Yedo' starts with his description of the busy streets on the day of the Japanese New Year. His eyes take in the variety of the people in the street: an old gentleman and his suite in their ceremonial dress, a group of merry girls playing in their brightest holiday kimonos, a couple of wandering mummers in shabby court robes.[47] He then explains the origin of the custom of New Year decoration of streets and buildings using branches of firs and bamboos, and gradually leads his readers to the city's history with the rise and fall of many Shoguns.[48] He then recounts his visit to the graves of the Shoguns in the temple of Zôjôji.[49] Close to the burial ground, Mitford finds a famous Shinto shrine, Shinmei, and he invites his readers, following *Edo hanjô ki,* to share the preoccupations of such worshippers as a young girl praying for a new gold hairpin for herself, a young man suffering from love-sickness, or a merchant praying for a sudden rise in the price of his stock.[50] Outside the shrine, he finds a space for various entertainments and the serving of tea: 'In Japan, religion and amusement, tea and prayers, always go together'.[51] His 'Ride' embraces every detail of life in the city. The daimyo's residential quarters are also visited and he mentions the tasteful interior of their traditional houses.[52] The topic about which Mitford becomes most enthusiastic is Asakusa, 'the most bustling place in Yedo'. Mitford contends that 'nowhere else can you see Japanese life in such perfection'. He introduces his translation of the relevant parts of *Edo hanjô ki* and *Edo meisho zue* to the readers. There is 'a lively and joyous scene' in a broad space called Okuyama near the temple of Asakusa: 'All sorts of sights are to be seen' there, including wild beasts, performing monkeys, automata, conjurers, jesters and fortune-tellers.[53]

An interesting feature of this part of Mitford's article is his severe criticism of Alcock's statement that the portraits of the most famous courtesans of Edo were hung each year in the temple.[54] Mitford could see no such pictures there and asked many Japanese about the matter, including the priests of the temple. He concluded that Alcock's tale was 'but one of the many strange mistakes into which an imperfect knowledge of the language led the earlier travellers in Japan', and maintained that 'in no country' was 'the public harlot more abhorred and looked down upon' than in Japan. His close association with the native intellectuals and sympathy with their way of thinking was, for Mitford, indeed a matter of importance. He was to take over the former authoritative position of Alcock in the minds of British readers who were interested in Japan.[55]

Mitford goes on to Saruwaka-chô, the theatre street, where he starts explaining the history of Japanese drama. He describes the history not as a unique phenomenon, but as one example common to the world: 'The origin of the drama in Japan, as elsewhere, was religious'.[56] He finds out that the ordinary Japanese dramas are enjoyed by the middle and lower classes of the population, and he distinguishes these from Noh, the 'classical severity' of which the noble and the military classes enjoy. His long 'Ride' ends with an extensive description of a performance of Noh drama in the palace of a prince when the Duke of Edinburgh visited Japan in 1869. 'So far as I know,' writes Mitford in a proud tone, 'such an exhibition had never before been witnessed by foreigners, and it may be interesting to give an account of it'.[57]

Compared with his 'Ride', Mitford's 'Wanderings' which appeared two years later in the *Cornhill Magazine* seems to show his more thorough sympathy with the minds of the people whom he met on the way. In his 'Ride', Mitford clearly differentiated his own description from that of the two Japanese guide books: 'The style will readily show where I am translating and where I am speaking in my own person.'[58] But in his 'Wanderings', it is obvious from his style that he smoothly shared the local people's interests and often did not care about distinguishing himself from them.

He visits the Shrine of Hachiman in Kamakura, which still stands as it did 'in the time of the splendour of Yoritomo', the first Shogun of the twelfth century. Having elaborated on the violent events of the Kamakura period with which the trees, shrines, stones and rivers of the place were closely associated, Mitford stands in front of 'a simple erection of largish stones in tiers'. This 'hidden and almost forgotten' monument itself marks the grave of 'the mighty Yoritomo'.[59] Mitford compares the grave with the richly ornamented 'grand temple' of the Tokugawa Shogun in Edo and concludes that in spite of the humbleness of the monument, the name of Yoritomo 'will live in Japanese history long after the grand cemeteries of Yedo shall have crumbled into dust'.[60]

Mitford was eager to accept any legend, history, or even superstition, as long as it was cherished in the minds of the Japanese. He refers to a popular story of the last months of Yoritomo, when the Shogun was haunted by the ghosts of the enemies whom he had destroyed:

> In justice to the character of the Japanese historical books, I should add that the story of the miraculous apparitions ... is based merely upon tradition, but it is treasured nevertheless in the memory of a marvel-loving people.[61]

In a mountainous area from where one can see the 'glorious cone' of Mount Fuji 'towering above the rugged outline of the Hakone range, and the wilds of Mount Oyama, dark, gloomy, and lowering, a sacred haunt', Mitford starts talking about a Japanese demon, Tengu – 'Dog of Heaven, a hideous elf, long-clawed, long-beaked, winged, loving solitude', and the 'terror of naughty children'. Surrounded by such natural settings, he confesses:

> ... the pilgrim ... will understand how superstition has peopled haunts more beautiful, more wild, and more lonely than usual with a race of fairies and demons fairer or more terrible than the children of men.[62]

Mitford was confident that he could understand the minds of the Japanese. His notions about the Japanese people's beliefs, therefore, were a long way from those of most British writers on Japan in the 1860s, who would have labelled Japanese religion as 'idolatry' and simply called the Japanese 'pagan'. For instance, Mitford discoursed in detail on each warrior deity of Shintoism adored by the people in Kamakura, and many old heroes' relics treasured by them. Mitford regarded the belief there as 'a form of hero-worship'.[63] At this remark, some readers might well have compared this in their minds to the hero-worship custom of ancient Greece.

It seems that Mitford, in the course of his eager study of Japan, developed a belief in the universal homogeneity of mankind. It was revealed in his, probably conscious, avoidance of the word 'singular' when explaining the manners and customs of the Japanese. This belief of his was, however, more clearly demonstrated in his bold and confident style of using metaphors and similes from the West to describe things Japanese. But here it would be useful to consider the writings of his contemporary, Sir Rutherford Alcock. In 1872, Alcock contributed an article on Japan to the *Edinburgh Review*. There he discussed the similarity between Britain and Japan, in terms of their geographical location, both facing a continent across a narrow body of water, and the 'marvellous likeness' of plants in the two countries.[64] He furthered his argument by stating that if the two peoples 'of the rising and setting sun' were 'brought in close comparison – not in the nineteenth, but in the tenth or twelfth centuries – numerous points of resemblance might be traced in their social, economic and political institutions'.[65] Alcock's tone in dealing with Kaempfer had changed since his writings of the early 1860s, when he had sought to achieve 'photographic accuracy'. Now calling Kaempfer 'the most painstaking and conscientious of chroniclers',[66] Alcock supported Kaempfer's mode of explaining the former Japanese political system with close reference to the medieval European concept of the dual government by two emperors, and also asserted that the Shoguns were 'the exact counterparts of the Mayors of the Palace under the Merovingian sovereigns'.[67] However, Alcock was well aware of possible criticisms against such an old fashioned analogy and, therefore, added an apologetic note: 'we advert to these parallel periods and facts in the history of western nations to save time'.[68]

Mitford's style was different from Alcock's which was, in short, to show a possible similarity between Britain and Japan. On the contrary, Mitford, in his 'Wanderings in Japan', described the historical effect of the birth of the Shogunate in 1192 in these words:

> From that time forth until the year 1868, the Emperor, or Mikado, became a cypher, the executive being in the hands of his commander-in-chief, and so it was that we heard many fallacies about spiritual and temporal emperors.[69]

To Mitford, Kaempfer's theory was just ridiculous. Mitford referred to the Japanese diviners called *ichiko*, who would profess to give tidings of the dead, in a decisive analogy: 'The *ichiko* exactly corresponds to the spirit medium of the West.'[70] He also tried in a light-hearted way to translate place-names in Japan into a very English style upon which no other Victorian writers had ventured. For example, 'Yedo' in 'Musashi no Kuni' was changed into 'Riverdoor' in the province of 'Armsburry'.[71]

There is one illustrative paragraph in Mitford's 'Wanderings in Japan' which shows one of his experiences of discovering the basic similarity between East and West. He found in a temple in Fujisawa two Chinese characters, *'Shen Tien'* (God's Field), on a stone lantern, and exclaimed: 'What an exact reproduction of our expression "God's Acre!" '[72] It was astonishing for him 'to find how the minds of men have hit upon the same expressions of thought', and he dwelled on the fact that 'almost all the proverbs of China and Japan have their fellows in our European languages'.[73] If one takes into account such an idea of the universal homogeneity of mankind in Mitford's mind, one can see how smoothly he could use metaphorical expressions to explain some of his observations in Japan. For example, when the inhabitants of the old castle-town of Odawara were surprised at their first sight of Mitford's horse, which was much larger in size than the native horse, he observed that his horse 'created as much astonishment as a giraffe might in a Yorkshire village'.[74]

It could be said that in Mitford's case each metaphor, simile, or analogy was an act of confession of his sympathy with Japan, through which he could maintain a sense of closeness to a geographically remote country, not only in his own mind but in the minds of his British readers. In fact, when he introduced one of Shibata Kyûô's *Dôwa* (Moral Tales) to British readers, he translated the word *dôwa* into English as 'a Japanese sermon'. By this title, his readers might have been guided to remember the familiar scenes of Christian sermons at home, though for many Victorians it was not an easy task to consider religious activities in non-Christian areas on the same terms as their own. But Mitford boldly compared the two types of sermon, in the East and in the West:

> The text is taken from the Chinese Classical Books, just as we take ours from the Bible. Jokes, stories, and pointed applications to members of the congregation are as common in those sermons as dry, rigid formality is with us.[75]

When Mitford's articles were appearing, in the two or three years around about 1870, there were few others writing about Japan in popular periodicals who shared his somewhat cosmopolitan idea of human homogeneity. One of the exceptional cases was an account of a

Japanese theatre published in the *Cornhill Magazine* in September 1872.[76] The author was Edward Howard House (1836–1901), an American drama critic, who had been employed by the Japanese Ministry of Education as Lecturer in English language and literature since 1871. House, writing just as if he had been guiding his readers into the theatre, suggested that they should 'fold' themselves 'together upon the matted floor', in a stall or box. They were to follow all the performances for as long as 'one uninterrupted day' since it was a Japanese custom to enjoy day-long performances.[77] After the curtain closed upon the climax of one of the plays of the morning, they were given 'a privilege' of going behind the scenes. Soon they found themselves 'in the midst of that familiar confusion and disorder', which House supposed, 'must always be the same whenever the theatre flourishes':

> Are we really in Japan? Why, this might be an entr'acte in any Metropolitan theatre where pure English is supposed to be spoken.

He felt 'entirely at home' there.[78] From such experience House offhandedly judged that, 'taken as a whole, the Japanese comedians . . . are on a level with those of any Western nation'. Apparently, his judgement had been reached merely by the standard of Western theatres, but one must not miss the abstract qualifying phrase which he attached to his judgement: 'as illustrators of the manners and feeling of their countrymen'.[79] He did not demand that foreign drama should be performed in the same way as that of the Western theatres, clearly judging the Japanese theatre on a certain universal standard. In this respect, House was free from the popular preoccupation of the time in Britain with the notion of 'singularity' in perceiving traditional things Japanese.

House's argument was, however, confined to the narrow range of the Japanese theatre. In Mitford's case, the belief in human homogeneity was to govern his judgment of all things Japanese upon which he chose to reflect. Also, if such a belief was developed to its logical conclusion, as was the case with Mitford, one would attain an open-minded viewpoint *vis-à-vis* Japan as well as Britain. Comparisons between the two countries, therefore, often led him to serious reflection on, for example, sexual morals in Japan. He was much concerned with the unfair and persistent 'sweeping attacks'[80] on the Japanese with regard to their alleged 'licentiousness'. He criticised, for example, the general charge that in Japan 'men of position and family often chose their wives among prostitutes in such places as "The Three Seacoasts" '. Mitford asked: 'Are not such things known in Europe?' He confessed that '*mésalliances*' were 'far rarer in Japan than with us'.[81] Mitford emphasised the clear separation in Japan between the world of prostitutes and the rest of society. With the help of an official guidebook he studied the details of the renowned Yoshiwara quarter of Edo, and maintained that 'the gulf between virtue and vice in Japan' was 'even greater than in England' because 'the Eastern courtesan' was 'confined to a certain quarter of the town'. He concluded:

> Vice jostling virtue in the public places; virtue imitating the fashions set by vice . . . these are social phenomena which the East knows not.[82]

In the interests of accuracy, one should note that the segregation of the courtesan quarter in Edo was made stricter than before by the Tempô Reform of the early 1840s; Mitford was generalising on the basis of a phenomenon which had recently developed.

What about the custom prevalent among lower-class people in Japan of bathing in public bath-houses, often without separation of the sexes? This custom was something which caused much astonishment and curiosity among Victorian visitors and, according to Mitford, even 'spread abroad very false notions upon the subject of the chastity of Japanese women'.[83] Mitford considered that those people were 'so poor' that they could not afford 'a bath at home', and that, as they had been 'used to the scene from their childhood', they saw 'no indelicacy in it'. He frankly concluded: 'it is a matter of course, and *honi soit qui mal y pense*'. He reminded his readers of 'the promiscuous herding together of all sexes and ages which disgraces our own lodging-houses in the great cities'.[84] Mitford also castigated those popular opinions held by the British, such as: 'It is no disgrace for a respectable Japanese to sell his daughter' or 'up to the time of her marriage, the conduct of a young girl is a matter of no importance whatever'.[85] He explained that it was 'only the neediest people' who sold their children to be prostitutes.[86] Mitford was conscious of the importance of an observer's own character in presenting ideas about foreign countries, and concluded his criticism with a telling suggestion:

> These charges of vice and immodesty [should] . . . rather recoil upon the accusers, who would appear to have studied the Japanese woman only in the harlot of Yokohama.[87]

Furthermore, he bitterly regretted that the 'corrupting influence' of the foreigners upon the women in the open ports was undeniable: 'Strange as it seems, our contact all over the East has an evil effect upon the natives'.[88]

These high-toned, irritated lines of Mitford might reveal the fact that his view of Japan was not likely to be accepted smoothly by the general public in Britain of those days. He published his *Tales of Old Japan* in two volumes through Macmillan & Co. in February 1871, adding more of the popular stories and folk-tales of the country. In this work Mitford tried deliberately to present the variety of Japanese culture, the manifestations of which, he thought, differed according to social classes. In the preface, he explained that he had searched 'diligently' but in vain for any story in which the emperor or *gôshi*, that is the farmer-samurai, played a conspicuous part. 'With these exceptions,' Mitford declared, 'I think that all classes are fairly represented in my stories'.[89] It was Alcock himself who had called in 1861 for an examination of manners and customs 'in all different classes' of the Japanese.[90] However, Alcock, in spite of his intention, had only introduced a fairly general idea about the Japanese; the savage rulers and the civilised people. Mitford's work invited the readers to understand sympathetically not the Japanese in general but individual figures who would represent each class in Japan. Things and thought in Japanese society were always shown through the eyes of its members against the background of Mitford's philosophy about basic human homogeneity.

When this work appeared two diverse responses were expressed in Britain: a few writers agreed with it, but others showed pronounced resistance. An example of the former was the response of Alexander Innes Shand (1832–1907): journalist, critic, a fine rider, shot and angler and a friend of John Blackwood. In his anonymous article, 'The Romance of Japanese Revolution' published in *Blackwood's Magazine* in June 1874, he briefly mentioned Mitford's work:

> But of the works that have been written, there is none, perhaps, that gives a more thorough insight into Japanese society than one of the lightest and least pretending – Mitford's '*Tales of Old Japan*'.[91]

However, Mitford's method of understanding Japanese people required much energy and time in addition to learning the Japanese language. Although Shand appreciated Mitford's work, when Shand himself described contemporary Japan, he could not but produce a compilation of various traditional ideas about the country, as will be shown later.

Perhaps, even among Western residents in Japan, few people were

In Quest of the Inner Life of the Japanese

qualified to follow Mitford's method. As Mitford recalled later, it was Minister Sir Harry Parkes who much encouraged his writing of *Tales of Old Japan*.[92] Basil Hall Chamberlain (1850–1935), the first Professor of Japanese and Philology at the Imperial University of Japan, suggested in 1893 that the members of the British Legation at that time were outstanding among all the foreign residents there in terms of studying the country. According to Chamberlain, Parkes 'founded a school' in the Legation:

> His stimulating influence raised the members of the consular service to the position of chief authorities on all subjects connected with Japan.[93]

It is thus fairly understandable that in the summer of 1871, a guest of the British Legation at Tokyo witnessed its members struggling with one another for the single copy of *Tales of Old Japan* which had recently arrived from London.[94]

The reception of the book in Britain was not always that enthusiastic; besides Shand's remark, the anonymous article ' "Ours" in Japan' in the May 1871 issue of *Fraser's Magazine* was one of the few articles which may have been written under the influence of Mitford's work.[95] The article was a review of a 'droll volume'[96] entitled *Our Life in Japan* published by two young British soldiers[97] of the 9th Regiment, which had been stationed in Japan since 1866. The reviewer tried to show his readers the highly refined features of Japanese life, rearranging the fragmented information presented by the soldiers out of their casual interest in emphasising the 'most peculiar and sensational' facts of Japanese life.[98] The reviewer showed his great concern, like Mitford, with 'the legendary lore of the country',[99] and with the samurai's mind on the occasion of an execution,[100] and concluded that 'the normal life of the people' in Japan had 'reached a height in social relations, in manners and in art, far beyond what some of their inherited customs . . . would seem to indicate'.[101] Then he considered the quality of life of those soldiers in Yokohama in contrast with this 'polished' society in Japan:

> As reflected in this Japan mirror, the life and interest of our English youth may be classified under the following heads: Fox-hunting, Horse-racing; Practical joking; After-dinner toasting, and responding; Drinking soda and B.[102]

Considering those soldiers to be 'fair chips of [off?] the British block',[103] the author expressed a vague anxiety about the future of

Britain if the energy and spirit of its youth were thus wasted and its government was unable to recognise 'the further destinies of the country'.[104] When this article appeared in Britain, the Paris Commune was in its final stage of collapse, and British intellectuals who had been anxious about its possible impact on the lower classes in Britain were in a mood resembling that following a nightmare. The writer presented an unhappy image of the contemporary British populace:

> Crowded and cramped in our overgrown cities, forming centres of disease and moral corruption, turning the struggle for existence into a chronic war of class against class – here are the people.[105]

It could be argued that if one developed a belief in the homogeneity of two peoples, one would naturally compare the lives of the two in terms of their outer forms rather than their substance. In such a case of comparison, 'refinement' was the notion which tended to emerge. Already, in 1857, Whitwell Elwin, the editor of the *Quarterly Review*, had discussed the refined characteristics of the life of the Chinese people in the countryside. This was in his review of the accounts of travel and residence in China by Robert Fortune, by Sir John Francis Davis (the chief British diplomatic figure in China in the 1840s), and by Évariste Huc.[106] Elwin's point in this article was to show that 'the better they [the Chinese] are known, the more apparent it becomes that man in China is much the same as man elsewhere'.[107] He argued this way:

> The assertion that the Chinese are a semi-barbarous nation is denied by almost every traveller who has penetrated beyond their ports and lived freely among the people.[108]

Elwin concluded:

> In the refinements of life, in courtesy, humanity and domestic affection, they are at least our equals, and in some respects, our superiors.[109]

However, this article on China was fairly exceptional among the mass of unsympathetic writings about the country which were published in Britain in those days. It seems that any information from an old resident who seriously studied Far Eastern countries was almost destined at home to be treated in an unsympathetic way. The *Saturday Review*, one of the most influential weekly reviews of the time, published a note on Mitford's work on 11 March 1871.[110] The anonymous writer interpreted Mitford's messages about the homogeneity of

Japanese culture with those of other countries as indicative of Japan's 'strangely imitative' character. In this writer's eyes, most of the stories and folk-tales which Mitford had endeavoured to introduce to British readers lacked in originality. He pointed out similar folk-tales in Russia, Germany, Ireland, Spain and Brittany and boasted that originality came from the West, maintaining that the Japanese had 'borrowed' ideas in a 'wholesale manner' from foreign sources. In the twentieth century, scholars have become interested in the coincidental world-wide distribution of certain patterns of folk-tales,[111] but for the above writer it was inconceivable that the Japanese folk-tales could be equally original.

It seems that no serious criticism of this review was published. In fact, there was sufficient reason for the idea of 'the imitative Japanese' to prevail in Britain in the early 1870s. As Mitford himself admitted, his study actually dealt with the 'fast disappearing civilisation' of 'old Japan' which had endured for centuries up to just a decade before.[112] 'New Japan' was rapidly growing, being rooted in the open ports and Tokyo, the new capital undergoing the thorough Westernisation of *bunmei-kaika,* or the 'enlightened' movement of destruction of much of the indigenous culture of the country. It is ironic that British learning about Japan, like Mitford's, should have begun when the influence of Britain, or the West in general, began destroying indigenous features of Japanese society. It is true that Sir Harry Parkes' 'school' was to produce sound scholarship on Japan, with rich knowledge of the language and a critical spirit based on a broader knowledge of the humanities. Satow, W.G. Aston, and Chamberlain would become distinguished figures through their activities in the Asiatic Society of Japan, which was established at Yokohama in 1872 under Parkes' guidance. However, by the mid-1870s their writings had not yet been published in popular British periodicals. Despite Mitford's efforts to change popular British ideas about the Far East, a fresh trend was beginning to appear among British writings about Japan; that is, the rapid prevalence of the word 'singularity' as a label. At the beginning of the 1870s Westernisation became conspicuous even in the ordinary streets of Tokyo. Mitford was already expressing his disgust at the appearance of the soldiers of the new army, dressed in ill-fitting European garments, 'disfiguring into the semblance of apes men who really used to look well in their own national dress'.[113] The introduction of Western 'civilisation' to Japan, which must have been what many British writers had advocated, began to be realised in the embarrassing form of imitation. Complex arguments among British writers on New Japan started from around 1871. The notion of the 'remoteness' of Japan from the West seems to have been revived and reinforced in Britain, leaving in Japan only a few sympathetic British scholars.

The following is an episode which may illustrate the distance of Mitford from one of the leading men of letters in contemporary Britain with regard to their attitudes to Japan. In his 'Wanderings in Japan', Mitford, after explaining a splendid scene he had faced in a mountainous area one morning, wrote as follows:

> It is always a matter of regret to me that the beauties of Japanese scenery should have been done justice to by no gifted word-painter like John Ruskin.[114]

On the other hand, Ruskin was becoming rather hostile to the Japanese who came to Britain. Although Ruskin was one of the people who had revealed Japanese art to Britain even before the London International Exhibition of 1862, about the late 1860s he began criticising Japanese art in general terms. Having seen a performance by some Japanese jugglers, he wrote a letter to 'a working cork-cutter' Thomas Dixon, describing Japan as a country 'of partially inferior race':

> There has long been an increasing interest in Japanese art, which has been very harmful to many of our own painters.[115]

Mitford's view might have come closer to Ruskin's idea of Japan as a result of rapid changes in the country, but for some reason he stopped writing on Japan for a quarter of a century after 1872. He is said to have visited Japan a second time on his round-the-world tour in 1874, but he never wrote about the visit, which he made on his westward voyage from San Francisco.[116]

6 'The Strange History of this Strange Country'

At the end of the eighteenth century, Honda Rimei (Toshiaki), a mathematician in Edo, expressed a unilinear evolutionistic idea about the histories of nations and estimated the time-lag between the West and Japan as 4500 years, the former being ahead of the latter. However, Honda suggested at the same time that Japan would become as great an Empire as Britain within three hundred years if the ruler of Japan adopted his proposal to move the capital of Japan from Edo to the Kamchatka Peninsula – on the same latitude as London, and followed his special scheme of governing. Honda based his argument on his peculiarly flexible notion of time supported by his own mathematics which was not well understood either by his contemporaries or by later historians.[1] How is it possible for a country to catch up in a short period with a civilisation that has taken several thousand years to develop? Although Honda was serious when he proposed a new name for the future empire of Japan, 'Konippon' (Old Japan), thinking that Japan would soon become a very old country, he was laughed at as an empty boaster.[2]

However, less than three-quarters of a century later, a similar argument about the extraordinary speed of Japanese development became popular in Britain. This time the argument was not a mere forecasting of the future of Japan, but was concerned with the real political and social changes which had taken place in the space of only a few years following the imperial restoration of 1868:

> Four years ago we were still in the middle ages – we have leapt at a bound into the nineteenth century – out of poetry into plain, useful prose.

This was Algernon Bertram Mitford's brief statement of his feelings about the new Japan in 1872.[3] The idea that Japan's recent progress covered at one stride many centuries of Western history continued to prevail among British writers throughout the 1870s. In 1872, Sir Rutherford Alcock, who had retired from his diplomatic career as Minister at Peking in the previous year, made the same point:

> The Japanese are the only nation in the history of the world that has ever taken five centuries at a stride, and devoured in a decade all the

space dividing feudalism and despotism from constitutional government and the other developments, commercial and municipal, of modern life.[4]

Two years later, Alcock put even stronger emphasis on this point:

> It has been remarked that no other nation has 'ever before taken five centuries at a bound'. But with equal truth ten centuries might have been the term.[5]

Sir David Wedderburn (1835–82), sometime Member of Parliament for South Ayrshire, who became one of the 'circumnavigators', an emerging, fashionable category of mankind at that time,[6] made a similar point in 1878:

> In this country a few years have sufficed for effecting changes such as have elsewhere required many centuries.[7]

Wedderburn was conscious that he was a mere traveller. So he carefully supported his opinion with that of others:

> Even the best-informed of the strangers in whose presence these changes have actually been wrought are loud in their expressions of astonishment.[8]

It is notable that Alcock, supposedly one of the 'best informed', having been President of the Royal Geographical Society (1876–8), should have repeated this somewhat extravagant language even as late as 1880.[9] Had Honda heard these opinions, he would have smiled at the belated but enthusiastic confirmation of his own views.

Along with this particular way of describing the pace of change in Japan, British writers once more resorted to the use of the terms 'singularity' or 'strangeness' when discussing the character of the country. They emphasised that recent events in Japan would find no counterpart in human history. In 1872, Charles Lanman, American Secretary to the Japanese Legation in Washington, published a book[10] in New York and London on the Iwakura Mission, the first large delegation sent by the new government to the West during 1871–3. Alcock reviewed this work in the July issue of the *Edinburgh Review*, in which he interpreted the latest decade of Japan's history as 'a revolution so entirely unprecedented in its character, extent, and rapidity of consummation'.[11] In the concluding part of this article, Alcock called this 'revolution' 'one of the strangest revolutions in history'.[12] In the same year, Frederic Marshall (1839–1905), a British barrister who had lived in Paris for more than twenty years, forecast in

Blackwood's Magazine that the recent 'introduction of European education, laws, and usages amongst the Japanese' would 'lead to revolutions still more thorough than those which had already taken place'. Of the character of the social changes in Japan, he wrote:

> They are trying a grave experiment, of which the world offers no other example.[13]

In 1874, Alcock again stressed the uniqueness of 'this singular phase in the national life of the Japanese',[14] basing his argument on new information about Japan provided by the works of those who had recently been in the country, such as Samuel Mossman, a journalist covering the Far East and Australia; F. O. Adams, formerly First Secretary to the British Legation in Japan and J. F. Lowder, formerly Vice-Consul at Hyôgo and Osaka and from 1872 Legal Adviser to the Board of Revenue and Customs in Japan.[15] Wedderburn, in the article mentioned above, also observed that the recent history of Japan presented 'some of the most startling phenomena recorded anywhere in the authentic annals of the human race'.[16]

One can observe that the usage of the label 'singular' more or less summed up the difficulty faced by British writers when they tried to explain the reason for various rapid changes in Japan. In particular, the development of public works, such as telegraphic communication, the mint, lighthouses, railroads, and dockyards, was astonishingly rapid. W. G. Aston (1841–1911), one of the ablest linguists at the British Legation in Tokyo and interpreter for the Iwakura Mission, noted in his article in *Macmillan's Magazine,* another one-shilling periodical rivalling the *Cornhill Magazine,* that this 'progress in civilization' was 'astounding'.[17] Aston mentioned the many new developments which were taking place in Japan. The new Japanese army was drilled after the French fashion and the navy was trained by the British.[18] He wrote:

> One edict followed another; many privileges of the upper class were abolished, and the lower classes were raised in position . . . The Mikado, too, came out of his seclusion into broad daylight.[19]

It seemed to Aston that all the changes which took place were as if 'by magic':

> It seemed as if a sudden passion had seized upon the people to pull down and abolish everything that was old.[20]

At this time, British writers were raising such questions as the reasons for these changes, the identity of the real promoter of the revolution, the financial conditions for introducing so many European things, and so on, which they found difficult to answer.[21] Of all the social and political changes in Japan, the one which British writers thought most 'singular' was the spontaneous abolition of the daimyos' territorial rights, the lead for which had been given by the four powerful daimyos in south-west Japan during 1869–71. It is obvious that such 'extraordinary' events made British writers view the history of Japan with a renewed sense of wonder. Any 'strangeness' in its course was bound to be viewed in a fresh light. Marshall enumerated 'strange', 'singular' and 'incredible' facts in the recent history of the country such as this 'warlike nation's' peaceful reception of Commodore Perry's squadron without any fight, or the sudden cessation of the anti-foreigners movement after the bombardment of Kagoshima and Shimonoseki.[22] For Alcock, too, there were many things difficult to understand. For example, how did Iwakura Tomomi, although one of the leaders of the revolution, acquire his knowledge of men and affairs when he had lived in obscurity before the critical time?[23] 'A greater mystery' for Alcock was about 'the Mikado' who had been living 'the enervated and miserable life of forced idleness and seclusion':

> How has it been possible for such a youth, even under strong guidance, to accept the role he is now playing with apparently so much *aplomb* and satisfaction to himself?[24]

Another circumnavigator, Sir Charles Wentworth Dilke (1843–1911), the radical politician and the author of *Greater Britain*, wrote about the 'singularity' of Japan, after his second tour round the world in 1875.[25] He posed several questions about the participants in the Japanese revolution and the contemporary political and social situation in the country. Although he tried hard to find answers, Japan for him was, in the end, 'so strange a country'. He gave one example:

> What can be, or ever has been, in the history of the world, more singular than the combination of the extreme democracy of the spirit of its government with the blind tradition that is personified in the Mikado?[26]

Given their bewilderment, what kind of language did British writers use in describing events in Japan? A. I. Shand, in order to explain the sudden fall of Japanese feudalism, in 1874 used the familiar label of 'happy despatch':

> How came it that the victorious daimios were prevailed upon to

'The Strange History of this Strange Country'   113

execute a happy despatch – to part with their authority and their lands, and their formidable military following?[27]

Using these words, Shand may have imagined that his argument would be in tune with the British reading public who were supposedly ready to show enthusiasm for this type of rhetoric. Some writers resorted to other familiar metaphors. In 1879, a short account on Japan appeared in the *New Quarterly Magazine,* formerly Oswald Crawfurd's dilettante literary periodical, then owned and edited by Kegan Paul. The article was on a new English dialect 'Yokohama Pidgin' spoken by the 'Yokohamese'. In this article, the author C. G. Leland (1824–1903), the American ethnologist who was living in London and was the founder of the Labelais Club there, reviewed Hoffman Atkinson's humorous work, *Exercises in the Yokohama Dialect* published in Yokohama in 1874. Atkinson had been in Japan for several years and was then made Secretary to the American Legation at St Petersburg. Leland added further information from the manuscript collection entitled *Japoniana Curiosissima* made by Arthur Diósy (1856–1923), 'a student of Japanese', and a future important member of the Japan Society, London, about the turn of the century. Leland introduced his readers to the story of the rapid 'development at Yokohama of a new language' as a phenomenon comparable with popular tales of sudden growth such as *Jonah's Gourd,* or *Jack and the Beanstalk.* One can imagine that his language would excite sympathy from readers who shared the common wonder at the sudden change in Japan. Leland wrote:

> The world had acquired Japan, and with it a fresher instance still of a sudden growth, which is also in keeping with the age in this, that it is no story at all, but a plain fact.[28]

Wedderburn, in 1878, summarised his impression in the following simile:

> The political and social revolution which created modern Japan, has been as sudden and complete as a theatrical transformation scene.[29]

In emphasising the 'singular' characteristics of Japan, those who had not been to the country themselves were more radical and imaginative than those who had stayed there for a long period. Shand, for instance, used in 1874 the word 'mystery' for Japan in a more general way than did Alcock. Shand wrote:

> Japan has always been enveloped in mystery, thanks to its jealous

policy of exclusion; and now that its ports are thrown open to us, it is more of a mystery than ever.[30]

For Shand, the story of Western contact with Japan 'resembled in all respects a historical romance' with its abundant sensations and startling surprises.[31]

Is it really possible, however, to say that British writers were simply resorting to the old label of 'singularity' in explaining things Japanese during the 1870s? Underneath such reinforcement of the popular label for Japan, there was a growing complexity in the British way of perceiving the country. As has been shown at length, one thing which is obvious in these articles of the 1870s is that the word 'singularity' was used increasingly with such words as 'romance' and 'mystery'. In other words, the nuance of the label 'singularity', which could have been used within the basically neutral sense of uniqueness as was often the case in the previous decades, became more closely related to a notion of 'unreality'. Here the question arises: why?

It is undeniable that mutual contact between Britain and Japan increased to an unprecedented degree in this period. For example, during the one year 1870, 318 British vessels entered the harbour of Yokohama.[32] In 1873, Henry Reeve mentioned the Pacific liner service as 'one of the most extraordinary exploits of our age', and explained how its huge paddle-wheel steamer would reach Yokohama from San Francisco in twenty-four days 'with the punctuality of railroad', and how the company had enjoyed eighty voyages without any accident up to 1871.[33] The amount of information about Japan increased very rapidly in Britain, from the exchange of growing numbers of visitors, and from the development of technology in communications. In fact, many writers would have been able to present, had they so wished, substantial answers to the individual questions mentioned above about the recent changes in Japan. How then can one explain the contradiction between the growing idea of 'mysterious' Japan and the obvious progress in the knowledge of the actual state of the country? It could possibly be argued that an increase in the amount of information about a country does not always change the basic mental framework of others when perceiving the country. One should also bear in mind, as has been mentioned earlier, that British images of Japan could hardly have been separated from those of the British themselves. In order to understand the persistent prevalence of the label 'mysterious' in writings on Japan in the 1870s, it will be helpful to examine how much knowledge of contemporary Japan British writers

'The Strange History of this Strange Country' 115

thought they were able to enjoy, and in what ways the knowledge was interconnected with their ideas of Britain.

First, it is important to estimate the strength of British public interest in Japan at the time. Obviously, international exhibitions in Europe excited fascination among the general public for Japanese products, interest in which had previously been more or less confined to wealthy aristocratic society. Following the London International Exhibition of 1862, more Japanese products, many of them inexpensive, were exhibited and sold at the International Exposition at Paris in 1867. At the Vienna International Exhibition of 1873, the enthusiasm for the extensive collection of Japanese arts and crafts was even more evident, being helped by the general interest in the Eastern world stimulated by the geographical location of Vienna as the traditional European gate to the East. Also, on this occasion, people's interest in goods from China shifted to those from Japan because there was a delay in the arrival of Chinese cargo from Hong Kong. *The Times* reported how the visitors to the Vienna Exhibition expressed their eagerness to discover tasteful Japanese goods.[34] Already in 1870, Sir Matthew Digby Wyatt (1820–77) the architect and writer on art, formerly Secretary to the Executive Committee of the Great Exhibition in 1851, had explained the increasing interest in oriental art, particularly of the Far East, among Western artists and artisans.[35]

Of course, popular interest in Japan was not confined to the country's material culture. The long stay of the numerous members of the Iwakura Mission in Europe for their study of Western civilisation during the years 1872–73 excited public interest in Japan and the Japanese. From the end of 1871 to early 1873, *The Times* published some sixty long and short articles on the mission besides ninety other notes on Japan. This number demonstrates the extent of the interest which the mission created in Britain, if one compares it with the fact that the number of articles on Japan published in *The Times* during 1870 was only about twenty-five. Also, round-the-world tourists arranged their schedules to spend a large portion of time in Japan. In 1878, Wedderburn explained that there was a strong curiosity about Japan among the British public:

> A traveller returning home from a tour of circumnavigation will (if I may judge from my own experience) be asked more questions about Japan than about any other foreign land, and will hear the strongest expressions of a desire to visit that country.[36]

Supported by such popular zeal, information about the country was introduced to Britain through various media. Besides private correspondence from the extensive number of British residents in Japan, there were three new factors which influenced directly or indirectly the contents of articles on Japan in British periodicals in the 1870s: first, the appearance of the works of round-the-world tourists; second, the growth of the publication of English newspapers in Japanese treaty ports; and third, the progress of British scholarship on Japanese society and culture.

With regard to the works of round-the-world tourists, one of the earliest publications, and probably the most influential one in terms of generating ideas about contemporary Japan among British magazine and review articles, was Joseph Alexander von Hübner's *Promenade autour du monde – 1871*. This was first published in Paris in 1873 and its English version, *A Ramble round the World*, translated by Mary Elizabeth Herbert, was published in London in 1874. Von Hübner's work went into many editions both in France and in England, and by 1877 the sixth edition was in preparation in Paris.[37] Baron von Hübner, born at Vienna in 1811, had been an eminent Austrian diplomat. He spent his earlier career as an aide to his father by blood, Prince Metternich, and later represented Austria as Ambassador in Paris and at the Vatican. His *Promenade* aroused great interest among British writers on Japan, not only because of the fame of the author in Europe, but also because of the importance of the Japanese leaders with whom the author had had interviews. Also, it was clear to readers of his work that the author had been told much about contemporary affairs by several Japan specialists in the diplomatic corps in Japan. Henry Reeve published a review of this book in the *Edinburgh Review* in the summer of 1873.[38] Alcock also mentioned the book in the *Quarterly Review* the following year,[39] and Shand, too, used it in his article on Japan in *Blackwood's Magazine*, remarking that von Hübner's 'account of Japan was the best that has lately been published'.[40] Its fifth French edition was reviewed in the *Quarterly Review* by the barrister and essayist Abraham Hayward in 1877.[41] Von Hübner's estimation of Japanese leaders and their policies was widely accepted by British reviewers, as will be discussed later.

It was of no less interest for British writers who were concerned with Japan that since the 1860s several English newspapers had been founded in Yokohama. Earlier examples were Albert W. Hansard's *Japan Herald* (started in 1861), Raphael Schoyer's *Japan Express* (1862), Francisco S. da Roza's *Japan Commercial News* (1863), *Japan Times* by Charles Rickerby (1865), John Reddie Black and M. J. B.

Noordhoek Hegt's *Japan Gazette* (1867), and so on. In 1870, J. R. Black began the illustrated monthly magazine, *Far East*. Charles Wirgman was also active in the 1870s as the editor of *Japan Punch* (from 1862) and as the correspondent in Japan for *Illustrated London News*. The *Japan Herald* and William Dunston Howell and Horatio Nelson Lay's *Japan Mail* (1870) were the local periodicals which were often quoted by British writers during the early 1870s.[42] Quotations from the local English Press, however, appeared in British periodicals for only a short period in the first half of the 1870s. This may have been the result of Press censorship by the Japanese government, especially the strict measures issued in 1875 (*Zanbô ritsu*), which damaged the credibility even of the treaty-port newspapers. Although publications within the treaty ports were beyond Japanese jurisdiction, some foreign writers in Yokohama, such as J. R. Black, who were close to or employed by the Japanese government were partially restricted in their expression of opinion, and their papers declined in quality.

While newspapers degenerated in Japan, publications about Japan were steadily increasing in Britain during the 1870s. Adams published a comprehensive history of Japan in the years 1874 and 1875.[43] Mossman's work published in 1873 covered extensively the recent state of affairs in Japan.[44] In 1879, A. H. Mounsey's *The Satsuma Rebellion: An Episode of Modern Japanese History* appeared in London. The author had been First Secretary to the British Legation at Tokyo for two and a half years, since 1876. In 1880, Alcock reviewed this work, together with Adams' second volume, and wrote that both of them had 'left very carefully-written histories, derived from all the best sources, official and private'. He even added the following complimentary words: 'To them the reader may safely be referred as standard works of authority'.[45] In 1880, the Naval Architect Sir Edward Reed's work on Japan,[46] and the famous lady traveller Isabella Bird's *Unbeaten Tracks in Japan* were published.[47]

Along with this type of endeavour, a genre which was of a specialised character also appeared in national magazines and reviews during the latter half of the 1870s. This consisted of articles written by linguists living in Japan. Before discussing these articles, however, one must mention the effort made by the Reverend James Summers (1828–91), Professor of Chinese at King's College, London, to encourage young linguists to produce scholarly writings on Japan. During the years 1864–65, Summers had already published in his *Chinese and Japanese Repository* a few articles on the language and literature of Japan by Ernest Satow and F. V. Dickins (1838–1915), a medical officer of the Royal Navy who had been stationed in Yokohama from about 1863 to 1866. After this periodical ceased publication in 1865, Summers started a new magazine in 1870: *Phoenix, a Monthly Magazine for China, Japan & Eastern Asia*. Until it ceased publication in June 1873, Aston, Satow and some Japanese abroad, such as Kikuchi Dairoku, then a student at Cambridge, contributed their writings on things Japanese. This magazine also reprinted articles extracted from the Yokohama Press.[48]

Although Summers' endeavours were rarely acknowledged in the articles on Japan which appeared in national periodicals, it is probable that some writers, such as Alcock, were reading them minutely. The *Phoenix* certainly paved the way for those young linguists to contribute their writings to more popular periodicals in later years.

During the years 1876 and 1877, Basil Hall Chamberlain published two articles in the *Cornhill Magazine*. In the first article, written with the assistance of Aston, he introduced his readers in great detail to the world of Noh theatre.[49] The second article was entitled 'Japanese Miniature Odes', and in it he revealed the condensed universe of Japanese classical short poetry (*waka*).[50] These articles may be classified as a development of the scholarship on the inner life of the Japanese which had been started by Mitford in the late 1860s. Japanese ethics were also studied in various ways. For example, Charles Hamilton Aidé (1826–1906), the novelist and composer, introduced the readers of the *Cornhill* to the ethics of *Jitsugokyô*, the popular Buddhist preaching which was said to have been written by the ninth-century priest Kûkai.[51]

In addition to these works, during the 1870s some writers were able to contribute to British magazines articles on Japan which had been written on the basis of close co-operation with Japanese intellectuals who were staying in Europe. For example, the popular author, Robert Louis Stevenson (1850–94) introduced the life of Yoshida Shôin, the eminent martyr of the Japanese revolution, to British readers. His account was based on what Masaki Taizô, one of Yoshida's disciples, had told Stevenson.[52] An extraordinary case of co-operation is the article by Frederic Marshall (1839–1905) which was published under the title 'Japan' in *Blackwood's Magazine* in September 1872.[53] Judging from a file of fragmentary manuscripts entitled 'Zaigai kôkan gaikokujin koyô kankei zakken (Miscellaneous Documents Relating to Employment of Foreigners at Japanese Diplomatic Establishments Abroad)' in the Archives of the Japanese Ministry of Foreign Affairs,[54] it seems that he was employed by the newly-established

Japanese Legation in Paris on a part-time basis during August–September 1871, and in the autumn of the next year, when the Iwakura Mission was staying in Britain, he was given a full-time post at the Legation. Later, in 1875, he was officially made Honorary Secretary, and then in 1881 Honorary Advisor to the Legation. He made a considerable contribution to Japanese diplomatic efforts to secure revision of the treaties between Japan and European countries. His contract was renewed twice after his retirement in 1888 and his relationship with Japanese diplomatic agencies in Europe lasted until his death in Brighton in 1905.[55]

Marshall was a friend of John Blackwood and an extensive contributor to *Blackwood's Magazine*. His first article appeared in the magazine in July 1871 under the title 'History of the Commune of Paris'. This was one of the early critical and detailed accounts of the commune which were written for British readers by British residents in Paris. By the time Marshall contributed the article on Japan to the magazine in 1872 he had become an established writer on the political and social aspects of France. One of his letters to Blackwood shows that in mid-July 1872 Marshall suddenly wanted to cancel one article on French home life which was due to appear in the September issue, and to substitute an 'Article on "The State of Japan" '.[56] This was partly at the request of the Japanese Minister Sameshima Naonobu (1846–80). Marshall wrote to Blackwood:

> Sameshima is very conscious that, at the moment when the great special Japanese Embassy is on the point of arriving in England, a clear statement should be given of what Japan now is.[57]

Marshall went on to explain his special qualifications for the work:

> I have of course information that no one else possesses & I think the paper may be made very interesting.[58]

The subsequent letters from Marshall to Blackwood show that the article completed was, in fact, a product of painstaking collaboration between Sameshima and Marshall. On 6 August, Marshall wrote:

> This Japanese article has been very difficult to progress. I have had to extract nearly all of it (for very little authentic information exists in books) out of Sameshima's head or out of Japanese documents which he has translated to me. As his current of thought is not the same as mine you may imagine the labour and the fatigue that all this has involved.[59]

In his letter of several days later, Marshall explained the situtation about the 'terrible Japan article':

> I am at it literally for ten hours a day, but the difficulty of worming accurate information out of people who are afraid of making the most trifling error . . . is really very great . . . And then when I think I have got it quite right, have written a couple of pages as hard as I can scribble . . . and read it to dear, good Sameshima, he gently says, three times out of four, 'no, that is not it at all', and I have to begin all over again.[60]

However, Marshall in some respects seems to have enjoyed his discussions with Sameshima:

> There is an amusing side to it, however; he is so intensely desirous to be correct, that he discusses the correct meaning of a word for half an hour, with a severity and an earnestness which we Europeans never reach.[61]

The manuscript was at last completed following Marshall's own rearrangement of its parts. It was just in time for the September issue of the magazine, and it certainly contained much new information which no one else could provide at that time. Reactions to this article will be discussed later.

It would appear, then, that British writers in the 1870s felt they knew Japan fairly well. Henry Reeve's remark in 1873 probably expressed the common feeling of those who were interested in Japan concerning the amount of information about the country in Britain:

> Considering the short period which has elapsed since Lord Elgin's memorable visit in 1858 . . . it is surprising how familiar we have already become with Japanese life.[62]

As early as 1871, Alcock had already emphasised that, owing to steam navigation and the telegraph, 'a great mass of well-digested information' concerning China and Japan did exist, 'only waiting to be analysed and reproduced in a more readable form than blue books usually supply'.[63]

Given their belief in their familiarity with things Japanese, the prevalence among these writers of the idea that Japan was 'mysterious' strikes the observer as very puzzling. Even Marshall mentioned the strangeness of Japan in the article he wrote with the help of Sameshima. After elaborating on the recent history of Japan with a good amount of understanding of its characteristics, he concluded:

'The Strange History of this Strange Country'

Such is, in the shortest words, the strange history of this strange country.[64]

One wonders whether there might be a psychological explanation for this puzzling tendency. An answer can be obtained by examining how these writers tried to change first-hand data about the recent Japanese revolution into 'a more readable form' for their readers, and then how those paradoxical perceptions were interconnected with their ideas of Britain and the British themselves.

Among the popular arguments about Japan in the 1870s, a most conspicuous topic was to ask who were the real promoters of the revolution. For this question, von Hübner's book provided British writers with a decisive answer. The account of his visit to the palace of the Mikado to obtain an audience with the 'divine' figure attracted attention in Britain. Following the audience given in 1870 to William Henry Seward, the former Secretary of State of the United States of America, von Hübner's audience was only the second one that had ever been given privately to a foreign individual.[65] In 1873, in his article in the *Edinburgh Review*, Reeve quoted several pages from von Hübner's book to illustrate the ceremony.[66] Von Hübner was accompanied by Adams and Satow of the British Legation. They were first 'received by Sanjô [Sanetomi], the first-minister, by Iwakura [Tomomi], and three confidential ministers, Kido [Takayoshi], Ôkuma [Shigenobu] and Itagaki [Taisuke]; the delegates of the Chôshiu, Hizen and Tosa clans, who with Saigô [Takamori], the delegate of the Satsumas, not then present, made the revolution of 1868'.[67]

In von Hübner's eyes, these figures could be regarded either as 'the regenerators or the destroyers of Japan'. The old diplomat judged each one's character from the features of his face. Both Iwakura and Sanjô looked like the 'great nobles' that they were, but the others with their background of lower social status before the revolution did not look graceful. 'Their recent greatness,' wrote the baron, had 'not polished their manners'.

> [Their physiognomy] bears the stamp of intelligence and daring, and also of the confidence of the gambler, who, feeling himself in luck, is decided to risk his all.[68]

Von Hübner elaborated further on their vulgarity:

> No doubt their finger-nails were neglected, and their gestures,

rather *brusque* and awkward, want the graceful ease of Japanese high breeding.[69]

After a while, they met 'the Son of the Gods' in a summer house of 'bewitching beauty'.[70] The room was dark but 'by a fortunate accident, a sunbeam struggled through the blinds and chinks in the paper screens [and] threw a radiance on the person of the Emperor'.

> The features of Mutsuhito bear all the marks of the Japanese race – a broad and rather flat nose, a sallow complexion, but keen and brilliant eyes in spite of the fixity prescribed by etiquette.[71]

Von Hübner also mentioned the plainness of the Emperor's dress; wearing no jewels and in a dark blue tunic and very full scarlet trousers. However, his headgear with 'an enormous aigrette composed of bamboo and horsehair, which rose above the right ear vertically to at least two feet and a half' was extravagant enough to be 'the emblem of his exalted rank'.[72] They then started a conversation, the system of which von Hübner described as follows:

> Conformably to etiquette, the Emperor in speaking muttered between his teeth inarticulate sounds, hard to be understood. Sanjo repeated them aloud, and the dragoman of the palace rendered them in English. Our answers were translated into Japanese by Mr Satow.[73]

It was through Reeve's extensive quotations from von Hübner's work that the 'adventurous' faces of the real promoters of the Japanese revolution became first popularly known among British readers. Before Reeve had introduced them in 1873, most discussion in Britain of the revolution had focused on the Mikado himself and presented him favourably. Mitford's report about the Emperor in 1870 was one such example:

> Unlike the Emperor of China, he is surrounded by men of advanced and liberal views, who encourage him in his desire to learn to become a ruler. He is said to be industrious and eager to improve himself.[74]

Also in 1872, Alcock quoted at length from the *Japan Herald* to show the 'praiseworthy routine' of the Emperor's daily life.[75] However, Marshall's above-mentioned article on Japan, although it appeared only a few months later than Alcock's, revealed the first glimmerings of the notion that the Emperor was in reality only a nominal ruler:

The Mikado is, theoretically, an absolute sovereign, who reigns and governs; but the work of government is done for him by the 'Great Council'.[76]

With the publication of von Hübner's book, the image of the Mikado as the ruler declined further, and Reeve summed up the Emperor's institutional character this way:

> He is, in fact, a talisman, and no more, but he serves the purpose of those who keep him there.[77]

In December 1873 Marshall began an eight-part satirical series on diplomatic formalities in Europe in *Blackwood's Magazine* and this is revealing of contemporary perceptions of the Mikado. The idea of writing this series, 'International Vanities', occurred to Marshall after he had written numerous reports about the mechanics of Western diplomacy for Sameshima.[78] Judging from the letter Marshall sent to Blackwood on 5 October 1873, Blackwood was in the beginning rather reluctant to approve Marshall's idea,[79] even though Marshall had promised the editor that he would not offend the diplomatic establishment in Europe:

> I am not such a furious, uncompromising Tory as you are, and, possibly, I have not the same deference for ancient usages; but I promise you to be respectful enough towards these old fancies.[80]

Marshall was increasingly open-minded towards the custom and ways of thinking of the Japanese, which were in his eyes different from those of the Europeans. Therefore, he thought that if the series could be worked out from a non-European point of view, like that of the Japanese, it would certainly become amusing and instructive for British readers.[81] In Blackwood's view, however, such an approach towards the European world was not at all suitable for his conservative magazine. Nevertheless, at Marshall's repeated urgings, the series was finally published. It was to consist of the following articles: I. Ceremonial; II. Forms; III. Titles; IV. Decorations; V. Emblems; VI. Diplomatic privileges; VII. Alien laws; VIII. Glory.[82] Blackwood, having read Marshall's early manuscripts, became interested in the amusing aspect of the series, and even encouraged Marshall to add more 'funny' passages; an idea which Marshall resisted:

> For two reasons I have not *tried* to make these articles manifestly funny. The first is that I do not want to seem to be animated by a parti pris of scorn for all these things (there is some good in them,

after all). The second is that my nature rather shrinks from pulling in jokes by the ears merely for the sake of provoking.[83]

However, Blackwood was delighted at Marshall's manuscript of the third part, 'Titles', in which Marshall discussed the development, refinement and accumulation of so many extravagant categories of titles in Europe as well as in Africa and Asia, and even in the United States. Marshall then turned to Japan:

> ... there exists a master who has held one unvarying rank since the time of Nebuchadnezzar; who would regard as a degradation any addition to the single quality by which more than a hundred and twenty of his fathers have been known before him ... Ten-o ... 'Heaven-Highest' ... is the one title of the sovereign of Japan.

Marshall observed that this 'solitary appellation' was 'far away the grandest' and surpassed 'all our vain attempts at glory'.[84] When Marshall added in conclusion that 'we' were 'not a model for other people' and that Japan was 'far more worth copying than we' were,[85] he might well have meant it. Blackwood's response to the manuscript of this article reveals his amusement over the apparently harmless comparison between Britain and Japan. He wrote to Marshall:

> I send proof of your pleasant & curious paper on Titles. They do look very funny when plainly written down & brought together.[86]

An appeal based on the existence of a different type of sovereign was to Blackwood tolerable so long as it was in a remote corner of the globe. The Japanese emperor weighed so little in his mind that he could accept Marshall's message as a light satire upon European 'vanities'. Blackwood, as editor, probably represented more or less the general feeling of the readers of his magazine. At this stage, Marshall and Blackwood were apparently in harmony.

Alongside changes in the general image of the Japanese sovereign, it became clear that the revolution had not been a popular one against a military aristocracy. According to Reeve, 'it was really made by the chiefs of the four great clans'.[87] In 1874, Alcock made this point in a more detailed manner, emphasising the important political role played by the retainers of those chiefs of the four clans rather than that of the chiefs themselves.[88] After the Emperor, the noble Iwakura's image was also found to fade, and names like Kido and Ôkubo became eminent in British magazines and reviews as the real leaders who wrote the scenario for the revolution.[89] Furthermore, the faces of these newly unveiled leading figures were not unique to Japan, but reflected a kind of political daring which could commonly be found in similar critical situations in the world. In the 1870s, British writers showed little sympathy with these 'adventurous' figures, and often demonstrated a degree of cool detachment from them. Von Hübner made an allusion in order to express his impression of the Court of Japan:

> I do not think I shall ever forget the scene of this morning; that fairy garden, those mysterious pavilions, those statesmen in full dress, pacing with us in the shrubbery; this oriental potentate who looks like an idol, and believes and feels himself a God, are things which surpass the Arabian Nights' Entertainments.[90]

This allusion must have given British readers a fresh sense of distance from Japan, since they had been rather accustomed to the usage of analogies or metaphors derived from medieval Europe for describing the political institutions of Japan.

It might have been interconnected with such cool attitudes towards the new Japanese leaders that many British writers reported the material progress of Japan without much enthusiasm. It is true that there were some British writers who were enthusiastic about Japanese 'progress'. Marshall's article of September 1872 in *Blackwood's Magazine* was to draw a favourable general picture of the new stage in Japanese history as it was meant by his collaborator Sameshima to be an advertisement for the Japanese government. Marshall not only enumerated various successful public works in Japan, but also mentioned the good relations between the government and the hired Western specialists (*oyatoi gaikokujin*).[91] Perhaps Mossman's book of 1873 and Reed's of 1880 were the two conspicuous examples which gave British readers very favourable images of Japanese progress and its promising future.

But all these works were strongly criticised by the majority of reviewers. In 1874, Alcock wrote that Mossman's work was 'altogether *couleur de rose,* as was Mr Oliphant's attractive narrative of Lord Elgin's first visit'.[92] In order to support this point, Alcock mentioned the insurrections of 'discontented parties' in Japan, the inefficiency in administration, problems in foreign relations and other difficulties resulting from the sudden social changes. Seven years later, he repeated a similar point, criticising Reed's work in contrast to Bird's detached observation of Japanese public affairs. According to Alcock,

Reed's three-month stay in Japan as 'the honoured guest of Ministers' was bound to give his observation a bias favourable to the Japanese point of view.[93] On the other hand, Bird, argued Alcock, had been 'under very different circumstances':

> – a lady, making her way with a single native attendant into the most inaccessible regions, she would . . . be less disposed to see with Japanese eyes, and more likely to be impartial in her judgement.[94]

In this article, Alcock himself presented a detailed account of 'the outcome' of the 'great national struggle' in Japan.[95] His way of introducing his readers to 'achievement' in the field of public works was sober. He detailed minutely the number of works, even sometimes including the number of workers involved, with a close eye to the financial conditions of the Japanese government, examining the various reports which had been published by the government itself. In the same year, 1880, F. V. Dickins reviewed the works of Reed, Bird and Mounsey in the *Quarterly Review*. Among the three authors, Dickins in particular thought highly of Bird's account:

> Miss Bird has given us the fullest as well as . . . the most impartial account we have yet met with of the actual condition of the Japanese people.[96]

Dickins was eager to emphasise whatever Bird mentioned as showing the backward state of Japanese society. It is noteworthy that Dickins, for his review, had not read the last part of Bird's book, in which she mentioned the progress that had been made in the area of public works. He had written to John Murray in the summer of 1880:

> I shall be shortly ready with my review of Mr Reed's book and Miss Bird's Unbeaten Track. Out of the latter I only possess sheets to p.305 of 2nd vol. The rem[ainde]r, indeed, from my confidence with Miss Bird.[497]

Generally speaking, the space within British review and magazine articles which was devoted solely to the topic of material progress in Japan was very small in spite of the fact that one of the major trends in Japanese history at that time was the zealous introduction of Western engineering. A possible reason for this phenomenon is that most of the public works were started under the guidance of foreign engineers. British writers focused their attention on the relative importance of help from different countries in different fields. Although the number of Western advisers was decreasing towards the end of the 1870s, these writers kept on mentioning the 'English Influence' in Japan, and reporting the low qualifications of native engineers.[98] Therefore, in articles in British periodicals, most of the attainments in Japanese public works were likely to be attributed to the efforts of foreigners. On the other hand these writers were interested in the financial conditions of the Japanese government, considering that, as regards public works, financial affairs were the only things with which the Japanese government were able to deal without any help from foreigners.

It was as late as June 1873 that the first budget table was published by the Councillor Ôkuma Shigenobu. For some years previously, British writers had been trying to discover this aspect of the new government, but mostly in vain. Perhaps the sole exception was Marshall's case. Thanks to Sameshima, he was able to present in his *Blackwood's* article a Japanese budget for 1872 with the special comment that it had been 'a document unknown either in Europe or in Japan'.[99] However, the new information about Japan which Marshall provided was not welcomed. Perhaps urged on by Sameshima, who was so interested in publicising Marshall's article as to seriously consider that a reprint of it be sold in 'a six penny pamphlet for the railway stalls', Marshall suggested that Blackwood draw the attention of Delane of *The Times* to what he had written.[100] Delane seems to have taken some interest in the article, and published on 5 September a short synopsis of Marshall's article, omitting all the expressions Marshall had used to praise Japanese progress.[101]

However, Aston, who had been impressed by the Japanese government's reticence in financial matters, could not help expressing his suspicions about Marshall's account and he wrote a short article and visited Alexander Macmillan, the proprietor of *Macmillan's Magazine*. Macmillan sent Aston's manuscript, with a short accompanying note, to the editor of the magazine, George Grove, on 14 September:

> I enclose an exceedingly bright little article – would make 6 pages – on Japan. It is brought me by an able young fellow who is now interpreter to the Japanese Ambassador [Iwakura]. He has lived six years in Japan. He married the daughter of an old School fellow of mine & that is how I came to know him . . . It looks just the sort of article that would be extensively quoted.[102]

Grove published this article in the October issue of the magazine. In the article, Aston criticised Marshall:

... it seems hardly to have occurred to the writer of the article [in *Blackwood's Magazine*] that this 'unknown document' may have been given to him for a purpose which he is to be the innocent means of carrying out.[103]

It was from 1874 onward that British writers began to write slightly favourable accounts of the financial condition of the Japanese government, always noting, however, the possibility that they might have been given inaccurate figures by officials.[104] What is important here, however, is that attention had shifted in British periodicals from improvements of the roads and harbours of Japan to narrower questions of finance. Certainly, this change of emphasis affected the general tone of articles on the New Japan, making it less enthusiastic than it had been earlier.

In addition to material changes, there was an enormous range of social changes in Japan, which British writers could not neglect. Certainly, Victorian advocates of 'civilisation' tended to emphasise the importance of social and spiritual progress over material progress. In the case of magazine and review articles on New Japan, perhaps this general tendency was reflected in the weight given to the subject matter of the articles. In 1872, for example, Alcock stated that the study of the 'vast changes' in Japan should be comprehensive, including studies of both institutions and people.[105] Also in 1880, he suggested that the 'progress' of a nation should be considered in three dimensions: 'the material and intellectual advancement of the nation and the development of its resources'.[106] Among the topics on non-material change in Japan, British writers seem to have been most concerned with changes in religious life, the decline of samurai privilege, and progress in national education.

In March 1868, the new government of Japan established Shintoism as the national religion, establishing the priestly office of *Jingikan* to direct the 'clear separation' of Shintoism from Buddhism.[107] Often Buddhist temples had had Shinto shrine annexes, and the rituals of both religions had been generally amalgamated. In the first half of the 1870s, inspired by the purist ideals of the Hirata school, the most influential patriotic group at the time, the fanatical destruction of Buddhist temples and images erupted in many parts of Japan. Finally a special government decree on religious freedom was issued to each religious sect in 1875. In May 1872, during the chaos created by aggressive Shintoists, an imperial edict to abandon Japan's traditional anti-Christian policy was announced. The notice boards prohibiting Christianity which had been found all over Japan were to be abolished from February 1873.

Alcock was puzzled at the 'two opposite courses' within Japanese policy towards religion: one to disestablish Buddhism because it was 'a foreign belief' and to return to the old form of native religion; the other to tolerate Christianity 'though admittedly foreign'.[108] Informed by von Hübner's work, Reeve presented to his readers a concrete idea of the 'disestablishment' of Buddhism in Japan; the violent striking down without hesitation of the 'whole ecclesiastical structure by the reforming government'.[109] Reeve expressed his hope that the 'Daiboudhs', the big image of Buddha in Kamakura had not yet been destroyed, reminding his readers of Aimé Humbert's beautiful drawing in his *Le Japon illustré*.[110] As Reeve had criticised idolatry in Japan in the 1860s,[111] his reaction to this movement was rather complex. On the one hand he regretted 'the destruction of what is beautiful and interesting in art', but on the other, it was 'impossible' for him 'not to feel that this stern overthrow of the idols of a degrading superstition' was 'eminently significant of a return to a purer faith'. Reeve then left this dilemma and turned his attention to what he considered to be a remarkable phenomenon: the general indifference of the Japanese population to 'the destruction of their false gods'.[112]

In 1875 Dilke experienced the last stage of this 'vandalism'. In an article published in 1876, he spoke of the 'shameless' neglect on the part of the new government of 'reverence for the past'. He also reported that a certain apathy towards religion dominated Japan.[113] Towards the end of the 1870s, discussions about Japanese religion almost disappeared from British magazines and reviews, except in religious periodicals such as the *Church Missionary Intelligencer and Record* which began issuing regular reports on religious affairs in Japan from 1872.[114] Probably, the idea of 'the general indifference to religion' was in many British minds a familiar label to attach to the Japanese since it had been revived during the 1850s on the basis of Kaempfer's work, and had been mentioned occasionally during the 1860s.

In addition to the problems faced by the Buddhists, another conspicuous social change was the denial of many privileges to the samurai and the eventual decline of the majority of this class. In 1870, Mitford observed that the 'great gainers by the revolution' were 'the people', and that 'the servile obeisances of the feudal system' were 'a thing of the past'.[115] Two years later, Alcock could not hide his amazement at the fact that the levelling of Japanese society had been broadly effected in only a couple of years, since such a transformation could not but 'try the power and the influence of the strongest governments in all countries'.[116] From 1870 onwards, the Japanese government issued a series of decrees prohibiting all but officials from owning swords. The culmination of these efforts was the coercive edict of March 1876, which banned the traditional custom of bearing swords among all samurai, except for high officials on the occasions when they wore ceremonial court attire, and for soldiers and policemen.

However, such a change in the external appearance of the samurai was not such a serious matter as their drastic economic decline. After the abolition of daimyo domains in 1871, the Japanese government, which had been encouraging daimyo retainers to 'return' to farming or to begin trading, started efforts to abolish their hereditary stipends. In 1876, the government granted to the former samurai interest-bearing bonds which would be converted into cash only gradually during the period from 1881 to 1906. As the interest they received each year was much lower than their stipends had been, and as most samurai had been brought up to be contemptuous of commercial activity, the majority were unable to make a living and suffered economic decline.

In 1874, Alcock reported that the great frustration of former samurai was connected with increasing agitation for Japanese action against Korea and Formosa.[117] During the years 1872 and 1873, Saigô Takamori was the main figure in the government who represented the bitter feelings of these former samurai. Saigô's plan to invade Korea was rejected by Iwakura, Ôkubo and Kido in 1873, causing the resignation of Saigô's party. However, the idea of annexing Korea and Formosa had already been a kind of national dream expressed in many popular books in the late Tokugawa period.[118] This dream had been given theoretical support by nationalist writings and was encouraged, in a way, even by the government, which was obliged to meet the practical necessity of utilising the expanded, frustrated imperial army after the civil war of 1868–9. The expedition to Formosa in 1874 was one of the outcomes of their policy. According to Robert Kennaway Douglas, then Assistant Librarian of the Chinese Library of the British Museum, and a prolific writer on China, this expedition attracted 'considerable attention' in Europe, since it was 'the first trial of the new military system and weapons' of Japan.[119] In 1875, the Japanese navy caused the Kanghwa Island Incident in Korea and early the next year forced the opening of secluded Korea in a manner similar to that in which the Western powers had approached Japan two decades before. In early 1876, Cyprian Arthur George Bridge (1839–1924), then a commander in the Royal Navy, reported in the *Fortnightly Review* on his recent visit to Korea. In the concluding part of his report, he explained critically how the Japanese were thinking about going to war with *'un cœur léger'*:

> The restless party in Japan, which has run such a headlong course on the path of Europeanisation, is said to purpose an attack upon Koreans, simply to 'keep in wind' the samurai.[120]

Since 1874, many insurrections of former samurai had occurred in Japan. Hayward mentioned some of those in Kumamoto, Fukuoka and Hagi in the autumn of 1876, which were also reported in *The Times*.[121] The Satsuma Rebellion in 1877, led by Saigô, was the last and longest in the series of such insurrections. In 1878, Wedderburn described the fall of Saigô in an emotional tone:

> All hopes of immediate constitutional reform have perished with the gallant Saigo, whose voluntary death by the sword of his best friend was that of a true Japanese gentleman, and who may bear in future the title of the Last of the Samurais.[122]

In 1880, Alcock described the rebellion as one of the recent expressions of the 'spirit of ferocity' shown by the samurai in conflict since the days of the struggle between the Minamoto and Taira during the twelfth century.[123]

Whether Saigô was admired or not, one thing which became clear was that in the course of Japanese history during the 1870s, the class called samurai disappeared from the centre of the stage. Even that distinct mode of dying associated with the samurai, which had been described by earlier Victorians as a 'happy despatch', was vanishing rapidly, as Wedderburn reported:

> It is a remarkable fact that since the Japanese authorities were induced by Sir H. Parkes to substitute death by the hands of the executioner for 'seppuku,' as the punishment of any Samurai who might be convicted of a murderous attack upon a foreigner, there has not been a single instance of such an attack being made.[124]

Whenever British writers referred to the samurai, their prose revealed an increasing sense of remoteness from this once feared class. In many

Victorian minds, the Japan represented by the samurai was fading away – and was not to be revived until two or three decades later, when the Sino- and Russo-Japanese Wars broke out.

If the samurai were in decline, the people at large were by contrast benefitting from the establishment of educational institutions throughout the country. Wedderburn noticed the change in the countryside:

> In country villages the one large building is generally the new school, and where a modern house in European style has not been built, it is usual to find the residence of a Samurai, or even of an ex-Daimio, appropriated for tuition.[125]

From the early 1870s, the topic of the development of national education in Japan was reported in numerous British periodicals. In 1872, Marshall reported that the newly established Ministry of Instruction had 'got on very well' since the previous year:

> Public primary schools are increasing rapidly, especially in the towns; but the movement is far more marked in the western provinces and on the coast than in the interior . . . Private schools are more abundant still . . . they spring up with facility wherever they are wanted.[126]

Marshall explained the 'feverish' desire for knowledge, especially in the towns, and pointed out that the publication of books and newspapers was growing rapidly:

> Even arithmetic is beginning to be generally taught, in spite of the horror of it which the Samurai have long felt, as being one of the elements of trade.[127]

In 1874, Alcock quoted extensively from the *Japan Weekly Paper*, which was, according to Alcock's judgement, 'a journal evidently possessing means of obtaining authentic information'.[128] This weekly was reporting that the goal of establishing '53,000 schools, or one for every 600 of the computed inhabitants of Japan', as set forth by the Education Law of 1872, had almost been attained. The report also mentioned that Western-style instruction was increasing, with pupils sitting on chairs, using tables, handling knives and forks and wearing uniforms. The report also criticised a popular false idea that 'the Japanese mind was incapable of advancing beyond a certain point in the acquisition either of European language or of European science'.[129] In 1880, Alcock again reported on the development of education in Japan as the field in which 'the greatest progress' had been made. He gave detailed figures for elementary and middle schools, both public and private, teachers, pupils and foreign instructors on the basis of 'the latest Annual Report of the Ministry of Education published in 1879'. He also described the Imperial University at Tokyo, founded in 1877, and some other colleges for training teachers. Lastly, he attached a detailed table of expenditures on the publicly financed school system, including salaries, rent, books, apparatus, fuel and light.[130]

Towards the end of the 1870s, as the educational system of Japan was following the general trend towards Westernisation, the tone of British writers became less and less enthusiastic when explaining the condition of education in Japan. These writers seemed content to present relevant figures supplied by the Japanese government. Certainly, the Westernised schools were more or less similar to any school in Europe as a whole, and any comparisons with the West in this field seems to have confined themselves to statistics.

'Out of poetry into plain useful prose' – this phrase which Mitford had uttered in the early 1870s[131] proved a prophetic expression of the sober feeling which most of the British writers on Japan shared when they dealt with Japan's Westernisation during the 1870s. It has become clear that this feeling resulted from their close studies of the Japanese social revolution. Also, new information, however precise it may have been, was not always accepted smoothly in journalistic circles. But even if they accepted this information, the more they knew the facts of various aspects of the New Japan, the more detached their feelings became. Eventually, some writers, particularly those who had no experience of Japan themselves, tended to resort to earlier clichés about Japan, as was shown in Reeve's explanation of Japanese attitudes towards religion. The changes in the image of the Mikado also illustrated this tendency. It was, therefore, no coincidence that the idea of British familiarity with Japan and the idea of its singularity were to be found side by side in British magazine and review articles. But how was it that such contradictory perceptions of Japan were able to coexist for so long when more and more information about Japan was becoming available? We may have a better idea of how to answer this question once we have considered how the writers of these articles allowed their perceptions of their own country to influence their descriptions of Japan.

7 The Expanding Gulf

It was in June 1874 that Alexander Innes Shand published his article, 'The Romance of Japanese Revolution' in *Blackwood's Magazine*.[1] In this article, as was shown in the previous chapter, Shand generally emphasised the mysterious and romantic characteristics of the country. He had never been to Japan, and it was at the Vienna International Exhibition of 1873 that he had become deeply interested in things Japanese. He arrived in Vienna just in time for the opening of the exhibition on 1 May 1873, and stayed there for several weeks as a special correspondent of *The Times*, an arrangement he had made with Delane.[2] According to Shand's letter to Blackwood of early March the following year, he had 'already written a good many passing articles' on Japan.[3] He revealed in this letter, in which he proposed a paper on Japan for 'Maga', that his major concern was to obtain 'the key to the mystery of the sudden revolution, & the self denying conduct of the great daimios'. For Shand, what had happened was a striking repetition of the 'old romances of Mitford's "Tales of Old Japan" '. Shand also disclosed the sources he would draw on:

> I should draw for facts chiefly on Baron Hübner's book, & the one that Mossman has just published, & on my own observations of the Japanese Collection at Vienna, with the letters I wrote about it to the Times.[4]

In another letter which he sent to Blackwood on writing up his Japan article, Shand further explained that his sources included such items as 'some Japanese *brochures*' given to him at the exhibition, talks with Japanese 'travellers', and even 'the Yokohama press'.[5]

Although he was eager to emphasise that he tried to place himself 'in the judicial & impartial standpoint', Shand was at the same time most anxious to make his article readable and to 'avoid making it a dull *précis*' of the recent history of Japan. He wrote:

> I . . . have merely made history the groundwork of an article which regards the changes from the picturesque point of view & speculates in the future as on the coming *dénouement* of a romance.[6]

The personal impressions of individual Japanese which he had formed at the time of the exhibition were, therefore, to play an important role in the compilation of the article. In fact, he made these impressions 'the key' to open up the 'mystery' of the revolution.

In order to symbolise contemporary Japan, Shand reminded his readers of certain scenes in Vienna at the time of the exhibition:

> . . . there was one strange type of nationality you met at every turn – small, slight-made men, with olive complexions and black twinkling eyes slit almond-fashion. But on their way to Vienna they had probably passed by Paris, and were dressed in such garments as are able to be procured at the Belle Jardinière or the Bon Diable, with tall chimney-pot hats that came well down upon their foreheads. They had taken wonderfully kindly to these new clothes of theirs, and yet there was something about them that told you that they were masquerading cleverly.[7]

Shand presented a detailed account of their behaviour in Vienna. In his eyes, those 'sprightly children of "the Land of the Rising Sun" ' were disturbing the traditional European image of Orientals:

> They hopped on behind the crowded tramway cars with an utter absence of the dignity we regard as the birthright of oriental blood; they submitted to be jostled and trodden upon with as little sign of temper or prejudice as the good-humoured Viennese themselves.[8]

Shand described how busy they were with studying men and things in the city, keeping their spirit 'always willing'.[9] He considered that they made an enormous contrast to high-cast Hindu and Chinese, who were clung tenaciously to their traditional mode of life even when abroad. The Japanese, wrote Shand, 'behaved themselves in every respect like easy and liberal men of the world'.[10] Their conspicuous behaviour obliged him to compare them with English and French setting foot for the first time in a foreign city. An Englishman would go about 'half shy, half suspicious' and 'in a chilling atmosphere of repulsion' which would numb 'his good-fellowship and facilities' and obscure 'his vision'. Frenchmen might be 'more versatile and impressionable', yet 'fugitive impressions' would 'disappear from their casing of vain self-complacency, like breath from a plating of polished steel'. By contrast, wrote Shand, 'surprises stimulated instead of stunning' the minds of Japanese abroad.[11]

Shand elaborated the image of these 'sprightly children' as the very symbol of New Japan:

> The imitation of externals came naturally to them . . . they were learning from everything around them, without an appearance of

effort – and under their *insouciant* exterior, they were remodelling their minds with marvellous rapidity.[12]

He concluded that the Japanese were 'the genuine representatives of that spirit of progress or innovation'. There were, however, limits to his enthusiasm and he pointed out a paradoxical feature of the exhibition, where the Japanese 'were playing a game of cross-purposes with the most advanced nations of the Western world':

> While they were doing their best to denationalize themselves with astounding success, we Europeans were servilely copying their arts, and humbly confessing that our attempts at imitation were failures.[13]

Shand could not help expressing his doubt about whether 'minds so mobile, and made of material so plastic' were 'the best materials for forming a great nation and founding a stable power'.[14]

He might have expected ready sympathy with his argument from many people in Britain who would share more or less similar feelings about Japanese visitors to Europe. At least, Blackwood seems to have shown his ready approval of Shand's manuscript of the article and to have sent him his compliments.[15]

However, as Shand also wished to make his article 'judicial', he sent his proofs to Frederic Marshall, whose acquaintance Shand had made just about ten days before through Blackwood's introduction.[16] Marshall was, in the eyes of both Blackwood and Shand, the authority on Japan at that time. According to Shand's letter to Blackwood of 12 May 1874, Shand sent the proofs to Marshall, 'begging him to read them or not as he preferred, according to whether he thinks he may be compromised or not'.[17] Judging from Marshall's letter to Blackwood of 17 May, it seems that Blackwood had also sent another set of Shand's proofs to Marshall,[18] but for some reason Marshall declined to make any observation on them, knowing that they contained factual inaccuracies.[19] Marshall might have felt that he knew too much about Japan to suggest a few alterations to Shand's general account of the country. Marshall wrote to Shand:

> I have nothing to say about it, except that I have read it with great interest. All the English books about Japan are incomplete or inexact. Mossman's and Adams's are no exceptions to this rule.[20]

Thus Blackwood and Shand lost the chance of giving the article a more 'judicial' character, and it was duly published on 1 June. However, it was certainly a more readable and less controversial article than Marshall's 'Japan' which had been published in the same magazine about two years before.

In the previous chapter, it was argued that a certain feeling of remoteness from Japan was increasingly prevalent among British writers as a result of their studies of various aspects of the revolution. This cool attitude towards Japan was closely connected with their embarrassment at the external imitation of Western things which was pursued so zealously in New Japan. Drawings of Japanese gentlemen dressed in the most unseemly and comical sets of Western clothes had often appeared in *The Illustrated London News* since 1866.[21] As has been already shown, Mitford was one of the early writers who expressed resentment of the Western style adopted by Japanese soldiers. The 'nondescripts' was the label which Mitford applied to those people in Japan who were innocently proud of their new garments.[22] Edward House also noted:

> The Japanese samurai, in his transition state from nobleman's retainer-at-large to national-guardsman, is as far as possible from an object of beauty.[23]

Not satisfied with changing merely their dress, some Japanese nobles started building their houses following what they thought was the Western style. In 1878, Bridge reported on the abode of the famous ex-Prince of Chôshû. Although the site where it stood was beautiful, the house itself was to Bridge's eye 'an ugly building with the hip-roof and bay-windows of a "villa residence" of a suburban house-agent's list'.[24]

Whenever British writers wrote about Japanese imitation of the West, they tended to judge the new Japanese taste very harshly, exaggerating their own excellence and so creating a vast gulf between Japan and the West which was impossible to bridge. In accordance with this phenomenon, any Japanese who was against the so-called 'enlightening' government was treated very warmly in British magazine and review articles. A good example was the case of Shimazu Hisamitsu, the chief figure on the Satsuma side in the Anglo-Satsuma War of 1863. Dilke was one of the writers who showed ready sympathy with this ex-lord who was, in Dilke's words, 'so violent a Tory'.[25] Dilke referred approvingly to the following episode, which had taken place 'the day after the first intimation of the desire of the Government that officials should wear European dress' had been made:

He came down to the Council of State with the hair [on] the sides of the scalp more firmly gummed up over the shaven part than ever, with one coolie to carry a mat for him to sit on among his colleagues (who of course were all seated in high velvet chairs), another coolie to pull out over his feet the brocaded trousers, which train behind a Japanese gentleman of the old school.[26]

Dilke, the famous Victorian radical, was very critical of the 'shameless' radicalism of the Japanese government, as he thought it did not show any 'reverence for the past'. Therefore he wrote:

... any Englishman, whatever may be his politics, cannot fail to feel much sympathy with the Japanese Conservatism.[27]

It seems that the dislike which British writers expressed towards Japanese Westernisation was to a great extent reinforced by their anxiety about the results of the too-speedy social changes in Japan. In 1872, Alcock used the analogy of the risks of a direct transplantation of a Western plant to Eastern soil in order to explain the enormous danger in introducing Western institutions to Japan. 'Steady progress' rather than 'undue speed' was his suggestion for the Japanese.[28] Aston also asked in 1872:

Is not the pace too great to last, and is there no fear that the speedy horse may break down when pressed so hard?[29]

Aston was particularly worried about the lack in Japanese government of a conservative element which seemed to him 'so necessary in such a crisis'.[30] Even Marshall, towards the end of his *Blackwood's* article of September 1872 which sought on the whole to present a favourable account of Japan, expressed pessimism about the country's future, in particular, about the likelihood of some sort of drastic reaction against change. Marshall compared the Japanese with the French to support his uneasy forecast:

... this is doubly true of such a race as the Japanese who are as emotional, as impulsive, and as wayward as the French.[31]

Two years later, 'the symptoms' for the future of Japan were, to Shand's eyes, still 'very ominous'. He was also forecasting the danger of reactionary movements in the near future.[32]

On the other hand, the general anxiety about the dangerous future of Japan also nurtured a notion that Japan might one day adopt

Socialism or Communism. Marshall worried about the consequences of the 'levelling tendencies' in Japan:

> With all the prudence of the Government, and all the present good intentions of the inferior population, the latter may perhaps some day imitate the example which their superiors have already set them; may let themselves, in their turn, be run away with by feeling, and by the thirst for novelty, and may try Socialism and an Eastern International.[33]

Alcock, in his article published in the *Quarterly Review* in 1874, compared the Japanese revolution with the French and American revolutions. He considered 'the passion for an impossible equality' in the histories of France and America:

> Of democracy there is enough and to spare in both countries; but it remains yet to be determined, in France at least, whether this is to lead to some ungovernable, and impracticable theory of Socialism and Communism, with a levelling downwards, and an equal division of property or a monarchic revival based upon hereditary succession, and not upon the mobile and uncertain plebiscite of a whole people.[34]

In Alcock's eyes, Japan had more or less entered upon the same 'career' which France had begun, *'de cœur léger,* some eighty years' before.[35] Although Alcock admitted the 'political sagacity' of the Japanese in having 'retained hereditary succession and a monarchy as steadying powers', and avoided the 'appeal to the "will of the people" ',[36] it seems that he was somewhat worried about the influence of American diplomacy, which, in his eyes, was always imposing on the Japanese 'a good many American notions' like 'equality' or 'political freedom'.[37] It is undeniable that the emergence and the drastic fall of the Paris Commune in 1871 induced these British writers to look upon the Japanese revolution with great anxiety. It was particularly so with Marshall, as he had had the terrible experience of having one of his daughters killed in the confusion of the Commune.

To the actual question of whether the revolution in Japan had successfully settled into permanence, British writers continued to present negative answers until well after the suppression of the Satsuma Rebellion in 1877. Despite occasional references to the 'marvellous aptitude' of the Japanese,[38] and the traditional 'gentle obedience' of the lower classes,[39] most writers refrained from any explicit remarks on the success of the revolution itself. Abraham Hayward was an exception. In 1877, he implied the general success of the Japanese revolution:

> So rapid have been the changes, that reforms which hardly three years since struck us as revolutionary and unsafe, have since been quietly and effectively completed.[40]

The dominant note of most British writers about the revolution was less optimistic. In 1878 Wedderburn was anticipating 'a certain amount of reaction' towards the 'too vast and too rapid' changes in Japan.[41] In 1880, Alcock still had reservations about the rosy picture of the New Japan presented in Reed's book.[42]

Judging from articles on Japan in British periodicals of the time, one of the main reasons for such scepticism was the fact that British writers concerned had met many Japanese students in Europe whom they considered uncontrolled and immature; yet they knew that these young people would become national leaders on their return home. British writers started discussing this question as early as 1872.[43] In 1876, Dilke wrote that Japanese conservatives must be 'in the highest degree' offended by 'the students trained in England and America'.[44] He also mentioned the 'corruption' and 'conceit' of young Japanese officials, and introduced his readers to a new notion about Japan: 'prigs' paradise'. This was an idea which was frequently mentioned by European residents in Japan who were 'groaning under the somewhat ignorant Radicalism of the newly appointed local officials',[45] and their complaints must certainly have reached Britain in their letters home.

Along with the popularity of descriptions such as 'prigs' paradise' for Japan, 'Young Japan' was conspicuously used to sum up the country during the 1870s. For example, in 1878, Wedderburn expressed his personal impression of the Japanese:

> The entire Japanese nation is still in its early youth, emerging for the first time upon the wide world, with no experience beyond the limits of its own home, eager for knowledge, eager for amusement, with a firm belief in the superior power and capacity of its elders, and a determination to imitate them now, in the hope of rivalling them hereafter.[46]

Many British writers did not hesitate to express the uneasy feelings which they had whenever they faced a 'youth' with such enormous potential for good or ill. A writer in the *Japan Weekly Paper*, whose

The Expanding Gulf

account Alcock quoted for his article in the *Quarterly Review* in 1874, was no exception:

> A people amiable, clever, and very impulsive, but which has little or no hold either on any religion or on any philosophy – which suddenly rushes forth, as it has done once before, in pursuit of the acquisition of a foreign civilization – what is to be said of it? There is no problem in the world's previous history, which can help us to foresee the end.[47]

Expressing such anxiety, British writers tried in their magazine and review articles to re-examine the early progress of the revolution and to find its real causes. During the 1860s, they tended to discuss the role of Britain and other Western countries in causing the drastic disorders in Japan. However, entering the 1870s, the tone of their arguments changed; they became more interested in emphasising indigenous causes for the revolution rather than pressures from foreign powers. In 1874, Alcock pointed out that the general discontent against the extended espionage system and 'iron rule of repression' of the Shogunate had been undermining 'the spirit of loyalty' of the ruled, and that such a rule was bound to become 'sooner or later' 'intolerable' to those who could resist.[48] For Alcock, the unpopular monopoly of foreign trade by the Shogun and the disturbing advent of foreign merchants were not the basic reasons for the revolution.[49] He quoted from Adams's *History of Japan:*

> Indeed, when the foreigners appeared on the scene, everything was already ripe for a revolution.[50]

In Adams's eyes, the government of the Shogun had been so 'imperfect' in dealing with 'the new order of things' which the conclusion of treaties with the West brought forth, that 'the fall of the Shogunate became a mere question of time' when the treaties came into force.[51] The idea that the Western powers had just given a mere tap to the rotten pillar of the Shogunate became stronger in the latter half of the 1870s. It was in 1878 that Wedderburn tried the following analogy in order to make a similar point:

> One thing is evident, that a slight external impulse only was required to topple down the existing fabric of Japanese society at the time when foreigners forced their way into the country producing an effect analogous to that of a solid dropping into a fluid on

the verge of crystallization, and converting it suddenly into a solid mass.[52]

There was another question to which British writers wanted to find the answer: the reason for the smooth speed of social change in Japan. Marshall tried a sociological analysis of Japanese history. He argued in his *Blackwood's* article in 1872 that the key to understanding the pattern of change in Japanese history was that its whole society was under the strong influence of 'feelings' of the nation:

> There never has been a country in which sentiments and emotions have exercised greater influence than in Japan, or where the connection between the feelings and the history of a nation has been more complete.[53]

Marshall asked why the measure of expelling Europeans from Japan in the early seventeenth century had become 'permanent and durable' throughout the Edo period, 'instead of being purely temporary'.[54] According to him, 'once the opinion against the foreigners had 'sprung up', it 'grew rapidly into a national conviction', acquiring such a permanent strength as 'an article of faith from generation to generation'. He attributed this radical process of faith-making to the Japanese system in which 'national opinion was formed by the upper classes only'.[55] Then why were the suppression of the Shogunate and the introduction of Western culture effected in so short a period? According to Marshall, it was because of 'a rapid and very general waking up of the population' to what they thought to be the merits of the West. Marshall wrote:

> Feeling, in this new direction, was once more carrying Japan away . . . Sentiment ran away again with reason; and though this argument was abundantly employed to prove the necessity of doing the exact contrary of what everybody had up to that moment done, argument was quite useless; its work was in reality performed by emotion and by infused faith.[56]

He also explained the sudden self-sacrifice of the daimyo in abandoning their territorial rights as arising from 'pure patriotic feeling':

> . . . the whole interior government of the country was blown away in three months by a gust of feeling.[57]

In 1880, Alcock introduced his readers to a new interpretation of the suddenness of the revolution. On the one hand, he presented a careful analysis of the causes of the revolution, drawing a delicate balance between domestic and foreign factors.⁵⁸ On the other, he argued that the real state of affairs in Japan had not changed as a result of the revolution. Alcock elaborated on how 'the actual power of the Shoguns' and 'the business of the clans under their respective chiefs or lords' had fallen 'into the hands of any clever men or set of men of the lower ranks about them', through the course of the Tokugawa period.⁵⁹ The positions of the Shogun and the daimyo had therefore been in decline well before the period of the revolution. Alcock then presented the following view:

> The sacrifice of land and revenues and the pomp and state of princes was more apparent than real.⁶⁰

In Alcock's eyes, both the smoothness and suddenness of the changes in Japan were quite natural because their major characteristic was the readjustment of social and political theories to reality rather than a change of society itself:

> Only thus can many of the chief incidents of the five years preceding the fall of the Shogunate, in 1868, and the otherwise inexplicable acts of renunciation and self-effacement of the whole Daimios on the Mikado's resumption of the reins of government, be understood.⁶¹

Dilke also pointed out the unchanged aspects of Japan before and after the revolution. For instance, he discussed the 'pliancy' of the Japanese, asserting that 'the leading men of the Tycoon's government' had been 'very generally employed by the government which succeeded to the imperial power'.⁶² He mentioned the illustrative case of Enomoto Takeaki, formerly the Commander in Chief of the last army of the Shogun, and later Japanese Ambassador at St Petersburg.⁶³ Thus both Alcock and Dilke extended the scope for argument about the indigenous causes of the overthrow of the Shogunate by pointing out the persistence of old elements after the revolution. In sum, British writers' discussions in the 1870s about the causes and character of the Japanese revolution tended to give the impression that most of the political and social changes in Japan had not been caused by the West, but had happened more or less spontaneously in that remote corner of the globe. Alcock was certainly aware of this kind of sentiment among his readers when he made the following recommendation of Mossman's book to non-specialist readers, even though he was well aware of the small inaccuracies in it:

> Mr Mossman tells in a single volume all that the general reader usually cares to know of so distant a country.[64]

The phrase 'so distant a country' to describe Japan could well have been a sincere expression of the sentiments of Alcock himself when he wrote it in 1874. At any rate, ideas about Britain which were directly or indirectly expressed in magazine and review articles dealing with New Japan were quite complacent during the 1870s. In particular, confronted by the Japanese zeal for Westernisation as well as their demands since 1868 for revision of the unequal treaties with the Western powers, British writers tended to demonstrate 'the greatness' of Britain, and emphasise the insuperable barrier between themselves and the Japanese. For example, in 1872, Aston mentioned the Iwakura Mission's grand tour of Britain in a patronising tone:

> Its members have a golden opportunity which they should not lose. They have already inspected our Fleet, our dockyards, and been present at a portion of the autumn manoeuvres. They doubtless have every facility afforded to them for visiting the great centres of our trade. They can examine our factories, our machinery, and all the various industries for which we are famous.[65]

Then Aston added one sentence: 'They can thus learn the source of England's greatness'.[66] He reminded his readers that the 'greatness' was 'the result of perseverance and hard toil' for many years, and suggested that such a thing could not possibly be attained by any sudden change in Japanese society.[67] If someone is conscious of being imitated by others, it is often natural for him to accentuate the features which seems to attract others. This may have been particularly true in the case of Anglo-Japanese relations, since the shrewdness of the Japanese in acquiring whatever they considered good had been a familiar notion since the early 1860s among British writers interested in Japan. Those writers felt, therefore, much flattered by the Japanese zeal for imitating things British.

The confident self-image of the British was also shown when they were discussing illustrious figures of their empire in this period. In early 1873, Henry Reeve published his review of the compilation of Lord Elgin's letters edited by Theodore Walrond.[68] This book contained many chapters of Lord Elgin's personal records of his diplomatic activities outside Europe, and one chapter dealt with those in Japan. In his article, Reeve described Lord Elgin in the following manner:

The governor goes out to a young and half-civilized country, invested with a dignity of an ancient sovereignty and a great power.[69]

Reeve's first point was about the power of the glorious past of Lord Elgin's family:

He takes with him, amongst a people of equal rank, the rank of some race as ancient as the Bruce, and the highest traditions of station and honour.[70]

Then Elgin's personal qualifications:

He takes with him the education of our universities, the polish of our manners, the experience of our public offices of government, the eloquence of our political assemblies.[71]

In sum, Lord Elgin was, in Reeve's words, 'the representative of whatever is best in the nation quite as much as of the majority of the Crown'. Reeve made these points under his belief that Britain was the model of civilisation. He added the following lines:

. . . and [Lord Elgin] conspicuously supplies precisely that in which a young people, struggling with the powers of nature, intent on material gain, and separated by oceans from the civilization of Europe, is necessarily most deficient.[72]

No wonder Japan was, in Reeve's mind, one of those 'young' peoples in this context. This seems to have been a basic as well as a common sensation which affected many British writers who were feeling an increasing sense of remoteness from New Japan.

It is not surprising, therefore, that British writers at the time expressed little concern about the Japanese request for the revision of their treaties with the West, that is, the request for revision leading to tariff autonomy and to abolition of consular jurisdiction by foreign countries in Japanese treaty ports. The sole exception in the first half of the 1870s was Marshall. Owing in part to his close co-operation with Sameshima, he maintained in his *Blackwood's* article that the government of Japan should be treated as an 'organised and civilised Government' equal to those of Western powers.[73] To other writers this idea was out of the question. As for Marshall's support of the Japanese claim to the sole administration of justice within her territory, Aston was prompt in criticising Marshall in his *Macmillan's* article, saying that 'it would be the height of folly to grant such rights to a nation which at the present moment' possessed 'no civil code at all, and whose system of criminal procedure' was 'still barbarous and tainted with cruelty'.[74] Aston added a few more lines in a somewhat paternalistic tone:

> No nation, we are sure, is more ready than our own to see equal rights accorded to Japan, when she can and will dispense full justice and afford full protection to foreigners.[75]

In the same year, Alcock said that foreign countries required from Japan 'something more solid than empty privileges' with reference to the issue of treaty revision. He enumerated their wants, such as liberty of travel in the interior, improved Customs administration, improved Courts of Justice, a civil code, a settled currency, the abolition of the old vexatious system of official surveillance and interference with foreigners, some check on the corruption of all the official classes, encouragement of facilities for the introduction of foreign enterprise, and so on.[76] However, Alcock was reluctant to urge the Japanese government to adopt in a short time new institutions to fulfil those requirements:

> These institutions, which it has taken European nations many centuries to work out and establish, cannot, without great danger, be suddenly transplanted in their full exotic growth to the soil of Japan.[77]

However, Marshall and Sameshima sought to pursue as best they could their campaign for Japan's better treatment by the West. On 1 January 1874, Marshall wrote to Blackwood asking whether he would publish as an article in *Blackwood's Magazine* 'the paper on Consular Jurisdiction'.[78] One week passed, but there was no reply from Blackwood, so Marshall wrote again:

> The article on Consular Jurisdiction – which I think I shall call 'Justice Abroad' – will be finished in 4 or 5 days. Will you have it? I fancy it will print about 14 or 15 pages of Maga.[79]

Still Marshall received nothing from Blackwood for the next week, but he chose to send the completed manuscript of his article to the publisher on 14 January, considering it might be possible that Blackwood would include it in the 1 February issue of the magazine. Marshall also sent a letter on the same day from the Japanese legation in Paris, implying that the publication of the article was expected by all the people at the legation:

I am afraid you will not get it in this month, but if you can we should all be glad here.[80]

The next day, Marshall became so impatient at Blackwood's long silence that he wrote another note:

> Are you ill, my dear Blackwood? I hope not. I am wasting all my efforts of imagination in attempting vainly to conceive why you have not written to me for a month.[81]

Finally, a letter dated 20 January came from Blackwood, in which he suggested that he might make room for the paper in the 1 February issue of the magazine. In reply, Marshall explained the reason why he had been pressing Blackwood over the matter:

> Cartwright [William Cartwright, MP for Oxfordshire], who is here again, expects that Richard – the peace society man – will bring forward a motion for the suppression of Consular jurisdiction; if so it will be useful to get the start of him. Anyhow the question is in the air, and I hope to lead Japan to take action about it. I know this article is aggressive; I made it so on purpose, supposing that vigorous denunciation is more likely to attract notice than mild discussion.[82]

However, in the end, Marshall's plan did not work. The 1 February issue of *Blackwood's Magazine* appeared without his 'Justice Abroad'. The publisher did produce the proofs for the 1 March issue and Marshall duly corrected it, but somehow Blackwood abandoned his idea of publishing it. He wrote to Marshall explaining his view of the matter:

> Reading over the paper after the corrected proof came back I felt that your proposal to bring in Public Opinion to act upon minute questions in remote parts as to which only those on the spot in authority or otherwise could judge was practically impossible. Do you not feel this yourself?[83]

Blackwood may have been concerned about antagonising the readers of his magazine. At any rate, Japan was to him, as the editor of the magazine, too 'remote' a country and its problem was too 'minute' to be discussed in public. He also expressed his belief that 'on the whole' the British behaved 'wonderfully well to the nations' such as the Japanese and that should any misconduct occur on the part of British agents abroad, they would 'speedily meet with punishment from home'. Thus Blackwood decided not to publish Marshall's paper in his magazine:

> I feel that in publishing it I might be making a hit in the dark on a point which I did not understand.[84]

Marshall's disappointment was deep. He wrote to Blackwood on 19 February:

> I am sorry you don[']t like Justice Abroad, very sorry. But, as I have written it for a purpose, to serve a cause which, in my conscience, I believe to be an honest one, I do not see my way to altering it. May I then ask your permission . . . to publish it elsewhere?[85]

John Morley's radical periodical, the *Fortnightly Review*, published Marshall's 'Justice Abroad' several months later, in July 1874.[86] In this article, Marshall explained the history of European consular jurisdiction in the East from the sixteenth century and demonstrated England's current hypocritical usage of the word 'justice' in Asian countries, which, in his eyes, implied 'a protection for oneselves but not as a guarantee for others'.[87] Carefully avoiding the appearance of speaking on behalf of Japan, he argued the theoretical invalidity and unfairness of the system of consular jurisdiction. Finally he introduced his readers to a lengthy imaginary 'protest' from abroad to the British government supposedly printed in *The Times*. For the sender of the protest, Marshall chose a figure who, he thought, could be an analogy to the sovereign of Japan – 'the king of the Gobi Desert'.[88] Marshall certainly tried his best to attract the attention and sympathy of his readers, but his very effort at achieving readability created a paradox: the introduction of the metaphor of the sovereign of a desert kingdom was at that time most likely to make his readers feel even more detached from the issue.

Perhaps the general feeling of remoteness from the country was much stronger in the public mind than in the minds of the writers who knew something of Japan. If so, British writers may have been aware of this popular attitude and adjusted their prose to accommodate this in their writings. This tendency in their prose, to emphasise, consciously or unconsciously, the remoteness of Japan from Britain, was obvious throughout the 1870s, but it was particularly strong in the earlier years of the decade.

Somewhat paradoxically, however, the more remote they felt Japan to be, the freer some observers of the country felt to describe it in whatever way they liked. By the mid-1870s, the earlier goal of presenting Japan in magazines and reviews as truly and objectively as possible had faded. This tendency was clear both in Marshall's attitude towards Shand's writing and in Alcock's attitude towards Mossman's in 1874. A new type of writing on Japan became dominant, taking full advantage of this decline in realistic concern with the country: the romantic accounts of Japan by tourists. They were the people who could freely extend the image of a 'strange and remote' country to an even more unreal realm, and it seems that such writings were welcomed not only by the British reading public but also by those writers who were fairly well informed about the country.

Some of these tourists, such as Dilke and Wedderburn, studied the literature about Japan before and after their visits to the country, and included in their writings what they had learned from others. But the dominant tone in their own general accounts of Japan was unmistakably different from the critical and detached tone in the articles written by such people as Alcock and Aston.

8 Victorian Travellers in the Japanese 'Elf-land'

In 1880, Rutherford Alcock observed that it was important to 'be in a position to understand' what Japan had been 'in the old time' in order to 'rightly understand the New Japan'.[1] He seems to have felt that sufficient time had elapsed since the revolution to enable him to approach Japan's past objectively. The idea that Britain had obtained fairly solid knowledge of Tokugawa Japan was advanced by British writers who had a keen interest in Japan. Not only institutional, political and economic aspects but also the spiritual and cultural life of traditional Japan were steadily revealed to the British reading public, as has already been discussed in Chapter 6. However, the idea of 'Old Japan' which became dominant in British magazine and review articles during the 1870s was not produced by such writers as Alcock or Chamberlain, but rather by those who came for brief visits to Japan from either Shanghai or Hong Kong or on round-the-world tours and provided highly coloured accounts of their experiences.

One can note certain characteristics which these British visitors shared. First, they tried to visit the interior of Japan. The brevity of their journeys in these areas did not matter, and the more traditional the area seemed, the more pleased they were. Second, they called these areas 'Old Japan', idealised as a paradise. Third, they demonstrated a strong distaste for 'New Japan'; that is, the treaty ports and Westernised quarters of the large cities.

From the early 1870s, there was a vague but rather persistent anxiety in Britain that traditional Japanese culture might almost have disappeared. In 1878, Wedderburn expressed this common feeling. According to him, even 'persons generally well-informed' would ask:

> Will not the distinctive charms of Japanese life and manners within a few years disappear for ever beneath the monotonous surface of modern civilization?[2]

Naturally, a traveller who was about to visit Japan shared this anxiety and therefore was most eager to certify that 'Old Japan' was still alive and well in the interior. Wedderburn pointed out the great difference between his impressions of the treaty ports and of rural Japan. He mentioned with delight how conservative the country people were 'of their costume, their language, and their religion'.[3] 'Even in the great cities,' said Wedderburn, 'political and social changes [had] failed to destroy the characteristics and colouring of Japanese life, and [had] produced upon the mass of the people but little visible effect.' Dilke, too, was interested 'to note how far foreign influence' was to be witnessed outside the treaty ports. He wrote that the changes in the countryside were less than a visitor from a treaty port would expect:

> You no longer meet two-sworded warriors; you no longer see the people bowing to the earth before their princes; – that is all.[4]

He was rather surprised at the unchanging features of the countryside:

> Even the hats and boots and umbrellas of the treaty-ports have not yet appeared, and clogs or sandals, picturesque top-knots, and cotton head-rags, and pretty paper sunshades are still the order of the day.[5]

Until the early 1870s, it was difficult for foreigners to travel beyond the limits of the treaty ports. Only diplomats, official employees, and those who, like von Hübner in 1871, could take advantage of diplomatic connections could manage to enter the interior. However, enforcement of the regulations about the so-called treaty limits, the boundaries beyond which foreigners' visits were prohibited, had gradually eased in the late 1860s. For example, since 1869, foreigners who had been considered ill enough to be obliged to resort to hot springs had occasionally been given permission to visit Hakone, Atami and other places. In 1872, a considerable change was introduced by admitting foreign visitors to the exhibition of art and industries in Kyoto. It was in May 1874 that the government inaugurated a more general rule which was called '*Gaikokujin naichi ryokô injun jôrei* (The Regulations on Foreigners' Travels outside the Treaty Ports)' and started issuing special passes to foreign residents and visitors who wanted to travel into the interior.

However, generally speaking, even after 1874, the 'interior' which was easily accessible for tourists, was limited in practice to the rather flourishing areas along the major highways connecting Tokyo, Yokohama, Kyoto, Osaka, Kobe and Nagasaki. The most convenient spots where they could enjoy 'Old Japan' were the castle grounds of former daimyo. Their eagerness to be absorbed into an imaginary traditional world was so strong that it did not matter to them that in many cases the main buildings and the moats had been demolished at the time of the abolition of daimyo-domains in the early 1870s. For example, Cyprian

Bridge of the Royal Navy, who was then stationed in China, visited the castle town of Imabari on the north-western coast of Shikoku, and wrote that he was 'brought face to face with the Middle Ages' there:

> Three years and a half only have passed since the abolition of the feudal tenures and dominion. The retainers still bear upon their sleeves the cognizance of their feudal lords . . . Those long white buildings within the castle walls must have re-echoed time after time to the tramp and hum of armed vassals and retainers of *samurai* and *yaconins* [*yakunin*, i.e., officials].[6]

Dilke also visited a castle-town called Akashi to the west of Kobe, and stood in a forgotten 'lovely park' within the deserted castle grounds, and admired the garden there which showed the Japanese love of 'the picturesque'.[7]

Villages along the routes were of no less attraction to these travellers than were the castle grounds. Bridge, on his second visit to Japan, managed to visit Kyoto. On his way to the city from Osaka, he passed by numerous villages where people were drying crops in their gardens. He enjoyed 'a cheering air of comfort about the villages and cottages' and noted his impressions of them:

> All seemed to have enough to supply the simple wants of a people yet uncontaminated by intercourse with the more self-indulgent strangers from other lands.[8]

To Bridge, everything appeared to be going well in the countryside. 'Misery and beggary in this favoured country,' he wrote, 'still hang closely to the outskirts of the treaty ports'.[9] He described the 'happy' people he encountered:

> Chubby children and rosy maidens crowded the village streets, happier than their peers in those more 'civilized' countries in which woman and child must labour in the fields.[10]

In touring the country, Kyoto was an essential stop as the capital of 'Old Japan'. It was von Hübner who had been the first tourist to enter the city after the fall of the Tokugawa regime. In 1871, this retired diplomat successfully used his old skill at negotiation to obtain special permission from Iwakura Tomomi to visit the outer precincts of the old palace of the emperor. But, being curious to see the inside, he started another negotiation on the spot with the officials of the prefecture, and managed to get through many gates until he reached one of the innermost parts of the palace. His description of this charming city excited great curiosity among the readers of his travelogue. Reeve, in his review of this book, summarised the author's impressions of Kyoto:

> ... a sort of mysterious awe still hangs about the deserted palaces, once the abode of the descendant of the gods; and Kiyoto [sic] is still the seat of the best productions of Japanese art and industry, if it has ceased to be the abode of rank and fashion.[11]

When Bridge visited the city in the latter half of the 1870s, he was struck by the 'regularity and compactness' with which the city had been built. Except for 'a few unsightly masses of stuccoed brick designed on the model of foreign buildings', all the houses were of wood and 'toylike tininess', and the streets were 'straight, very wide, and scrupulously clean'. Bridge enjoyed the contrast made by the bright colours of the clothes worn by the young ladies against the general sombre colours of the street.[12] The capital of 'Old Japan' was still there. Bridge was delighted by the little schoolgirls of Kyoto:

> A troop of maidens coming home with cheerful chatter from some of the numerous schools throws a gleam of brightness over many a street picture that but for their presence would be dull and sombre.[13]

In early 1872, the citizens of Kyoto were ordered to keep their streets and drainage ditches particularly clean in order to impress foreign visitors to the exhibition. This was exactly a repetition of the traditional decree which local authorities used to issue whenever important guests were expected from outside. The governor of Kyoto prefecture even gave them ample funds to effect their cleaning operations. Moreover, the citizens, including children and servants, were instructed to behave properly in front of foreign visitors. The main point of the governor's decree was as follows:

> Many [foreigners] are to enter Kyoto soon. At this moment if we should be in any state which they criticize as barbarous or mean, it would not only be the shame to Kyoto but to the whole country, Japan.[14]

During the 1870s, not only in Kyoto but in many country districts in Japan, the authorities were trying hard to prevent trouble between the inhabitants and foreigners. But the foreign visitors were unaware of these efforts and innocently enjoyed their excursions to these newly opened areas and encounters with well-instructed citizens and villagers.

An itinerary for touring 'Old Japan' soon became well established, and British visitors, encountering more or less similar scenes, produced more or less similar descriptions of what they saw. One is struck by the pleasant tone in which they wrote of their experiences. In 1878, Wedderburn introduced his readers to the highway of Nakasendô, or the 'Central Mountain Road', in the summer season. He was much impressed by the beauty and variety of the scenery en route which was 'highly cultivated and richly wooded, with glassy rushing rivers and flowery hills'.[15] Tiny gardens in villages also attracted him:

> Trim little gardens, some not much larger than a table cloth, exhibit the fondness of the Japanese for flowers and dwarfed shrubs; and each garden has its tiny pond full of goldfish.[16]

Tea-houses and traditional inns were other delights which foreign travellers enjoyed and wrote about in their travelogues. Wedderburn, too, was duly welcomed into a tea-house with a 'chorus of "Ohaio!" [Good morning!]'. He described his reception there:

> When disposed to rest you kick off your shoes and step upon the spotless matting, where the first thing brought to you is fire for your pipe, the second is water for your feet, and the third is tea. All these services are performed by neat-handed smiling maidens, tastefully attired in scarlet or purple sashes, hopping about, bird-like, with rapid movements and pleasant chirping voices.[17]

Wedderburn concluded:

> . . . any one who enjoys roughing it a little, with complete change of life and scene, will find few pleasanter places for an excursion than the uplands of 'Dai Nihon', or Great Japan.[18]

The good manners of the country folk was another theme these visitors spoke of with delight. For example, Bridge passed groups of people on the road to Imabari and was impressed by their bearing:

> All, even peasants, charmed the strangers by their pleasing and graceful manners. Natural good-breeding is a characteristic of even the lowest of the Japanese. It is not merely the civility of the people, but their politeness and grace which so win the strangers' hearts.[19]

No doubt smiling villagers and their children were the most agreeable companions for a foreign visitor who was not able to speak the native language. Wedderburn wrote that the traveller could not 'help feeling at home' in Japan where 'every one seems delighted to see' him, where 'the very dogs' were 'too well-mannered to bark at a stranger', and where he is 'welcomed with friendly salutations of "Ohaio!" by all, from the village patriarch down to the smallest urchin'.[20] Particularly, the 'plump, rosy, and clean' children of Japan looked delightful to Wedderburn:

> Babies, carrying still smaller babies on their backs, greet the passing stranger with a gracious bow, and if he seats himself, collect around, silently surveying him with an intelligent interest.[21]

According to him, 'even a street boy is a little gentleman'.[22] The coolies of Japan who pulled *jinrikisha* (rickshaws) were also very popular among these travellers because of their cheap fares, endurance, politeness and good-humour.[23]

Reading these accounts, one is struck by the similarity between these images of the amiable common people of Japan and those which had been presented by Kaempfer, William Adams, or even by Jesuit missionaries centuries before. To be sure, Kaempfer's accounts had been revived in many ways during the 1850s, and much reinforced by Oliphant in the early 1860s. However, during the 1860s, when Japan underwent much political turmoil and most samurai were intensely hostile to the West, Kaempfer's favourable views about the Japanese were not so popular. Alcock was the leading figure in criticising Kaempfer in those days.[24] Also, the appearance of various articles on the new revolutionary Japan in popular magazines and reviews in the early 1870s weakened the influence of older images of Japan as a 'happy country'. However, the sketches by the tourists during the 1870s revived those old ideas vividly. For example, Wedderburn summarised his impressions of the country at the end of his article, 'Modern Japan, II':

> Japan seems to be a country where men never lose their temper, where women and children are always treated with gentleness, where common labourers bow and beg pardon of each other if they happen to jostle accidentally, where popular sports do not inflict suffering upon the lower animals, where a paper screen is a sufficient protection against all intrusion – even that of burglars, and where cleanliness takes a high rank among social virtues as to be carried almost to a ludicrous excess.[25]

As accounts such as these proliferated in the late 1870s, the general tone of writings about Japan began to change. Even Alcock started praising Kaempfer in 1880. Speaking about contemporary works on

Japan, Alcock argued that it would be 'a great injustice to pass over [Kaempfer] without mention'. In Alcock's opinion, Kaempfer was 'the most painstaking, intelligent, and honest of students in the field of Japanese history', and he frankly admitted that Kaempfer's work had 'long formed the quarry, from which all compilations relating to Japan' had been 'taken, with or without acknowledgement'.[26]

Many writers revived the time-honoured discussion about the differences between China and Japan. Bridge, for example, presented an impressive contrast between the general atmosphere of a Chinese city and that of the areas surrounding the Inland Sea of Japan. The former he described in the following lines:

> The air is laden with sickening stenches, the beauty of buildings is obscured beneath the accumulated foulness and neglect of years. Filthy animals almost dispute the narrow ways with the passer-by. Hunger and fatigue must be excessive to make a stranger . . . enter the vermin-infested dwellings to seek refreshment or repose.[27]

And, the Japanese scene:

> The scenery is truly lovely: a Devon foreground set in a background of the Alps.[28]

The Inland Sea stretching in front of him 'bask[ed] in a climate almost perfect in its serenity and freedom from extremes'.[29] In the city of Nagasaki, 'physical cleanliness, at all events, reigned supreme'. The traditional English idea of the foul and fusty China in contrast to the clean and serene Japan was now much reinforced. The argument about racial differences between the Chinese and the Japanese was also revived. Wedderburn was much inspired by the research of Charles Wolcott Brooks about many Japanese junks which had been stranded on the coast of North America and on the Hawaiian or adjacent islands. Brooks, Japanese Consul at San Francisco, had published his research in the *Proceedings of the California Academy of Science* in 1875.[30] In 1878, Wedderburn asserted that the Black Current of the North Pacific connecting the Philippines, Japan, Aleutian Islands, the American coast and the Hawaiian Archipelago, determined the racial kinship of the Japanese with the stock of southern areas.[31] Although he admitted the cultural influence of China on Japanese life, he thought the two peoples must be very different in their origins:

> The natural genius of the Japanese people, their language, features, and habits, all are perfectly distinct from those of the Middle

Kingdom, and seem to indicate Malay or Polynesian rather than Mongolian affinities.[32]

Wedderburn enumerated several of 'the many points of difference' which he himself observed and considered seriously as proof of the theory. Among them were the use of chairs in China, but not in Japan, different hair styles for men, and different clothing habits among women.[33] More detailed differences were now being cited than in Kaempfer's time, but the traditional pattern of differentiating the two peoples in favour of the Japanese persisted throughout the 1870s.

Travellers to Japan during the 1870s did not merely revive certain traditional ideas about Japan, they also revealed some new characteristics in their observations and writings. Many of these visitors possessed pre-conceived images of Japan and the Japanese when arriving in the country, and once there, they went off in search of scenes which confirmed these ideas. Some may have got the images from reading books, but it is more likely that they got them from Japanese prints, or from the decoration on the Japanese porcelain and lacquerware which was increasingly abundant in European drawing-rooms in the 1870s. One of the travellers who showed such a tendency very clearly was von Hübner. The ideas about Japan which had pre-occupied him before his visit to the country were the picturesqueness of Japanese scenery and the grotesque bodies of the Japanese. The former impression had been gained from Japanese woodblock prints and the latter from ceramic and lacquer works in which fanciful figures of the people had been humorously represented. When he saw near Mount Fuji that village girls carried their babies on their backs with 'their hands folded backwards', he said that 'grotesqueness' was a characteristic of both men and things in Japan, and that he had seen it in specimens of Japanese art 'a thousand times'.[34] Reading some of Bridge's descriptions of Japanese scenery, one might argue that the images presented in those passages were not too different from what one could imagine as a typical Japanese scene through the prints of Hiroshige or Hokusai. Here is one example, a description he wrote when he was on the road from Kobe to Osaka with the Rokkô hills on his left and the blue waters of the inland sea on his right:

> Mountain, stream, cascade, and sea; grove and copse; golden grain and brilliant flowers in middle distance and foreground; deep-blue waters fading into a pale horizon, shadowy peaks melting into the violet distance.[35]

Perhaps because of such interplay between their descriptions of Japan and Japanese images represented in arts and crafts imported to Europe from Japan, these travellers tended to describe things Japanese as if they had been totally unreal, emphasising to an unusual extent their mysteriousness or strangeness. For example, Dilke called Japan 'the traveller's paradise',[36] and observed about the inhabitants there:

> It is impossible to realise that the Japanese are real men and women. What with the smallness of the people, their incessant laughing chatter, and their funny gestures, one feels one's self in elf-land.[37]

The over-mystification of things Japanese was a tendency which von Hübner also manifested in some parts of his book. Reeve was much impressed by one of them and translated it extensively in his review:

> The sky was pink, with light blue clouds, floating about it. Only at Yokohama, and but rarely there, have I witnessed such effects of light. I imagined myself in an ideal world, in some enchanted region; and in my dreams I rejoice to see over again the strange, mysterious, and poetic scene of the Great Temple of Yoshida.[38]

Although von Hübner was not, in this passage, evoking Japanese mysteriousness in such a sweeping way as was the case with Dilke, both of them were excessively romanticising the country. Perhaps they did so in response to the desire among the British reading public to see in Japan something extraordinary and mysterious. As was conspicuous in Shand's case, there was a tendency even among those writers who had not been to Japan to exaggerate the mysterious or romantic aspects of Japan. Stevenson's article on Yoshida Shôin, which appeared in the *Cornhill Magazine* in 1880, showed this same tendency. Yoshida was a radical patriot, who had been executed in 1859 at the age of thirty-one. The promising young novelist introduced this figure to his readers as a representative of 'a heroic people' in the East:

> A military engineer, a bold traveller (at least in wish), a poet, a patriot, a schoolmaster, a friend to learning, a martyr to reform – there are not many men, dying at seventy, who have served their country in such various characters.[39]

Stevenson was also impressed by the verse which another patriot named Kusakabe had uttered just before his execution:

> It is better to be a crystal and be broken, Than to remain perfect like

a tile upon the housetop.

Stevenson's point was to use the experiences of those 'great-hearted gentlemen' to urge his English readers to reflect upon their daily lives. For this purpose, he romanticised their behaviour:

> Only a few miles from us, to speak by the proportion of the universe, while I was droning over my lessons, Yoshida was goading himself to be wakeful with the stings of the mosquito; and while you were grudging a penny income tax, Kusakahé [sic] was stepping to death with a noble sentence on his lips.[40]

An extreme case was Dilke who compared rural Japan with Lewis Carroll's fictitious kingdoms, as if the fact that Japan actually existed had made no difference to him:

> All who love children must love the Japanese, the most gracious, the most courteous, and the most smiling of all peoples, whose rural districts form, with Through-the-Looking-Glass-Country and Wonderland, three kingdoms of merry dreams.[41]

The question raised in Chapter 6 as to why British writers were inclined to emphasise the mysteriousness of Japan despite their increasing familiarity with the country can be answered, on the one hand, by their feeling of extreme remoteness from New Japan as was shown in Chapter 7, and on the other hand, by this desire, shared by British visitors to Japan and non-visitors alike, to make Old Japan as romantic or unreal as possible. But why did such a desire exist? One finds a clue to answering this question if one looks at another aspect of the style these writers employed in presenting Japan to the public.

One conspicuous characteristic of their style was their use of metaphors drawn from ancient Greece and Rome. In 1873, when Reeve introduced one such expression used by von Hübner to the readers of the *Edinburgh Review*, they might have been led into a new fantasy about Japan. The part Reeve translated was the author's account of a Shinto ceremony at the 'Temple of Yoshida'. A high priest's performance on the occasion deeply impressed the visitor:

> Words fail me to describe the play of his features, the classical beauty of his attitudes, the striking effect of the music, the noble and mysterious majesty of the scene. The attitudes of the priest were, I repeat, classical, but not only in a general sense; one could not fail to perceive in them a likeness to the well-known examples of Greek sculpture of the best period.[42]

During the previous two decades, such expressions had been employed very infrequently in periodical articles. For example, in the late 1850s, Osborn once compared Japanese junks to Roman galleys,[43] but it was only a brief comment which had little significance in the whole context of his writings on Japan. Entering the mid-1870s, however, whenever British travellers tried to explain 'Old Japan' to their readers, the ideal world of classical Europe was bound to appear in their descriptions. Even Alcock, a careful writer on Japan, became influenced by this trend:

> The mode of life of a Japanese, whatever his rank, was very simple; the Daimio, in his castle, was accustomed to Spartan fare of rice and fish chiefly.[44]

As has already been shown, the general image of Japan in those travellers' minds was so freely idealised and made so abstract that it seems to have been almost natural for them to connect their 'Japan' directly to the classical world.

From the late eighteenth century, there had been a gradual revival in Britain of interest in the ancient Graeco-Roman world, a trend visually manifested by many architects in the early nineteenth century and by pre-Raphaelites in the latter half of the century. During this time, people educated in public schools became more conscious of the accomplishments of these 'pagan' civilisations.[45] For Victorian visitors to Japan, ancient Greece and Rome were the world which should be compared with their 'Japan'. The Setouchi, or the Inland Sea of Japan, with its numerous tiny isles, strongly reminded them of Mediterranean scenes, and in their imaginations they were transported into ancient times when Greece and Rome had flourished. A good example was Bridge. In 1875, he explained what he had felt in the Setouchi:

> Those who land for the first time in the more remote parts of Japan find themselves transported not so much to a new world as to a different age. Immediately after having entered the Inland Sea the voyager is brought face to face with scenes and customs irresistibly recalling what is known of those of ancient Greece and Rome.[46]

The shape of the boats there had, according to Bridge, 'the same rig, the same single sail, with *antenna* and *ceruchi*'; 'Dodona and the shrine of the Tyrian Astarte are recalled by the sacred groves which wave on every island'.[47] Even the garments of the inhabitants were no exception:

The flowing robes of the comfortable classes in the streets of towns closely resemble the toga of the Romans, but not more closely than does the short tunic of the women, the *chitôn* of the Greeks.[48]

In Bridge's travelogue, almost every impressive figure in Japan was metamorphosed into an inhabitant of the classical world. At an entrance to Imabari, many citizens came out to see Bridge's excursion party:

> Women, girt with broad zones of brilliant hue, seductive as the cestus of Venus herself in their exposure of the form and their coquettish fastening behind, soon joined the crowd which was quickly collecting in the strangers' wake.[49]

It often happens that when a certain type of language is established firmly for describing a country, it assumes a kind of life of its own, and seeks its own proliferation. Bridge, on another visit to Japan, went even further than before in his own metaphorical style of describing the country. The image of a farmer working in a field near Osaka was superimposed by Bridge with the image of a Roman politician:

> A grave husbandman guiding a simple plough of wood tipped with iron, in his loose gown edged with a broad fold or a stripe as ample as the *laticlave,* his stature increased to the Western standard by the thick sandals on his feet, might pass for an Oriental Cincinnatus tilling his patrimonial fields.[50]

In Kyoto, he saw an evening entertainment, *odori,* or dance, and was much impressed:

> Such pantomimic dancing might have been performed in days of old by hands of modest Dorian youths and maidens in honour of the far-darting Apollo.[51]

It is worth considering the impact of such a flood of Graeco-Roman metaphors on Bridge's readers. Had they had no previous knowledge of Japan, Bridge's rhetoric must have played a decisive role in forming their images of Japan. Nor was Bridge unique – Wedderburn frequently used a similar style. Not satisfied with indulging in mere rhetoric, Wedderburn even started a serious comparison between the Japanese and the ancient Romans:

> They are a *gens tagata,* long-robed and bareheaded. Their delight is in the warm bath. They practise cremation; they celebrate funeral games in honour of slain heroes.[52]

These references to the classical world may have enabled British writers to discuss openly certain topics about Japan, which were taboo under Victorian notions of 'respectability' and 'decency'. One such topic was the manner in which Japanese common people exposed their bodies in the hot season. As was pointed out earlier, this was something which British writers often cited during the 1850s and 1860s to prove the 'low' stage of 'civilization' in Japan. But Bridge and Wedderburn were inclined to compare half-naked Japanese with the plump and healthy people of classical days. Wedderburn noted that the favoured sports of the Japanese were 'contests of naked athletes'.[53] Bridge described Japanese farm labourers this way:

> . . . the men exposing nearly the whole of their thick-set muscular bodies to the sun, and the women as lightly clothed as the 'single-garmented' Spartan maidens.[54]

In their romanticisation of Old Japan, one finds a strong tinge of antipathy towards modernity. Indeed, their love of Old Japan was counterbalanced by their hatred of New Japan, which was, in their eyes, not at all Japan but industrialised Britain or, in more general terms, modern European civilisation itself. In 1878, Bridge wrote in a tone of sorrow:

> Such ideal parallel [between Japan and the world of the Classics] would soon be dispelled. A line of railway, not long completed, seams the fair champaign with an ugly scar of 'Western Progress' – the shibboleth of New Japan.[55]

Bridge went on to explain what had happened to the interiors of Japanese office buildings:

> The cleanly matted flooring of the rooms has been replaced by one of planks, befouled by the boots . . . The neat lacquered writing tables, some three inches high, at which Japanese accountants kneel, have given place to ungainly copies of European desks and chairs.[56]

In Bridge's view, such buildings suggested 'an irruption of Birmingham into Arcadia'.[57] He saw in the changing scenes in Japan the victorious face of modern Britain, which was nothing but a 'vulgar common-place'.[58] The distaste for the unseemly industrialised big cities in the Midlands was fairly commonly shared by British intellectuals at that time, and this tendency seems to have become more intense among those who visited Japan.

At that time, particularly among British liberals, there was growing anxiety about Britain's 'Mission of Civilization' in the Far East. This feeling was acute in the case of China, as it was perceived that the British position in diplomatic negotiations was often influenced by the opium trade. In 1875, John Henry Bridges, the Comtist philosopher, revealed his concern about images of Britain and observed that 'the noble result of Western Civilization' in China since the late 1860s had been to increase the opium trade on the land route across Yunnan.[59] He was afraid that British diplomats might use the recent murder of a British subject, Augustus Raymond Margary, as leverage in negotiations for a new commercial treaty.[60] In the next year, Dilke expressed more or less similar criticisms in his article on China published in *Macmillan's Magazine*.[61] The same type of argument was presented by Wedderburn when he criticised the Foreign Office's previous negotiations with the government of the Shogun over the affairs of Kagoshima and Shimonoseki in the early 1860s. In the former case, he believed that the indemnity supposed to atone for the murder of a British merchant, Lennox Richardson, by retainers of the Shimazu of Kagoshima raised serious moral questions:

> There is too great an appearance of truth in the accusation that a private crime was made pretext by a powerful nation for extorting money from a feeble one.[62]

There was also a different type of anxiety which began to be expressed by some specialists in Far Eastern affairs. It was about the future security of the British position in the Far East in view of the possible war between an Eastern country, most likely China, and Britain. Alcock was among those who were concerned with this question at an early stage. In 1874, in a signed article published in *Macmillan's Magazine*, he warned his readers that it was 'a very common mistake to consider the Chinese hopelessly anti-progressive and sluggish',[63] and outlined the possible danger which lay ahead:

> It depends not a little upon the Western Powers themselves, and their represenatatives, political and commercial, in China and Japan, whether the result shall be the development of mutual interests and goodwill – or the more or less rapid adoption of all the material elements of our strength and civilization, only to be turned against Western nations and enable the Chinese to fight them with their own weapons.[64]

Against such a background, it is understandable that in the latter half of the 1870s visitors to Japan, such as Dilke and Wedderburn, were vociferous in expressing their opinion that British extraterritoriality in Japan should be abandoned. Wedderburn was very sympathetic with the Japanese 'grievances' over the matter,[65] and Dilke was worried about destroying Japan's goodwill towards Britain and with it the possibility of an Anglo-Japanese alliance in the future.[66]

During the latter half of the 1870s, liberal periodicals such as the *Fortnightly Review* published more articles on Far Eastern questions than those periodicals on the conservative side. For example, *Blackwood's Magazine* became less concerned with Japan in this period, publishing only one short article by the German novelist Rudolph Lindau (1829–1910), the former Swiss Consul at Yokohama, about a heart-broken British businessman in Japan and his faithful dog.[67] Lindau had published several articles on the country in the *Revue des Deux Mondes* before the Franco-Prussian War, but since then he had become interested in having his writings published in Britain. During the summer of 1878, Lindau was occupied with writing a paper on von Moltke, the strategist, but he managed to employ his very limited 'leisure hours' writing for Blackwood this little tale from Japan,[68] and Blackwood wrote to Lindau saying that he liked the tale because a part of it had appealed to his 'Scotch humour'.[69] It seems that there was little need for them to discuss matters concerning Japan itself. At the same time, Blackwood's activities had been curtailed since the spring of 1878 owing to lung and heart disease, which proved fatal the following year.[70]

But in the case of other more or less conservative periodicals, like the *Quarterly Review* and the *Edinburgh Review*, such a tendency could also be pointed out. Since 1874, Europe had undergone a serious economic depression. Certainly, questions concerning the Far East, particularly Japan, were less important in British magazine and review articles than those about immediate social and political questions in Europe. In Britain, Japan might have become too remote a country for conservative realists to take an interest in it; and too remote a country for romantic radicals to discuss. It is undeniable that diplomatic arguments about China and Japan by the radicals sometimes showed their shrewd calculations of future British interests in the region, and if they tended to discuss critically the 'sinful' face of Britain, it was often an image of their country devised for the sake of making their arguments successful.

However, when they discussed the British destruction of Old Japan, their perception of Britain was much less confident. It was based on the embarrassment which many British visitors to Japan felt when they discovered that their own country had been producing a mediocre and monotonous civilisation and passing it on to the much finer old civilisation of Japan. Such a discovery may have been the sort of experience which tended to affect a person's own identity. A similar feeling had already been expressed in Britain earlier concerning the arts and crafts of Japan. It was Wyatt who confessed a sincere admiration for the 'harmonizing', 'common-sense system' of Eastern design and proposed to promote exhibitions, schools and museums to enlighten the British public about the fine taste of the East, including Japan.[71] There was an idea prevalent in Britain during the 1870s that most of the Japanese products which were coming to Europe were specially made for the vulgar taste of the West and that the best things were never exported. At the time of the Vienna Exhibition, Shand reconfirmed this notion:

> The Mikado and the great nobles were not likely to strip their palaces and risk their most treasured objects on a perilous sea-voyage, even in order that they might raise the reputation of their country in the opinion of remote barbarians.[72]

But Shand was sufficiently impressed by the Japanese collection at Vienna to make the following observation about the civilisation of Japan:

> Such as the exhibition was, however, it showed you sufficient to indicate the existence of an old civilisation of a very high character; for when a country has made such advances in the arts, it implies a strong social organisation, refined tastes, and the leisure and security to indulge them.[73]

The Westernisation of Japanese art was, therefore, a matter of irritation for British people. It was in the middle of the 1870s that Dilke felt relieved when he found at one of the annual exhibitions held at the old imperial palace in Kyoto that Japanese art had 'not yet been killed by English "taste" '.[74] To his delight, many articles 'manufactured for the European market' could 'compare favourably with the productions of the best days of Japanese art'.[75] However, within a few years, Bridge, visiting a similar exhibition at Kyoto, noted that tasteful works of traditional art were mixed with 'imitations of foreign schools by native artists'.[76] He was irritated and wrote:

> That style of art which was founded on observation of Nature, which followed Nature in all the richness of her luxuriant variety, is now yielding to the assaults of the prim formalism of the West.[77]

With profound regret, he described what he felt to be the intrusion of Western bad taste on Japan:

> The artists whose delicate perception could seize the beauty of the soft-toned hues that dwell in the fleecy cloud or on the surface of the waving stem, and could transfer them to the *faïences* of Satsuma or Kyôto, now follow the rage for foreign models and produce jugs and bowls as prim and mean as any that emanate from Staffordshire or Delft.[78]

Bridge was very embarrassed by the fact that many Japanese craftsmen were becoming overwhelmed by a mistaken 'belief in the superior aesthetic development of the art-loving inhabitants of Birmingham or Massachusetts'.[79]

These comparisons between Japan and Britain, or the West in general, were not to be confined to the field of arts and crafts. Wedderburn, for instance, contrasted Japanese civilisation with that of Europe in general. In his mind, the spiritual qualifications which were required for the inhabitants of an advanced civilisation were as follows: urbanity, gentleness, consideration for others, together with courage, energy and intellect.[80] By such a standard, Wedderburn had to draw an unfavourable picture of his own society:

> Foreigners, after living in the interior of Japan for a considerable time, on returning into 'civilised society', have even stated that the manners of their own countrymen appear to them vulgar and almost brutal, accustomed as they have become to a courtesy singularly free from servile or mercenary considerations.[81]

'Gentle courtesy', 'natural politeness', and 'good breeding' were the characteristics which Bridge thought distinguished the Japanese from other peoples.[82]

These British writers had to admit, however reluctantly, that their own 'vulgar' civilisation was rapidly consuming the very features of the idealised Old Japan they cherished. Bridge suggested that 'those who would see anything of real Japan should visit the country without delay'.[83] It was a serious anxiety. Already twenty years had passed since the heroic Yoshida Shôin whom Stevenson had admired had been executed. Bridge saw the disgusting manners and bearing of

'*Occidentalised* natives', most of whom were former samurai. They had cleverly survived the overthrow of the Shogunate and now were proud of their 'brief authority of some post in the new fangled hierarchy of officialdom'.[84] British writers felt they shared a vicarious responsibility for all these changes, considering that Western influences were likely to bring unhappiness to the people of New Japan. A sense that Britain had made an irreparable commitment to the Westernisation of Japan was expressed in many articles in British magazines and reviews from the mid-1870s, and the writers of those articles often showed, explicitly or implicitly, their serious uneasiness about the British responsibility in this respect. This tendency seems to have been reflected even in the following passage by Alcock, in which he tried hard to calm such anxieties about the British commitment in the Far East and to rationalise all the difficulties that had emerged between Britain and Japan during the past few decades:

> It is hardly to be expected that the sudden contact of the two kinds of government and social organization, so widely different as the Japanese and the Western World presented, could take place without a collision and conflict.[85]

It was, in fact, rather convenient for Alcock's apology that he could regard Japan as so different a society from the West. Although his attitude towards Japan was not so romantic as that of travellers to the country, he was not entirely free from the general tendency among British writers to stress the singularity of Japan.

During the 1870s there was some tension between the British writers on Japan who had stayed in the country for long periods and those who had been there only as tourists. Between the two groups, however, there was a fairly extensive exchange of information about Japan, as Alcock observed in 1880:

> From the flying visits of travellers 'round the world', the no less ephemeral works which record them, and Reports of members of the Diplomatic Missions, there is much to be gleaned, though not without a process by which the chaff may be separated from the grain.[86]

At the same time, whenever these tourists wrote about New Japan, they did not hesitate to borrow information from the accounts written by those who had spent a long time there. The reason for this mixture of information from various sources appears to have been the lack of an authoritative writer in Britain, comparable to Oliphant in the early

1860s and Alcock in the mid-1860s, who could have given a lead to journalistic circles in discussions about Japan. There were some British authorities, such as Satow, Aston, and Chamberlain, but most of their scholarly activities were still confined to the Asiatic Society of Japan, based first in Yokohama and subsequently in Tokyo. In British popular magazine and review articles of the 1870s, there was little obviously direct influence from any of these writers' works, as these young authorities in the new field of Japanology may have been regarded as too highly specialised in journalistic circles.

Writers who had never been to Japan, such as Reeve, Marshall or Shand, enjoyed considerable freedom in presenting their own ideas of the country, producing mosaic-style works combining pieces of information which ranged from recent financial reports to old ideas which could be traced back to Kaempfer's time. In particular, Shand's article, 'Romance of Japanese Revolution', which appeared in *Blackwood's Magazine* in 1874, was notable among journalistic accounts of Japan in the 1870s, in depicting the general tendency to make loose patchwork compositions. It was in this paper that Shand used the notion of 'singularity' or 'mystery' in a more comprehensive way to describe the general character of the country, whereas earlier writers had often employed these terms to describe either the rapid speed of change or a particular incident in Japanese history. Shand's article proved the precursor in the 1870s of subsequent articles on Japan by tourists. These visitors were enthusiastic about their discoveries of what they had expected to find in Japan. They changed their cool sense of detachment from New Japan, which had been prevalent in Britain, into an unrealistic strong hatred for Western civilisation in the context of New Japan, and imposed on traditional Japan more mysterious images than did earlier writers.

Thus the world of images of Japan in the 1870s increasingly showed a paradoxical tendency to consume, if necessary, any amount of new information from Japan simply to enrich the mystification of the country. Obviously, this conversion process was supported by two kinds of emotion: feelings of remoteness from New Japan and the desire to idealise and mystify Old Japan. But the real promoter of this process of mystification seems to have been anxiety: an anxiety that unpleasant aspects of contemporary Britain might be suggested by realistic descriptions of the New Japan.

Many Japanese intellectuals at that time were much concerned, in their zeal for Westernisation, about the opinion of British intellectuals about Japan. But some British intellectuals also became much concerned with their own identity, as they faced the image of their own country which was inevitably reflected in the mirror of Japan.

Conclusion

The three decades from 1850 witnessed the persistent reinforcement, in articles on Japan in British periodicals, of the idea that Japan was a singular and mysterious country. To be sure, there were conscious efforts to re-examine stereotyped perceptions of the country from the early 1860s onwards. Alcock became an advocate of 'photographic accuracy' as a new standard for writing on Japan. Young Mitford demonstrated his insight into the inner life of the Japanese and presented Japan not as a country inhabited by a quaint people but as a country which shared many cultural traits with Britain. Marshall tried to offer the reading public first-hand data about the current situation in New Japan. However, the thirty-year history of popular British perceptions of Japan proves to be a history of the incessant failure of such realistic approaches to the country.

Except for Mitford and perhaps a few others, every writer, even those who had experienced lengthy stays in Japan or had close acquaintances with Japanese intellectuals, committed himself to the idea of Japanese singularity. In other words this idea proved a strong and active stereotype which could digest, if necessary, various pieces of new information and perpetuate itself. After the Restoration, Japan's affinity to modern Britain was growing rapidly in terms of institutions, technology, and even of ways of thinking among intellectuals. The mid-century British ideal of introducing every nation to Christianity and commerce *was* being steadily realised on Japanese soil. Had writers of articles on Japan in British periodicals wished to emphasise Japan's increasing closeness to Britain, they could have done so. Instead they stressed Japan's 'remoteness'.

Raymond Dawson once 'tried to relate' certain popular European ideas about China 'to the factors that conditioned them', and argued that 'these factors have generally been events in European intellectual history rather than changes in the situation in China'.[1] To some extent this view is in harmony with our observations. Since the early 1850s, we have traced changes in British perceptions of their own civilisation in the context of writing about Japan. In the beginning, there was Knox's idea of British 'civilisation': this consisted of a number of values which Knox thought should be accepted universally. Evidently there was a mood of comfortable complacency among British intellectuals at that time. In the early 1860s, there was a vague consciousness among

British writers on Japan that in any civilisation the 'civility' of its members should matter most and we saw the early growth of satirical accounts of British civilisation in some articles on Japan from about the mid-1860s. In the early 1870s, there was a degree of boasting about British civilisation when Japan inaugurated its programme of zealous Westernisation, but it is striking how brief this tendency was: by 1873 symptoms of economic depression were abundant in Britain, particularly in agriculture. From the mid-1870s onwards, British miners and agricultural workers frequently resorted to strikes to resist reductions in wages. It is probably no coincidence that Dilke and others, conscious of the unrest in the British countryside, began to write about the paradisaical villages of Japan.

We have observed that the increase in anxiety about British civilisation in the minds of British writers on Japan was linked to the development of their sense of remoteness from Japan. Since the mid-1860s, it was always this growing sense of remoteness which supported the broader use of the 'singularity' label for Japan. This sense of remoteness was particularly strengthened when Japan began imitating modern Britain, as France, Germany and America had done in earlier times. The comment on Japan's 'lack of originality' in the *Saturday Review* in 1871 could be interpreted as an expression of defensive feelings in Britain. The reading public tended to become less open-minded towards other nations. The following episode from 1872 illustrates this trend: John Blackwood and Frederic Marshall had an argument about how to present the French habit of bowing in *Blackwood's Magazine*. The editor wanted a hilarious account for his readers. Marshall lost his temper at this request:

> I have tried honestly, five times, to carry out your wish of making more fun of the Frenchman's bow. But I have failed . . . [To laugh at] a bow is a prejudice, like all the rest; the people of Thibet [*sic*] pull their right ear and put their tongue out as a sign of reverence – Why not? All these things are but relative, our custom makes them. Everyday I see here the Japanese rub their knees and hiss, that is their fashion of saying good morning to each other.[2]

'All these things are but relative' – a message hard to accept for increasingly self-centred minds.

Up to this point, we have followed Dawson's view. Changes in the British intellectual climate were certainly related to the reinforcement of the stereotype about Japan, but this study has revealed a more complex mechanism of forming popular images about Japan in British periodicals. Our knowledge can bridge the gap between general aspects of British intellectual history and British ideas about a particular country – in this case Japan.

First, it is clear that changes in the situation in Japan influenced British perceptions. Knowledge in Japan of the effects of British power in China paved the way for smooth negotiations between Lord Elgin and Tokugawa officials. Besides, at that time, Japanese society reflected the long-term effects of the rigorous Tempô Reforms. In consequence, the style of life of the common people was somewhat subdued and British visitors' impressions must have reflected this. The subsequent 'anti-foreigners' movement and the next stage of rapid Westernisation, which owed much to fast developments in the technology of communications at that time, also influenced British perceptions of Japan. Tourists in the late 1870s were received by villagers and city residents in a manner more or less similar to that in which Lord Elgin's Mission had been received. All these factors should not be overlooked.

Secondly, it is clear that raw information about Japan never appeared in magazines and reviews in its original complexity. This feature can be examined in terms of the three major groups of authors of articles on Japan: residents of Japan; visitors to the country for short terms; and those who had never been to Japan.

In the first group, there was Alcock in the early 1860s, Mitford 1869–72 and Aston in 1872. We have observed how Alcock's initial call for factual accuracy in presenting Japan led to the paradoxical result of reinforcing old ideas about Japan's 'singularity' among writers in the third group. Also, Alcock's attitude gradually changed after his departure from Japan, as we noted in connection with his opinion of Kaempfer. In Mitford's case, his published account of Taki's execution was significantly different from his original report of the ceremony. But his writings had little influence on other writers and it is noteworthy that he stopped writing about Japan within a few years of returning to Britain. Aston's work appeared only once in *Macmillan's Magazine,* and his role was to criticise another well-informed writer, Marshall. In spite of Macmillan's expectations, there is little evidence that Aston's short article was quoted by other writers. On the whole, resident writers did not enjoy much influence in this field of publication. On their return home their attitudes towards Japan tended to become similar to those of the people who had never been there. Mitford's case illustrates this tendency. In the mid-1880s, W. S. Gilbert (1836–1911) used miscellaneous Japanese images in magazines

Conclusion 173

and reviews for a laughable entertainment and reflection upon Britain: 'The Mikado of Japan whose object all sublime'; the joyous 'three little maids from school'; the ever-bowing samurai; the custom of the 'happy despatch', and so on. At the Savoy Theatre, the chorus sang in the première of *'The Mikado, or the Town of Titipu'* on 14 March 1885:

> If you want to know who we are,
> We are gentlemen of Japan:
> On many a vase and jar –
> On many a screen and fan,
> We figure in lovely paint:
> Our attitude's queer and quaint –
> You're wrong if you think it ain't, oh![3]

It is remarkable that Mitford should have assisted in producing this operetta. In a letter dated 17 March 1885, Gilbert expressed his renewed thanks for Mitford's 'invaluable help' with the production.[4] The idea of 'the Japanese gentleman' and his *seppuku* seems to have changed in Mitford's mind.

The works of short-term visitors showed that they were strongly influenced by earlier travellers' accounts. Not only Osborn and Oliphant but also Dilke, Wedderburn and Bridge conveyed little original information about Japan. Their writings almost always resulted in the reinforcement of old ideas about a singularly happy Japan. One could attribute this phenomenon partly to the characteristics of the areas they visited in Japan. Had they been more curious, they could have seen different scenes, as did Isabella Bird. But most of the visitors at that time showed, at least in their writings, few realistic concerns with Japanese society, and their observations were under the strong influence of their preconceptions about the country. Writers in this group thus played an important role in reinforcing whatever popular ideas about Japan prevailed in Britain at that time; and, as experienced residents were few and without journalistic influence, short-term visitors were often prejudiced by the works of authors who had never even visited Japan.

The role of people who had never seen Japan in producing popular images of the country was thus very important. They were the writers who tended to exaggerate the singularity of Japan, using any information available, as we saw in the cases of Reeve, Shand, Knox and Russell. The lack of personal experience of Japan made them more ready to resort to old clichés and more susceptible to editorial influence, as was illustrated by White's case. Many in this group were prolific writers. It is clear that writers such as Reeve, Stephen, Tremenheere and Shand cared little about factual accuracy in articles on Japan, though they often claimed to do so. To many of them, minor errors were of no consequence as they were dealing with a 'remote' country. Marshall's case demonstrates the responsiveness of the language these writers used to the taste of readers as they perceived it. In the article he produced in co-operation with Sameshima, he summed up his account by emphasising the strangeness of Japan, and he was not much concerned when Shand requested that he improve the 'judicial' quality of his article. Alcock recommended Mossman's work to the general public in the mid-1870s, despite being well aware of its inaccuracies.

The active role of such non-visitors in creating popular ideas about Japan can also be explained by the fact that they were, in general, much closer to their editors. Some of the writers in this group were editors themselves, or on the editorial boards of magazines and reviews. Successful editors, whether they write articles themselves or not, are keen observers of the public interest, and in Victorian times as was shown in the case of Blackwood, editors' opinions often affected the tone of articles about Japan. Blackwood was fairly consistent in his desire, which coincided with his concern for sales, that articles on Japan be pleasant entertainment. Reeve used works by Oliphant, Alcock and von Hübner very effectively in producing his own extravagant pictures of the 'amiable', 'contradictory' or 'strange' features of Japan.

Nor should one overlook the reading public of magazines and reviews, who, in the eyes of these authors and editors, often seemed to insist on certain clichés about Japan, or to respond vividly to familiar metaphors and similes regarding things Japanese. It was through this dimension of language that the reading public was involved indirectly, but to a very high degree, in the formation of the stereotype of Japan. In the 1850s and early 1860s, when Japan's affinity with Britain was generally felt in Britain, non-visitors were most active in using European analogies to describe Japan for their readers. But from the mid-1860s, as feelings of remoteness from Japan grew in Britain, these writers began to use images of Japan to satirise Britain. Once this mode of dealing with information about Japan was established, the major concern in their articles gradually shifted from Japan to Britain, and it was through this type of writing that knowledge about Japan became subordinated to the concerns of the reading public as perceived by these writers. The intellectual climate of Britain was thus reflected in articles on the particular topic of Japan.

By the mid-1870s, 'Japan' became a means by which British journalism could express unrestricted opinions about Britain. This subtle change, first in Shand's article of 1874 and later in many other articles, was significant. The label 'the singular country' to describe Japan – in particular, the increased emphasis on Japan's general unreality and romance in contrast to contemporary Britain – could be interpreted as indicating the deep anxiety in British intellectuals' minds. Japan was a convenient peg on which to hang anxieties about contemporary Britain that might not have found such an opportunity for expression had it not been for Japan. The image of Japan in the late 1870s was thus a precursor of intense nationalism, the components of which were increasingly simple and symbolic images of the country in relation to the outside world.

From about 1880, the image of an unreal Japan became firmly established in Britain and began to exert a broader influence. For example, the image of 'a civilization without any originality', which was as romantic an idea as the tourists' idea of Japan as an elf-land, became an element in the way British intellectuals thought about Far Eastern questions in general. In 1880, F. V. Dickins, the former resident of Japan, emphasised this image in his review of Bird's work, which he wrote without reading her account of Japan's modernisation.[5] In 1900, Mitford published *The Attache at Peking*. In the preface to these memoirs of his early days in China, he made a notable statement. Criticising the unfairness of comparing China with Japan in terms of their speed at modernisation, Mitford defined Japan as a 'borrower' from other civilisations since the very beginning of its history. Mitford thought it would be easy for a borrower to cast away old traditions without suffering loss of pride and he wrote: 'It must be remembered that Japan has never originated anything'.[6] So the man who had once shown such great insight into Japanese culture, the expression of which he thought varied according to social classes, became a less sophisticated observer who attributed any characteristic of the inhabitants of Japan either to Japanese nationality or to the sweeping category of 'Eastern civilisation'. This was a notion on which Mitford and many of his contemporaries relied to defend the British Empire.

Notes and References

Introduction

1. Article published in 11 September 1886 issue of *Tokyo Nichinichi Shinbun*. See Kurata Yoshihiro, *1885–nen London Nihonjin Mura* (The Japanese Village in London, 1885), (Tokyo, 1983) pp. 164–7.
2. Gloucestershire Record Office, The Redesdale Papers, D 2002/c, 44/1: from 19 Harrington Garden, South Kensington, 17 March 1885.
3. As regards previous work on British ideas about Japan, one can point to the following major contributions: Edward Vivian Gatenby, 'The Influence of Japan on English Language and Literature', *Transactions and Proceedings of Japan Society*, vol. xxxiv (1936–37), pp. 37–64; John Ashmead, Jr. 'The Idea of Japan 1853–1895: Japan as Described by American and Other Travellers from the West' (Ph.D. thesis, Harvard University, 1951); Earl Miner, *The Japanese Tradition in British and American Literature* (Princeton, 1958); Jean-Pierre Lehmann, *The Images of Japan: From Feudal Isolation to World Power, 1850–1905* (London, 1978); Jean-Pierre Lehmann (ed.) 'Britain and Japan – Mutual Images', *Proceedings of the British Association for Japanese Studies*, vol. v, Part I, (1980), pp. 149–204, 227–8; Endymion Wilkinson, Gokai [Misunderstanding], *Europe versus Japan* (Tokyo, 1981). However, none had analysed British periodical articles on Japan as the major subject of study until the following brief essay appeared: Gordon Daniels, 'Contemporary British Assessments of Bakumatsu Japan: Major Books and Reviews', Ian Nish (ed.) *Bakumatsu and Meiji: Studies in Japan's Economic and Social History/International Studies* 1981/2 (London, 1982), pp. 77–89.
4. W. W. Rostow, *British Economy of the Nineteenth Century* (reprint edn, Oxford, 1961), p. 137.
5. Yokoyama Toshio, 'Shin koku e no michi' ('Towards the Divine Land') Hayashiya Tatsusaburô (ed.) *Bakumatsu bunka no kenkyû* (Studies of Japanese Culture in the Late Tokugawa Era) (Tokyo), 1978), pp. 41–8, 74–89.
6. W. G. Beasley, *Great Britain and the Opening of Japan, 1834–1858* (London, 1951), pp. 200–02.
7. Murata Fumio, *Seiyô Bunken Roku* (Records of My Experiences in the West), (Hiroshima; 1869–70); Nakai Ôshû, *Man'yû Kitei* (Records of my wanderings outside Japan), (Tokyo, 1876).
8. To locate relevant articles in these periodicals, a number of indexes and lists of contents were used. Among these, *The Wellesley Index to Victorian Periodicals 1824–1900* edited by Walter E. Houghton (Toronto, vol. I, 1966; vol. II, 1972; vol. III, 1979) has been of particular importance. The identification of anonymous contributors has also been based mostly on this index, unless otherwise mentioned.
9. The final issue of *Blackwood's Magazine* was no. 1982, vol. cccxxviii.
10. See *Wellesley Index*, vol. I, p. 8.

1 'This Singular Country'

1. Ann Lohrli, *Household Words, A Weekly Journal 1850–59, Conducted by Charles Dickens* (Toronto, 1973), p. 4.
2. H. Morley, 'Our Phantom Ship: Japan', *House. Words*, vol. iii (1851), pp. 160–7; identification of the author by Lohrli, *op.cit.*, p. 374.
3. Morley, 'Our Phantom Ship', pp. 161, 163.
4. Morley, 'Our Phantom Ship', p. 167.
5. Ibid.
6. *The Times*, 23, 26 and 29 March 1852.
7. *China Mail*, 13 May, 17 June 1852.
8. *Wellesley Index*, vol. II, pp. 11–13; C. W. Russell, 'Japan', *Dubl. Rev.*, no. xxxiii (1852), p. 267–92.
9. Ibid., p. 267.
10. C. W. Russell, 'The Lamas of Tibet', *Dubl. Rev.*, vol. xxxiii (1852), pp. 1–45.
11. Russell, *Dubl. Rev.*, vol. xxxiii, p. 270.
12. Mrs William Busk, or M. M. Busk, 'Manners and Customs of the Japanese. From recent Dutch accounts of Japan, and the German of Dr von Siebold', *Asiatic Jour.*, vol. xxix, new series (1839), pp. 181–99, 274–90; vol. xxx, new series (1839), pp. 32–42, 93–104, 185–95, 265–75; vol. xxxi, new series (1840), pp. 5–17, 108–17; vol. xxxii, new series (1840), pp. 240–51. The author's identification by *The British Library General Catalogue of Printed Works to 1975*.
13. *The History of The Times*, vol. II (London, 1939), pp. 133, 450.
14. A. A. Knox, 'Japan', *Edin. Rev.*, vol. xcvi (1852), pp. 348–83.
15. The number of copies printed of the review was, in 1852, 5750. RU, LA, 'Longman Impression Book' no. 12, p. 44.
16. The Hague, 1729.
17. Leiden, 1832–52.
18. London, 1817.
19. Paris, 1736.
20. London, 1745–47.
21. London, 1852.
22. Russell, *Dubl. Rev.*, vol. xxxiii, p. 271.
23. Charles MacFarlane, *Japan*, (London, 1852), Preface, p. viii.
24. *The Universal Library. Voyages and Travels* (London, 1853), vol. I, p. 146. By contrast, modern scholars almost unanimously deny the unchangeableness of Japanese society before the mid-nineteenth century.
25. For example, M[ark] P[rager] L[indo] 'Japan and its intercourse with Foreign Nations', *Fraser.*, vol. li (Feb 1855), p. 154.
26. Knox, *Edin. Rev.*, vol. xcvi, p. 348.
27. Ibid., p. 351.
28. Ibid., p. 356.
29. Russell, *Dubl. Rev.*, vol. xxxiii, p. 292.
30. For example, ibid., pp. 270, 286.
31. C. P. Thunberg, *Travels in Europe, Africa and Asia. Made between the Years 1770 and 1779* (2nd edn., London, 1795), vol. IV., Preface, p. vi: 'Japan is in many respects a singular country, when compared with the different states of Europe.'

32. Golownin, *Recollections of Japan* (London, 1819), for example pp. 81, 101; Mrs Busk, *Asiatic Jour.*, vol. xxx, new series, for example pp. 32, 93.
33. Russell, *Dubl. Rev.*, vol. xxxiii, p. 270.
34. MacFarlane, *Japan*, Preface, p. viii.
35. Knox, *Edin. Rev.*, vol. xcvi, p. 352.
36. Russell, *Dubl. Rev.*, vol. xxxiii, p. 285.
37. Ibid.
38. W. Elwin, 'Travels in China – Fortune and Huc', *Quar. Rev.*, vol, cii (1857), p. 153.
39. Knox, *Edin. Rev.*, vol. xcvi, p. 359.
40. Ibid.
41. Russell, *Dubl. Rev.*, vol. xxxiii, p. 292.
42. Ibid., p. 285.
43. Ibid.
44. Golownin, *Recollections of Japan* (London, 1819), p. 104.
45. MacFarlane, *Japan*, p. 331.
46. Ibid., pp. 329–31.
47. Ibid., pp. 351–2.
48. Mrs Busk, *Asiatic Jour.*, vol. xxx, new series, pp. 32–3.
49. Knox, *Edin. Rev.*, vol. xcvi, p. 355.
50. Ibid.
51. Ibid., p. 351.
52. Ibid., pp. 351–2.
53. Ibid., p. 353.
54. Russell, *Dubl. Rev.*, vol. xxxiii, pp. 285–6.
55. Thunberg, *Travels.*, vol. III, pp. 74–7; Golownin, *Recollections*, pp. 22–5.
56. Knox, *Edin. Rev.*, vol. xcvi., p. 351.
57. Ibid., p. 360.
58. Mrs Busk, *Asiatic Jour.*, vol. xxx, new series, p. 35.
59. Knox, *Edin. Rev.*, vol. xcvi, pp. 351–2.
60. Russell, *Dubl. Rev.*, vol. xxxiii, pp. 288–9.
61. Ibid., pp. 289–90; MacFarlane, *Japan,* pp. 171–3; E. Kaempfer, *History of Japan* (London, 1727), vol. I, p. 149. Kaempfer's information about the matter seems to have been derived mainly from the occasional Dutch reports of the sixteenth century collected in Arnoldus Montanus, *Atlas Japanensis . . .* (London, 1670; original Dutch edition published in Amsterdam, 1669). For a valuable account of mid-nineteenth-century Japanese Court life, see Zushoryô, *Bakumatsu no Kyûtei;* (The Court towards the End of the Tokugawa Period) (Tokyo, 1922).
62. Russell, *Dubl. Rev.*, vol. xxxiii, p. 289.
63. Ibid.
64. Ibid., p. 290.
65. Mrs Busk, *Asiatic Jour.*, vol. xxx, new series, pp. 93–5.
66. Knox, *Edin. Rev.*, vol. xcvi, p. 364.
67. Ibid., p. 368.
68. Ibid.
69. Ibid., p. 369.
70. Ibid.

71. Mrs Busk, *Asiatic Jour.*, vol. xxx, new series, p. 95. It seems that this information was based on von Siebold's misunderstanding that there was such a 'constitutional custom' in Japan. However, there had been some cases of the Shogun's abdication.
72. Knox, *Edin. Rev.*, vol. xcvi, p. 368.
73. Ibid., p. 371.
74. Ibid.
75. Ibid., p. 370.
76. Ibid., p. 371.
77. Ibid., p. 351.
78. *Wellesley Index*, vol. I, pp. 416–18.
79. Russell, *Dubl. Rev.*, vol. xxxiii, p. 292.
80. Golownin, *Japan and the Japanese* (London, 1852), vol. II, pp. 105–8.
81. Ibid., pp. 105–8; Russell, *Dubl. Rev.*, vol. xxxiii, pp. 286–8. It might be On'yôdô that would correspond to Golownin's fourth category. 'A sect' might have been a type of Shugendô that would correspond to Golownin's fourth category.
82. Ibid., p. 288.
83. Ibid.
84. *Wellesley Index*, vol. II, pp. 13–14.
85. Russell, *Dubl. Rev.*, vol. xxxiii, p. 288.
86. Knox, *Edin. Rev.*, vol. xcvi, p. 356.
87. Ibid.
88. Ibid., p. 351.
89. Ibid., p. 353. About the tenth century, the cultured élite in the Court of Japan believed that this romantic custom of using a shrub of nishikigi existed in the northernmost areas of mainland Japan. This notion eventually became a literary tradition and was probably confused with reality among those in the West who read carelessly the much simplified explanation of 'Nixiqigui' in the Jesuits' Japanese–Portuguese dictionary, *Vocabvlaro da Lingoa de Iapam* (Nagasaki, 1603), p. 184.
90. Russell, *Dubl. Rev.*, vol. xxxiii, p. 286.
91. Ibid.
92. For example, the footnote about *Ambassades Memorables* (Amsterdam, 1680) in Golownin's *Recollections of Japan* (London, 1819), p. 81; also another footnote in ibid., p. 32.
93. Kaempfer modestly tried to describe the Mikados as 'Popes by birth', but he never furthered this analogy, thus giving no significance to the rhetoric. See Kaempfer, *History of Japan* (London, 1727); vol. I, p. 149.
94. Knox, *Edin. Rev.*, vol. xcvi, pp. 364–5.
95. Russell, *Dubl. Rev.*, vol. xxxiii, pp. 288–91.
96. Ibid., p. 288.
97. Knox, *Edin. rev.*, vol. xcvi, p. 370.
98. Ibid.
99. Kaempfer, *History of Japan* (London, 1727), vol. I, p. 208.
100. Ibid., vol. I, p. 86.
101. Knox, *Edin. Rev.*, vol. xcvi, p. 355.
102. Ibid., p. 351.
103. Ibid.

104. Ibid.
105. For example, the popular reaction in Japan to the news of the Opium War in the early 1840s was contempt for the Manchu Government and not for the Chinese. See Yokoyama Toshio, 'Shin koku e no michi', pp. 53–60.
106. Knox, *Edin. Rev.*, vol. xcvi, pp. 352–3.
107. Morley, *House. Words*, vol. iii, p. 163. The remark in brackets may have been made at Charles Dickens' suggestion, as his editorship was notably thorough; Morley is said to have made many concessions to Dickens' editing. See Lohrli, *Household Words*, pp. 371–2.
108. Kaempfer, *History of Japan*, vol. I, p. 60.
109. Morley, *House. Words*, vol. iii, p. 160.
110. Knox, *Edin. Rev.*, vol. xcvi, p. 354. Modern scholars estimate that the former exceeded the latter roughly by ten million.
111. Ibid. This is still a difficult point to prove because statistics in both countries at the time covered only stable inhabitants.
112. Ibid., p. 357.
113. MacFarlane's book contained over twenty illustrations which were reproduced from the works of Kaempfer, von Siebold and others, but the pictures were much less faithful than in the original; often the people and architecture in them were Sinicised or Europeanised due to the ignorance of the engravers. *The Illustrated London News* contained fifteen illustrations related to Japan (mostly natural scenery) during the period 1853–55. Their quality was not so different from that of Mac-Farlane's.
114. 'Japan', *New Monthly Mag.*, vol. xcv (1852), p. 96. Dejima's size was about three acres.
115. Knox, *Edin. Rev.*, vol. xcvi, pp. 372–8.
116. Ibid., p. 374.
117. *New Monthly Mag.*, vol. xcv, p. 102.
118. Russell, *Dubl. Rev.*, vol. xxxiii, p. 278–80.
119. Ibid., p. 273.
120. Ibid., p. 292.
121. *New Monthly Mag.*, vol. xcv, p. 102.
122. Ibid., p. 101.
123. Ibid., p. 102.
124. Ibid.
125. Knox, *Edin. Rev.*, vol. xcvi, p. 383.
126. Ibid.
127. Ibid., p. 351.
128. Ibid., p. 354.
129. Ibid., p. 356.
130. Ibid., p. 382.
131. Ibid., p. 372.
132. Ibid., p. 381.
133. Ibid., p. 382.
134. T. Yokoyama, 'Shin koku e no michi', pp. 53–73.
135. See the replies of several daimyo and intellectuals to the President of the Council of State Abe Masahiro's inquiry concerning the United States'

Notes and References

demand to open Japanese harbours; Watanabe Shûjirô, *Abe Masahiro Jiseki* (Tokyo, 1910), vol. I, pp. 162, 170 and 172.
136. Knox, *Edin. Rev.*, vol. xcvi, p. 381.
137. W. G. Beasley, *Great Britain and the Opening of Japan, 1834–1858* (London, 1951), pp. 113–127 and 198.
138. H. Morley, *House. Words*, vol. xiii (1856), pp. 154–7 – identification of the author by Lohrli, *Household Words*, p. 150. This article was based on Paul B. Wittingham, *Notes on the Late Expedition against the Russian Settlements in Eastern Siberia; and of a Visit to Japan and to the Shores of Tartary, and of the Sea of Okhotsk* (London, 1856).
139. *New Quar. Rev.*, vol. v (1856), pp. 376–81.
140. W. E. Aytoun, *Blackw.*, vol. lxxxi (1857), pp. 702–18.

2 Japan and the Edinburgh Publishers

1. NLS, BP, MS. 4133, f. 27; Osborn to Blackwood, 20 September 1858.
2. See Mrs Gerald Porter, *Annals of a Publishing House, John Blackwood*, (Edinburgh and London, 1898).
3. See NLS, BP, Acc. 5643, D3, pp. 131–2: Blackwood to Oliphant, 9 May 1859, ibid., D2 pp. 389–90: Blackwood to Osborn, 30 November 1858.
4. S. Osborn, 'A Cruise in Japanese Waters', *Blackw.*, vol. lxxxiv (1858), pp. 635–46.
5. NLS, BP, Acc. 5643, D2, p. 389: Blackwood to Osborn, 30 November 1858.
6. Ibid., pp. 389–90.
7. Ibid., p. 390.
8. See NLS, BP, MS. 4141, ff. 219–21: Osborn to Blackwood, 14 February 1859; ibid., MS. 4135, ff. 67–8: Mrs Ashington to Blackwood, 2 March 1859.
9. The author of the article is yet to be identified. '*The Times* Archive Editorial Diaries' and other relevant documents in the archive do not show any name.
10. Ibid.
11. Ibid.
12. Kaempfer, *History of Japan* (London, 1727), vol. II, Appendix, pp. 52–75.
13. 'W.N.S.', 'The Empire of Japan', *The Times*, 20 November 1858, p. 12.
14. S. Osborn, 'A Cruise in Japanese Waters' [hereafter contracted to 'Cruise'] *Blackw.*, vol. lxxxv (1860), p. 394.
15. Ibid., p. 61.
16. Osborn, *Blackw.*, vol. lxxxiv, p. 645.
17. Osborn, *Blackw.*, vol. lxxxv, p. 52.
18. Ibid., p. 60.
19. Ibid., p. 51.
20. Ibid., p. 409.
21. Ibid., p. 57.
22. Osborn, *Blackw.*, vol. lxxxv, p. 57.
23. Ibid.
24. Ibid., p. 402.

25. Ibid., p. 538.
26. Ibid.
27. Osborn, *Blackw.*, vol. lxxxv, p. 537; W. Adams' letter no. 1 in Thomas Rundall (ed.) *Memorials of the Empire of Japon: in the XVI and XVII Centuries* (London, 1850), p. 32: 'The people of this Iland of Iapan are good of nature, curteous aboue measure, and valiant in warre'; 'I meane, not a land better gouerned in the world by ciuill policie'.
28. Osborn, *Blackw.*, vol. lxxxv, p. 57.
29. NLS, BP, MS. 4141, f. 217: Osborn to Blackwood, 23 January 1859.
30. Ibid., f. 218: Osborn to Blackwood, 23 January 1859.
31. See Jack J. Gerson's introduction to the reprint of Laurence Oliphant's *Narrative of Lord Elgin's Mission to China and Japan* (Oxford, 1970), vol. I, Introduction, pp. vii–x.
32. NLS, BP, MS. 4141, ff. 217–18: Osborn to Blackwood, 23 January 1859.
33. Ibid., ff. 219–21; Osborn to Blackwood, 14 February 1859.
34. NLS, BP, Acc. 5643, D3, p. 94: Blackwood to Osborn, 6 April 1859.
35. Ibid., D2, p. 416: Blackwood to Ashington, 29 December 1859.
36. Ibid., D3, p. 32: Blackwood to Ashington, 4 February 1859.
37. Ibid., p. 127: Blackwood to Ashington, 9 May 1859.
38. NLS, BP, MS. 4135, ff. 69–70: Ashington to Blackwood, 19 March 1859.
39. Ibid., f. 73: Ashington to Blackwood, 18 April 1859.
40. NLS, BP, MS. 4141, ff. 219–21: Osborn to Blackwood, 14 February 1859.
41. NLS, BP, Acc. 5634, D2, pp. 183–5: Blackwood to Oliphant, 8 January 1858.
42. NLS, BP, Acc. 5644, F4–F6.
43. NLS, BP, Acc. 5643, D3, p. 94: Blackwood to Osborn, 6 April 1859.
44. Ibid., pp. 141–2: W. Blackwood to Ashington, 1 June 1859.
45. NLS, BP, MS. 4135, ff. 77–8: Ashington to Blackwood, 3 June 1859.
46. NLS, BP, Acc. 5643, D3, pp. 146–7: W. Blackwood to Osborn, 9 June 1859. As regards the details of this decision-making process, see Yokoyama Toshio, 'Victoria-ki Igirisu ni okeru Nihon zô keisei ni tsuite no oboegaki (Some Notes on the Formation of Japanese Images in Victorian England) – I', *Zinbun Gakuhô* (Kyoto), vol. xlviii (1980), pp. 14–16.
47. NLS, BP, Acc. 5643, D3, p. 150: W. Blackwood to Ashington, 17 June 1859.
48. NLS, BP, MS. 4135, ff. 85–6: Ashington to Blackwood, 11 July 1859.
49. Ibid.
50. NLS, BP, MS. 4141, f. 222: Osborn to Blackwood, 28 July 1859.
51. Ibid., ff. 224–5: Osborn to Blackwood, 5 August 1859.
52. Osborn to Murray dated 'Thursday Night [1859]': a letter within the unclassified letters in the John Murray Archives at 50 Albemarle Street, London.
53. NLS, BP, Acc. 5644, F4, p. 383.
54. Ibid.
55. NLS, BP, MS. 4141, ff. 224–5: Osborn to Blackwood, 5 Aug. 1859.
56. Ibid., f. 225.
57. Ibid.

58. Ibid., ff. 233–4: Osborn to Blackwood, 6 September [18]59.
59. See for example, NLS, BP, MS. 4141, f. 218: Osborn to Blackwood, 23 January 1859; Ibid., Acc. 5643, D3, p. 215: Blackwood to Osborn, 21 November 1859.
60. See NLS, BP, MS. 4141, f. 245: Osborn to Blackwood, 4 November 1859.
61. NLS, BP, Acc. 5634, D3, p. 181: W. Blackwood to Osborn, 19 September 1859.
62. S. Osborn, *A Cruise in Japanese Waters* (1st edn, Edinburgh & London, 1859), p. 91.
63. NLS, BP, Acc. 5643, D3, p. 181.
64. NLS, BP, MS. 4141, fol. 241: Osborn to Blackwood, 21 September 1859.
65. S. Osborn, *A Cruise in Japanese Waters* (2nd edn, Edinburgh & London, 1859) p. 91.
66. NLS, BP, MS. 4141, f. 243: Osborn to Blackwood, 24 October 1859.
67. NLS, BP, Acc. 5644. F4, p. 383.
68. See, for example, NLS, BP, MS, 4141, f. 225: Osborn to Blackwood, 5 August 1859.
69. Osborn was acquainted with Captain John Hanning Speke, another important military writer for the Blackwoods. See, ibid., ff. 232–4; Osborn to Blackwood, 6 September 1859.
70. NLS, BP, MS. 4141, ff. 218 and 221: Osborn to Blackwood, 23 January & 14 February 1859.
71. NLS, BP, Acc. 5643, D3, p. 95: Blackwood to Osborn, 6 April 1859; also see Ibid., p. 132: Blackwood to Oliphant, 9 May 1859.
72. Ibid.
73. Hereafter contracted to *Narrative*.
74. See *Narrative*, vol. I, pp. 183–4.
75. NLS, BP, MS. 4141, f. 192: Oliphant to Blackwood, 19th of unknown month [1859]. Where incomplete dates for correspondence are provided here and in the following notes, further details were not available either in the letter itself or from any other source.
76. Ibid., f. 154: Oliphant to Blackwood, Tuesday [1859]; f. 186: Oliphant to Blackwood, 30th [1859]; f. 190: Oliphant to Blackwood, 15th [1859].
77. For example, ibid., f. 153: Oliphant to Blackwood, Monday [1859]; f. 160: Oliphant to Blackwood, Wednesday [1859].
78. Ibid., f. 156: Oliphant to Blackwood, Tuesday [1859]: 'I suppose some of my slips have gone there, as I find here one set the others being missing. That is all right however as Lord Elgin will have time to look over them and they require a good deal of amendment.'
79. Ibid., f. 145: Oliphant to Blackwood, Sunday [1859].
80. NLS, BP, Acc. 5643, D3, p. 220: W. Blackwood to Oliphant, 28 November 1859.
81. NLS, BP, MS. 4141, f. 149: Oliphant to Blackwood, Monday [1859].
82. NLS, BP, MS. 4141, ff. 143–4, 152–3, 174–5, 178 and 192: Oliphant to Blackwood, dated respectively, Sunday, Monday, Friday, Friday, 19th [1859].
83. Ibid., f. 147: Oliphant to Blackwood, undated [1859]; see also ibid., ff. 150 and 170: Oliphant to Blackwood, dated respectively, Monday,

84. Thursday [1859]: concerning the spelling of a Japanese word, 'Quanon'.
84. NLS, BP, Acc. 5643, D3, p. 180: W. Blackwood to Oliphant, 15 September 1859.
85. For example, NLS, BP, MS. 4141, f. 184: Oliphant to Blackwood, 3 [November 1859]; f. 192: Oliphant to Blackwood, 19 [October 1859].
86. Margaret Oliphant, *Memoir of the Life of Laurence Oliphant and of Alice Oliphant, His Wife* (Edinburgh & London, 1891), vol. I, p. 290.
87. Ibid., vol. I, p. 296.
88. See *Narrative*, vol. I, Preface, p. viii.
89. NLS, BP, MS. 4141, f. 164: Oliphant to Blackwood, Wednesday [1859]; Also see Ibid., f. 188: Oliphant to Blackwood, 9th [1859].
90. *Narrative*, vol. II, p. 494; see also, NLS, BP, MS. 4141, f. 158: Oliphant to Blackwood, Wednesday [1859].
91. NLS, BP, Acc. 5644, F4, pp. 36–7.
92. NLS, BP, MS. 4141, f. 249; Osborn to Blackwood, 17 November 1859: ibid., ff. 264–5: Osborn to Blackwood, Tuesday [1859]; ibid., Acc. 5643, D3, p. 211: Blackwood to Osborn, 9 November 1859.
93. NLS, BP, MS. 4141, ff. 138–9: Oliphant to Blackwood, 1 December [1859]; ibid., f. 140: Oliphant to Blackwood, [4 December 1859].
94. Ibid., f. 140.
95. NLS, BP, Acc. 5643, D3, pp. 220–1: W. Blackwood to Oliphant, 28 November 1859: ibid., MS. 4141, ff. 138–9; Oliphant to Blackwood, 1 December 1859; ibid., ff. 154–5: Oliphant to Blackwood, Tuesday [1859]. An American edition, however, was published by Harper & Brothers, New York, later in the following year.
96. NLS, BP, Acc. 5644, F4, p. 396.
97. Ibid., MS. 4141, f. 168: Oliphant to Blackwood, Thursday [1859]: 'I am glad to know that you expect to get some copies of the book out before Xmas.'
98. Ibid., Acc. 5643, D3, p. 273: Blackwood to Oliphant, 7 February 1860.
99. Ibid., p. 285: Blackwood to Oliphant, 23 February 1860.
100. Ibid., p. 239: W. Blackwood to Oliphant, 4 January 1860.
101. NLS, BP, Acc. 5643, D3, p. 273: Blackwood to Oliphant, 7 February [1860].
102. Ibid., Acc. 5644. F5, p. 301.
103. For example, ibid., Acc. 5643, D2, p. 184: Blackwood to Oliphant, 8 January 1858; ibid., D3, p. 248: Blackwood to Lady Oliphant, 13 January 1860.
104. Ibid., p. 313: Blackwood to Oliphant, 29 March 1860.
105. NLS, BP, Acc. 5643, D3, p. 295: Blackwood to Oliphant, 23 February 1860.
106. NLS, BP, MS. 4152, f. 33: Oliphant to Blackwood, 18 [February] 1860.
107. See *Narrative* (2nd edn), vol. I, Preface, pp. ii.
108. NLS, BP, MS. 4152, f. 36: Oliphant to Blackwood, 3 March [1860].
109. Ibid., f. 38: Oliphant to Blackwood, [5 March 1860].
110. NLS, BP, Acc. 5644, F4.
111. NLS, BP, Acc. 5643, D3, p. 265: Blackwood to Osborn, 27 January 1860.
112. Ibid., p. 266.

113. 'The Elgin's Embassy', *The Times*, 3 January 1860, p. 10. The identification of the writer both by NLS, BP, MS. 4141, ff. 276–7: Osborn to Blackwood, Friday [1859] and by a letter to T. Yokoyama from the Archivist of *The Times*, G. Phillips, dated 3 July 1982.
114. NLS, BP, MS. 4155, ff. 51–2: White to Blackwood, 15 January 1860.
115. Ibid., f. 53: White to Blackwood, 18 January 1860. 'Maga' was the popular nickname for *Blackwood's Magazine*.
116. NLS, BP, Acc. 5643, D3, pp. 263–4: Blackwood to White, 25 January 1860.
117. Ibid., p. 264.
118. J. White, 'Lord Elgin's Mission to China and Japan', *Blackw.*, vol. lxxxvii (1860), p. 255.
119. Ibid., p. 275.
120. Ibid., p. 276.
121. NLS, BP, Acc. 5643, D3, p. 290: Blackwood to White, 29 February 1860.
122. Ibid., Acc. 5644, F4. To be precise, this increase took place in February 1860. This might correspond with the fact that White's article was first planned for the February issue.
123. Ibid., Acc. 5643, D3: W. Blackwood & Sons to The Earl of Elgin, 24 February 1860.
124. Ibid., pp. 285–6: Blackwood to Oliphant, 23 Feburary 1860.
125. *Narrative*, vol. II, p. 51.

3 Britain, the Happy Suitor of a Fairyland

1. H. Reeve, 'Lord Elgin's Mission to China and Japan', *Edin. Rev.*, vol. cxi (1860), pp. 96–118.
2. *Narrative*, vol. II, p. 202; Reeve, p. 117.
3. *Narrative*, vol. II, p. 205; Reeve, p. 118.
4. *Narrative*, vol. II, p. 207.
5. Ibid.
6. C. W. Russell, 'Oliphant's Japan', *Dub. Rev.*, vol. xlviii (1860), p. 405.
7. *Narrative*, vol. II, pp 206–7: Russell, *Dubl. Rev.*, vol. xlviii, p. 406. One should note that Kaempfer stayed in Japan only two years.
8. For example, H. Morley, 'Far East', *House. Words*, vol. xiii (1856), p. 154; 'Epedition of an American Squadron to the China Seas and Japan', *New Quar. Rev.*, vol. v (1856), pp. 376–7.
9. Reeve, *Edin. Rev.*, vol. cxi, p. 118.
10. S. Osborn, 'A Cruise in Japanese Waters', *Blackw.*, vol. lxxxv (1859), p. 408.
11. Ibid.
12. *Narrative*, vol. II, 164–5.
13. Morley, *House. Words*, vol. xiii, p. 156.
14. Ibid.; B. Whittingham, *Notes on the Late Expedition against the Russian Settlements in Eastern Siberia; and of a Visit to Japan and to the Shores of Tartary, and of the Sea of Okhostk* (London, 1856), pp. 60–2.
15. White, 'Lord Elgin's Mission to China and Japan', *Blackw.*, vol. lxxxvii

(1860), p. 275.
16. F. M. Drummond-Davies, 'Japan', *Westmin. Rev.*, vol. xvii, new series, (1860), p. 540.
17. Osborn, *Blackw.*, vol. lxxxv, p. 51.
18. Ibid., p. 412.
19. J. M. Tronson, *Personal Narrative of a Voyage to Japan, Kamtschatka, Siberia, Tartary, and Various Parts of Coast of China; in H.M.S. Barracouta* (London, 1859), p. 256. When Tronson visited Japan, he was Assistant Surgeon of the Barracouta, *The Navy List* (London, 20 September 1854), p. 139.
20. *Wellesley Index*, vol. I, p. 663.
21. 'Japan and the Japanese', *North Brit. Rev.*, vol. xxxi (1859), p. 435.
22. Osborn, *Blackw.*, vol. lxxxv, p. 408.
23. Ibid., p. 61.
24. Russell, *Dubl. Rev.*, vol. xlviii, p. 414.
25. Ibid., pp. 414–5; see *Narrative*, vol. II pp. 213–6.
26. White, *Blackw.*, vol. lxxxvii, p. 273.
27. For example, the following reviews of *Narrative* shared explicitly this point: Osborn, 'China and the War', *Quar. Rev.*, vol. cvii (1860), pp. 85–118; 'Lord Elgin's Mission', *Bentley's Miscellany*, vol. xlvii (1860), pp. 136–43; Cooke, *The Times*, 3 January 1860, p. 10.
28. White, *Blackw.*, vol. lxxxvii, p. 256.
29. Osborn, *Blackw.*, vol. lxxxv, p. 644.
30. *Wellesley Index*, vol. II, p. 303.
31. M. P. L]indo⁻, 'Our New Treaty with Japan', *Fraser*, vol. lviii (1858), p. 658.
32. However, F. M. Drummond-Davies expressed an exceptional opinion at the time that the Japanese were probably a mixture between the Mongols and a primitive Malayan race. See Drummond-Davies, *Westmin. Rev.*, vol. xvii, new series, p. 521.
33. A. W. Habersham, *My Last Cruise: or, Where We Went, and What We Saw; being an account of visits to the Malay and Loo-Choo Islands, & C.* (Philadelphia & London, 1857).
34. Aytoun, 'American Exploration – China and Japan', *Blackw.*, vol. lxxxi, p. 717.
35. Osborn, *Blackw.*, vol. lxxxv, p. 54. In this passage, 'Semitic' was misprinted as 'Sinitic' but was corrected to 'Semitic' in the reprint editions. See *Cruise* (1st & 2nd edns), p. 47.
36. *North Brit. Rev.*, vol. xxxi, pp. 426–7.
37. Aytoun, *Blackw.*, vol. lxxxi, p. 709.
38. Osborn, *Blackw.*, vol. lxxxv, p. 410.
39. Ibid., p. 535.
40. White, *Blackw.*, lxxxvii, 257.
41. *North Brit. Rev.*, xxxi, 441.
42. Reeve, *Edin. Rev.*, cxi, 104.
43. See Yokoyama Toshio, 'Han kokka e no michi (Towards the Establishment of Han States)', Hayashiya Tatsusaburô (ed.) *Kasei bunka no kenkyû* (Studies of Japanese Culture in the Bunka and Bunsei Eras) (Tokyo, 1976), pp. 92–102.

44. See Yokoyama, 'Shin koku e no michi', pp. 41–53.
45. Shin Yoo Han, *Kai yû roku* (The Record of a Seaborne Journey), trans. Kan Je On (Tokyo, 1974), pp. 113–20, 136 and 313–14.
46. Osborn, *Blackw.*, vol. lxxxv, p. 410.
47. Yokoyama, 'Han kokka e no michi', pp. 108–9.
48. However, other decrees followed to change this point: one ordered merchants to hide from their shops certain goods such as swords, maps and plans of samurai's houses; the other prohibited the sale of particular kinds of cloth and paper which the Shogun had chosen as his souvenir to the Mission, 'Igirisu Ikken' (A Record of England), vol. jô-ii, in 'Kyû bakufu hikitsugi sho (The Papers Transmitted from the Shogunate). Kokkai Toshokan (The Diet Library, Tokyo), MS. 808/8.
49. *Narrative*, vol. II, p. 113.
50. *Bakumatsu ishin gaikô shiryô shûsei* (Collected Documents Relating to Japanese Diplomacy during the late Tokugawa and Restoration Period), ed. Ishin Shi Gakkai (Tokyo), vol. iii, 1943, pp. 203–7. Also, for details, see 'Igirisu Ikken', vols. jô-i, ii, chû, gé.
51. Osborn, *Blackw.*, vol. lxxxv, p. 532.
52. *North Brit. Rev.*, vol. xxxi, p. 426.
53. Ibid., pp. 425–6.
54. Aytoun, *Blackw.*, vol. lxxxi, p. 703.
55. Ibid.
56. Ibid., p. 718.
57. For example, *Narrative*, vol. ii. p. 113.
58. Tronson, *Personal Narrative*, pp. 342–4.
59. *North Brit. Rev.*, vol. xxxi, pp. 436–7.
60. Ibid., p. 437.
61. Ibid., p. 434.
62. Osborn, *Blackw.*, vol. lxxxv, p. 405.
63. Drummond-Davies, *Westmin. Rev.*, vol. xvii, new series, p. 534.
64. Osborn, *Blackw.*, vol. lxxxv, p. 405.
65. Morley, *House. Words*, vol. xiii, p. 156.
66. Reeve, *Edin. Rev.*, vol. cxi, p. 105.
67. Morley, *House. Words*, vol. xiii, p. 155.
68. Ibid., p. 154. The Governor was Hori Toshihiro (1818–60), whose kinship with the Shogun was, if at all, not close.
69. *Narrative*, vol. II, p. 104.
70. Reeve, *Edin. Rev.*, vol. cxi, p. 115–17.
71. Ibid., p. 117.
72. Morley, *House. Words*, vol. xiii, p. 156.
73. Reeve, *Edin. Rev.*, vol. cxi, p. 105. Italics added by Yokoyama.
74. Drummond-Davies used Rundall, *Memorials of the Empire of Japon*.
75. F. L. Hawks, *Narrative of the Expedition of an American Squadron to the China Seas and Japan, Performed in the Years 1852, 1853 and 1854 under the Command of Commodore M. C. Perry . . . by Order of the United States*, (Washington, 1856).
76. Drummond-Davies, *Westmin. Rev.*, vol. xvii, new series, p. 539.
77. Ibid., p. 509.
78. Ibid., pp. 536–9.

79. Ibid., p. 539.
80. Osborn, *Blackw.* vol. lxxxv, p. 403.
81. For example, ibid., 537.
82. *North Brit. Rev.*, vol. xxxi, p. 446.
83. *Narrative*, vol. II, p. 117; H. Reeve quoted these lines in his review of *Narrative*: *Edin. Rev.*, vol. cxi, p. 111.
84. Yokoyama, 'Han kokka e no michi', pp. 112–21.
85. Osborn, *Blackw.*, vol. lxxxv, p. 539.
86. Yokoyama, 'Shin koku e no michi', pp. 80–1; see also Hayashiya (ed.) *Bakumatsu bunka no kenkyû*, Appendix, pp. 5–7.
87. Osborn, *Blackw.*, vol. lxxxv, p. 645.
88. Reeve, *Edin. Rev.*, vol. cxi, p. 113.
89. Ibid., p. 114.
90. Katsu Kaishû, *Rikugun rekishi* (reprint edn, Tokyo, 1967), vol. I, p. 65: '. . . migi o motte eikan no chô sôgei no rei koto no hoka teatsuku, isu mo jôseki ni suhete toriatsukai kata ika ni mo teichô ni kore ari sôrô'.
91. Mathison's letter, read before the Royal Geographical Society of London on 28 Januray 1850, *Journal of the R.G.S.* vol. xx (1951), 136–7; see also Takahashi Kyôichi, *Uraga bugyô shi* (The History of the Uraga Magistrates) (Tokyo, 1974), pp. 738–40.
92. Kojima Matajirô, 'Amerika ichijô utsushi (A copy of a Record of America), MS. City Library of Hakodate; see also *Nihon shomin seikatsu shiryô shûsei* (Collected Documents from the Lives of Japanese Common People); ed. Tanigawa Ken'ichi (ed.) (Tokyo), vol. xii, 1971, pp. 251–75; also Yokoyama, 'Shin koku e no michi', pp. 66–9, 73.
93. Osborn, *Blackw.*, vol. lxxxv, p. 400.
94. Ibid., p. 539.
95. Ibid.
96. White, *Blackw.*, vol. lxxxvii, p. 276.
97. Reeve, *Edin. Rev.*, vol. cxi, p. 110.
98. *British Parliamentary Papers,* Japan 1 (reprint edn, Shannon, 1971), pp. 51–157: 'Reports, Returns and Correspondence Respecting Japan 1856–1864', in particular see Minister Alcock's despatch to Lord Russell, 7 January 1860.
99. Russell, *Dubl. Rev.*, vol. xlvii, pp. 404–5.
100. *The Times*, 1859–21 November, pp. 7 and 8; 22 November, p. 7; 7 December, p. 9; 8 December, p. 4; 20 December, p. 3; 1860–10 February, pp. 7 and 8; 11 February, p. 12.
101. PRO, FO, 46/16, ff. 1–2: E. Hammond to Oliphant, 5 January 1861; Ibid., ff. 5–6: Russell to Oliphant, 14 January 1861.
102. Royal Archives at Windsor: Russell to Her Majesty, 29 December 1860–quoted from Philip Henderson, *The Life of Laurence Oliphant, Traveller, Diplomat and Mystic* (London, 1956), p. 97.
103. NLS, BP, Acc. 5643, D4, pp. 16–17: Blackwood to Oliphant, 8 January 1861.
104. NLS BP Acc. 5644, F4, p. 397. During the one year they sold only 315 copies. See also ibid., F5, p. 233 and F6, p. 352. In 1873 the firm still held 1531 copies, and by 1881, 1347 copies had been sold to another publisher.

105. NLS, BP, Acc. 5643, D4, p. 17: Blackwood to Oliphant, 8 January 1861.
106. NLS, BP, Acc. 5643, D3, p. 273: Blackwood to Oliphant, 7 February 1860.
107. Ibid., p. 377: W. Blackwood to Oliphant, 18 July 1860.

4 Britain, the Suitor Disillusioned

1. R. Alcock, 'Japan and the Japanese', *Edin. Rev.*, vol. cxiii (1861), p. 45.
2. The wet-plate was the invention by Frederic Scott Archer in 1851 which superseded both Daguerre's and Talbot's processes by the 1850s. See The Arts Council of Great Britain, *'From today painting is dead', The Beginning of Photography* (London, 1972), p. 31.
3. Ibid., p. 33.
4. Alcock, *Edin. Rev.*, vol. cxiii, p. 45.
5. Oliphant, L. *Blackw.*, vol. xciii (1863), p. 405. According to the Consular Register in 1863, there were 140 British permanent residents in Kanagawa (incl. Yokohama), and in 1864 the number rose to 200 (*British Parliamentary Papers, Japan 4* (reprint edn, Shannon, 1971), pp. 91 and 110: 'Commercial Report on Kanagawa, 1863' and 'Commercial Report on Yokohama & Kanagawa, 1863–1864').
6. Oliphant, L. 'Political Tragedies in Japan', *Blackw.*, vol. xci (1862), p. 424.
7. The month of this work's publication is based on RU, LA, Divide Ledger, 7D, p. 191.
8. NLS, BP, Acc. 5643, D4, pp. 16–18: Blackwood to Oliphant, 8 January 1861.
9. *Edo meiji kawaraban senshû* (Selection from the One-sheet Illustrated Newspapers Published during the Edo and Meiji Periods), Nakayama Einosuke (ed.) (Tokyo, 1974), plates 12, 13 and 20; *Banzuke shûsei* (Collection of Miscellaneous Ranking Bills), Hayashi Hideo and Haga Noboru (ed.) (Tokyo, 1973), vol. I, pp. 193–212, and vol. II, p. 34.
10. Alcock, *Edin. Rev.*, vol. cxiii, p. 63.
11. See, for example, PRO, FO, 46/5, ff. 1–18: correspondence between E. Hammond and Student Interpreters, Jan., Feb., Sept., 1859, FO 46/9, ff. 1–25: ditto, Feb., Mar., June 1860. As regards the Japanese side, see Nihon no eigaku hyakunen Henshubu (eds) (The editorial board of the book as follows), *Nihon no eigaku hyakunen* (The Hundred Years of English Learning in Japan), Tokyo, (Meiji-vol., 1968).
12. R. Alcock, *Elements of Japanese Grammar, for the Use of Beginners* (Shanghai, 1861); Alcock also published *Familiar Dialogues in Japanese, with English and French Translation* (London, 1863).
13. Alcock, *Edin. Rev.*, vol. cxiii, pp. 33–73. The identification of the author by RU, LA, Box Longman, II/320.
14. *The Times*, 31 May 1861, p. 12 and 3 June 1861, p. 9. The number of copies printed of the Jan. 1861 issue of the *Edin. Rev.* in which Alcock's review of his own work was printed was 5750 copies. See RU, LA, Impression Book, no. 14, p. 12. This figure had been more or less consistent during the 1850s, but during the 1860s, it declined to less than

5000. See ibid., nos. 15, 16 and 17.
15. RU, LA, Divide Ledger, 7D, pp. 146, 484 and 646, and 11D, p. 96. By July 1863, 51 copies were presented, 1394 were sold. The ledger of the book ends in 1881.
16. For example, Oliphant, L. 'Sensation Diplomacy in Japan', *Blackw.*, vol. xciii (1863), pp. 397–413; H. Reeve, 'Sir Rutherford Alcock's Japan', *Edin. Rev.*, vol. cxvii, (1863), pp. 517–540; J. H. Tremenheere, 'Japan', *Quar. Rev.*, vol. cxiv (1863), pp. 449–80; J. F. Stephen, 'Japan', *Fraser.*, vol. lxix (1864), pp. 101–17.
17. Oliphant, *Blackw.*, vol. xciii, p. 398.
18. Reeve, *Edin. Rev.*, vol. cxvii, p. 518.
19. Alcock, *Edin. Rev.*, vol. cxiii, pp. 59–63.
20. Alcock, *The Capital of the Tycoon*, vol. I, Preface, p. xv.
21. Alcock, *Edin. Rev.*, vol. cxiii, p. 42.
22. Alcock, *The Capital of the Tycoon*, vol. I, Preface, p. xvi.
23. Alcock, *Edin. Rev.*, vol. cxiii, p. 50.
24. *British Minister's Correspondence respecting affairs in Japan. July to November, 1861. Presented to both Houses of Parliament by Command of Her Majesty* (London, 1862), p. 9: Alcock to Russell, 10 July 1861; J. H. Tremenheere, 'Japan', *Quar. Rev.*, vol. cxiv (1863), pp. 476–7: quotation from Alcock's above-mentioned correspondence.
25. Ibid., p. 453.
26. *Ishin shi* (The History of the Restoration), Ishin Shiryô Hensan Kai (ed.) (The Association for Compiling Historical Documents Relating to the Restoration) (Monbushô, or the Japanese Ministry of Education, vol. II, 1940), pp. 526–9: Imperial statement, 8th day, 8th month, 5th year of the Ansei Era (14 September 1858).
27. Alcock, *Capital of the Tycoon*, vol. I, P. 227. Alcock was not much mistaken, although Hayashi Daigaku, the then Principal Preceptor of the Tokugawa, had discovered in 1853 a precedent for the use of the title 'Tycoon' in the Shogun's correspondence of 1636 with the sovereign of Korea. For detailed information, see Haga Shôji, 'Washin Jôyaku-ki no Bakumatsu Gaikô ni tsuite' (Tokugawa Diplomacy concerning the Treaties of Peace and Amity, 1853–1858), *Rekishigaku Kenkyû* (Journal of Historical Studies, Tokyo), vol. cdlxxxii (July, 1980), pp. 1–13 and 52.
28. Alcock, *Capital*, vol. II, pp. 491–5: 'Titles in Japan' reproduced from the *Japan Herald*, a weekly started by the pioneer British journalist in Japan, Albert W. Hansard, in November 1861, with the editor-in-chief, John Reddie Black.
29. Reeve, *Edin. Rev.*, vol. cxvii, p. 520.
30. Tremenheere, *Quar. Rev.*, vol. cxiv, p. 451.
31. Ibid., p. 452.
32. J. F. Stephen, 'Japan' *Fraser.*, vol. lxix (1864), pp. 113–14.
33. Reeve, *Edin. Rev.*, vol. cxvii, pp. 525–7. See also Alcock, *Capital of the Tycoon*, vol. II, 237–40.
34. These observations by Alcock at that time were not very much mistaken. It was in late 1865 that the emperor finally gave the Shogun *Chokkyo*, or the imperial permission, for the treaties with the West.
35. Tremenheere, *Quar. Rev.*, vol. cxiv, p. 451.

Notes and References

36. Ibid., p. 452.
37. Ibid.
38. Oliphant L. 'The Moral and Political Revolution in Japan', *Blackw.*, vol. ci (1867), p. 429.
39. Reeve, *Edin. Rev.*, vol. cxvii, p. 531.
40. For example, see Tremenheere, *Quar. Rev.*, vol. cxiv, p. 457. In reality, the authority of those high officials did not correspond to the relatively small size of their incomes, and they could often exercise great power over feudal lords.
41. Oliphant, *Blackw.*, vol. xci, p. 424.
42. Ibid., p. 425.
43. Oliphant, *Blackw.*, vol. xciii, p. 406.
44. Ibid.
45. Stephen, *Fraser.*, vol. lxix, p. 102.
46. Alcock, *Edin. Rev.*, vol. cxiii, p. 45.
47. *The Illustrated London News*, 4 February 1854; Oliver Impey, *Chinoiserie, the Impact of Oriental Styles on Western Art and Decoration* (London, 1977), p. 186.
48. Ibid., pp. 188–9; M. Eidelberg, 'Bracquemond, Delâtre and the Discovery of Japanese Prints', *Burlington Magazine*, vol. cxxiii (1981), pp. 221–7.
49. Alison Adburgham, *Liberty's, a Biography of a Shop* (London, 1975), p. 14.
50. Gabriel P. Weisberg, 'Japonisme: Early Sources and the French Printmaker 1854–1882', G. P. Weisberg and others, *Japonisme, Japanese Influence on French Art 1854–1910* (reprint edn London, 1975), pp. 3–4 and 16–17.
51. See R. Alcock, *International Exhibition, 1862. Catalogue of Works of Industry and Art, Sent from Japan* (London, 1862).
52. Adburgham, *Liberty's.*, p. 13.
53. *The Times*, 5 December 1862, p. 5.
54. In this connection, more than twenty articles were published in *The Times* during the period from 29 March to 13 June 1862. See also *The Illustrated London News*, 12 April and 24 May 1862.
55. J. MacDonald, 'From Yeddo to London with the Japanese Ambassadors', *Cornhill*, vol. vii (1863), pp. 603–20.
56. *Wellesly Index.* vol. I, pp. 321–2.
57. Richard Altick, *The English Common Reader, A Social History of the Mass Reading Public 1800–1900* (Chicago, 1963), p. 359. However, its circulation was reduced to about 20,000 in the following few years. *Wellesley Index*, vol. I, p. 322.
58. Ishizuki Minoru, *Kindai nihon no kaigai ryûgaku shi* (History of Overseas Studies of Modern Japanese Students) (Kyoto, 1972), pp. 301–9. Ishizuki identifies about 110 students who went to Europe during the period, 1861–68.
59. See, for example, the four diaries of Satsuma samurai who fought against the British squadron in *Ishin sen'eki jûgunki* (Soliders' Journals from Battles during the Restoration Period). Sendai Kyodoshi Hensan Iinkai (ed.) (Committee for the Local History of Sendai in Kagoshima Pref.),

(Sendai, 1974), pp. 1–54.
60. Oliphant, *Blackw.*, vol. ci. p. 437.
61. Tremenheere, *Quar. Rev.*, vol. cxiv, p. 460.
62. Oliphant, *Blackw.*, vol. xciii, p. 406.
63. Alcock, *The Capital of the Tycoon*, vol. II. p. 438.
64. Alcock, *Edin. Rev.*, vol. cxiii, p. 64.
65. Stephen, *Fraser.*, vol. lxix, p. 115.
66. Oliphant, *Blackw.*, vol. xciii, p. 400; Alcock, *The Capital of the Tycoon*, vol. I, p. 240.
67. Reeve, *Edin. Rev.*, vol. cxvii, p. 517.
68. Tremenheere, *Quar. Rev.*, vol. cxiv, p. 458. See also Oliphant, *Blackw.*, vol. xciii, p. 410; Alcock, *Capital*, vol. II, p. 63. This point was over-simplified, and scarcely true throughout Japanese history. As regards cases in the Tokugawa period, see, for example, Morinaga Taneo, *Hanka Chô* (The Complete Record of Criminal Cases at the Court of Nagasaki) (Tokyo, 1962).
69. For example, Reeve, *Edin. Rev.*, vol. cxvii, p. 519; Oliphant, *Blackw.*, vol. xciii, p. 410.
70. Reeve, *Edin. Rev.*, vol. cxvii, p. 521.
71. Stephen, *Fraser.*, vol. lxix, p. 103–4.
72. Reeve, *Edin. Rev.*, vol. cxvii, p. 521.
73. A. Wilson, 'The Inland Sea of Japan', *Blackw.*, vol. xc (1861), p. 617.
74. Wilson, *Blackw.*, vol. xc, p. 623.
75. Oliphant, *Blackw.*, vol. xciii, p. 410.
76. Ibid., p. 411.
77. Ibid.
78. Stephen, *Fraser.*, lxix, 107.
79. Tremenheere, *Quar. Rev.*, cxiv, 458.
80. Oliphant, *Blackw.*, xciii, 404 and 412.
81. Tremenheere, *Quar. Rev.*, vol. cxiv, p. 478.
82. Reeve, *Edin. Rev.*, vol. cxvii, p. 523.
83. 'The Japanese Martyrs', *Frasers*, vol. lxvii (1863), p. 401.
84. These examples were quoted respectively from: Reeve, *Edin. Rev.*, vol. cxvii, pp. 518, 525 and 540 and Tremenheere, *Quar. Rev.*, vol. cxiv, p. 449.
85. Alcock, *Capital*, vol. I. p. 414.
86. Reeve, *Edin. Rev.*, vol. cxvii, pp. 520–1.
87. Alcock, *Capital*, vol. I, p. 414.
88. Alcock, ibid., vol. II, pp. 297–301.
89. Stephen, *Fraser.*, vol. lxix, p. 114.
90. Alcock, *Edin. Rev.*, vol. cxiii, p. 46.
91. Alcock, 'China and Japan', *Edin. Rev.*, vol. cxxii (1865), p. 196.
92. Alcock, *Edin. Rev.*, vol. cxiii, p. 67.
93. Ibid., p. 68.
94. Oliphant, *Blackw.*, vol. xciii, pp. 397–8.
95. Oliphant, *Blackw.*, vol. ci, p. 442.
96. Oliphant seems to have met Harris for the first time about the turn of the 1850s. See Margaret Oliphant, *Memoir of the Life of Laurence Oliphant* . . . (Edinburgh & London, 1891), vol. II, p. 2; Philip Hender-

son, *The Life of Laurence Oliphant* . . . (London, 1956), p. 145; Ivan Parker Hall, *Mori Arinori* (Cambridge, Mass., 1973), p. 98.
97. Tremenheere, *Quar. Rev.*, vol. cxiv, p. 464; Reeve, *Edin. Rev.*, vol. cxvii, p. 518; Wilson, *Blackw.*, vol. xc, p. 617.
98. Stephen, *Fraser.*, vol. lxix, p. 101.
99. *Nihon bôeki shinbun* (The Japan Trade News), nos 70 and 71, in *Bakumatsu meiji shinbun zenshû* (Collection of Newspapers Published in the Late Tokugawa and Meiji Periods) Kimura Ki (ed.) (reprint edn, vol, I, Tokyo, 1973), pp. 177–9.
100. Tremenheere, *Quar. Rev.*, vol. cxiv, p. 464.
101. Oliphant, *Blackw.*, vol. xciii, p. 404.
102. Ishii Takashi, *Meiji ishin no kokusaiteki kankyô* (The International Conditions for the Meiji Restoration) (enlarged edn, Tokyo, 1966), p. 324.
103. Reeve, *Edin. Rev.*, vol. cxvii, p. 536.
104. For example, ibid.; Oliphant, *Blackw.*, vol. xciii, pp. 404–5.
105. Masuda Takeshi, *Bakumatsu ki no eikokujin* (An Englishman of the Late Tokugawa Period) (Tokyo, 1980), pp. 106–25. See also PRO, FO, 46/42, ff. 201–2: Russell to Alcock, 26 July 1864. This instruction reached Japan on 28 September, more than twenty days after the victorious military operation by the allied powers.
106. Alcock, 'China and Japan', *Edin. Rev.*, vol. cxxii (1865), pp. 175–202.
107. Reeve, *Edin. Rev.*, vol. cxvii, 537. A similar opinion was expressed in Stephen, *Fraser.*, vol. lxix, p. 115.
108. Alcock, *Edin. Rev.*, vol. cxxii, p. 202.
109. Alcock, *Edin. Rev.*, vol. cxiii, 58 & 70–71. A similar view was shown in Tremenheere, *Quar. Rev.*, cxiv, 472–3.
110. Alcock, *Edin, Rev.*, vol. cxxii, p. 179.
111. Tremenheere, *Quar. Rev.*, vol. cxiv, p. 479.
112. Oliphant, *Blackw.*, vol. ci, p. 442.
113. Reeve, *Edin. Rev.*, vol. cxvii, p. 517.
114. Oliphant, *Blackw.*, vol. ci. p. 441.
115. Stephen, *Fraser*, vol. lxix, p. 113.
116. Ibid., p. 116.

5 In Quest of the Inner Life of the Japanese

1. Appointed Second Secretary in March 1868; see *The Foreign Office List–January 1872* (London, 1872), p. 143.
2. A. B. Mitford, 'A Japanese Sermon', *Cornhill.*, vol. xx (1869), pp. 196–204 (August); 'Another Japanese Sermon', ibid., pp. 356–62 (September); 'The Execution by Hara-Kiri', ibid., pp. 549–54 (November).
3. For details, see Kurachi Tadashi, *Kobe-jiken to Taki Zenzaburô* (The Kobe Incident and Taki Zenzaburô) (Okayama, 1938), Oka Yoshitake, *Reimeiki no Meiji Nippon* (The Meiji Japan in its Dawn) (Tokyo, 1966), pp. 7–10.
4. Mitford, *Cornhill.*, vol. xx, p. 549.
5. Ibid., p. 550.

6. Ibid.
7. Ibid.
8. Ibid., p. 551.
9. Ibid.
10. Ibid.
11. Ibid., pp. 551–2.
12. Ibid., p. 552.
13. Ibid., p. 554.
14. Lord Redesdale, *Memories* (London, 1915), vol. I, pp. 1–77.
15. E. M. Satow, *A Diplomat in Japan* (London, 1921), p. 285. Frank Ashton-Gwatkin mentioned the Redesdale family legend about A. B. Mitford's language ability at the 358th meeting of the Japan Society of London. See *Bulletin of the Japan Soc. of Lond.*, vol. xviii (1956), p. 8.
16. Lord Redesdale, *Further Memories*, Edmund William Gosse (ed.) (London, 1917), pp. 53–4. See also A. B. Mitford, 'Tales of Old Japan, No. II', *Fort. Rev.*, vol. viii, new series (1870), p. 143.
17. PRO, FO, 46/92, ff. 23–8; Mitford to Parkes, 3 March 1868.
18. Ibid., ff. 13–18: Parkes to Stanley, 11 March 1868.
19. PRO, FO, 46/92, f. 23.
20. *The Times*, 7 May 1868, p. 9.
21. The source was the *Owl*, a weekly journal of politics and society. See M. Wolff *et al. Waterloo Directory of Victorian Periodicals* (Waterloo, 1976), vol. I, p. 805.
22. E. M. Satow, A Diplomat in Japan (London, 1921), pp. 346–7.
23. Lord Redesdale, *Memories*, vol. II, pp. 429–33.
24. Mitford, *Cornhill.*, vol. xx, p. 552.
25. PRO, FO, 46/92, f. 25.
26. Mitford, *Cornhill.*, vol. xx, p. 550.
27. PRO, FO, 46/92, f. 26.
28. Mitford, *Cornhill.*, xx, 551.
29. PRO, FO, 46/92, f. 23.
30. Mitford, *Cornhill.*, vol. xx, p. 549.
31. PRO, FO, 46/92, f. 26.
32. Mitford, *Cornhill.*, vol. xx, p. 551.
33. Some documents relating to Smith, Elder & Co., the publishers of *Cornhill*, are kept at the John Murray Archives, and at the National Library of Scotland (Acc. 7212), but the magazine's editorial documents during the period 1869–72 are few and fragmentary.
34. *Wellesley Index.*, vol. II, p. 173.
35. A. B. Mitford, 'Tales of Old Japan, No. I', *Fort. Rev.*, vol. vii, new series (1870), pp. 668–84.
36. Ibid., p. 670.
37. Ibid., p. 669.
38. Ibid., p. 681.
39. Ibid., p. 684.
40. Ibid., p. 668.
41. A. B. Mitford, 'A Ride through Yedo', *Fort. Rev.*, vol. vii, new series (1870), pp. 505–35. Yedo, now Tokyo, was also spelled Edo or Yeddo at that time.

Notes and References

42. Ibid., p. 505.
43. Saitô, *Edo meisho zue* (Pictorial Guide to the Famous Spots of Edo), (Edo, 1834–36).
44. Terakado Seiken, *Edo hanjô ki* (The Record of Flourishing Edo), (Edo, 1832–36).
45. A. B. Mitford, 'Wanderings in Japan –I', *Cornhill.*, vol. xxv (1872), p. 196.
46. Ibid., pp. 199–200.
47. Mitford, *Fort. Rev.*, vol. vii, new series, p. 506.
48. Ibid., pp. 507–9.
49. Ibid., pp. 509–11.
50. Ibid., p. 512.
51. Ibid.
52. Ibid., pp. 516–7.
53. Ibid., pp. 521–3.
54. Alcock, *The Capital of the Tycoon* (London, 1863), vol. II, pp. 311–2.
55. Mitford, *Fort. Rev.*, vol. vii, new series, pp. 521–3.
56. Ibid., p. 523.
57. Ibid., pp. 528–35.
58. Ibid., p. 505.
59. Mitford, *Cornhill.*, vol. xxv, pp. 201 and 206.
60. Ibid., p. 206.
61. A. B. Mitford, 'Wanderings in Japan –II', *Cornhill.*, vol. xxv (1872), p. 305.
62. Ibid., p. 304.
63. Mitford, *Cornhill.*, vol. xxv, pp. 200–1.
64. Alcock, 'Reform in Japan', *Edin. Rev.*, vol. cxxxvi (1872), pp. 244–5. For his latter point, Alcock referred to the *Gardener's Magazine*.
65. Ibid., p. 245.
66. Alcock, *Edin. Rev.*, vol. cxxxvi, p. 246.
67. Ibid., pp. 257–8.
68. Ibid., p. 258.
69. Mitford, *Cornhill*, vol. xxv, pp. 200–1.
70. Mitford, *Fort. Rev.*, vol. vii, new series, p. 523.
71. Ibid., p. 507.
72. Mitford, *Cornhill.*, vol. xxv, p. 303. On this point, Mitford was excessive. '*Shen Tien*' [*Shin Den*] was not a graveyard but a field where rice is grown, partly as an agricultural ritual, and partly as one of the financial supports of the Shinto shrine.
73. Ibid.
74. Ibid., p. 308.
75. A. B. Mitford, 'A Japanese Sermon', *Cornhill.*, vol. xx (1869), p. 196.
76. E.H. House, 'A Day in a Japanese Theatre', *Cornhill*, vol. xxvi (1872), pp. 341–56.
77. Ibid., p. 341.
78. Ibid., p. 354.
79. Ibid., p. 353.
80. Mitford, *Fort. Rev.*, vol. viii, new series, p. 151.
81. Ibid., p. 149.

82. Ibid., p. 150.
83. Ibid.
84. Ibid.
85. Ibid., p. 149.
86. Ibid.
87. Ibid., p. 151.
88. Ibid., p. 140.
89. A. B. Mitford, *Tales of Old Japan* (London, 1871), vol. I, Preface, p. vi.
90. Alcock, 'Japan and the Japanese', *Edin. Rev.*, vol. cxiii (1861), p. 45.
91. A. I. Shand, 'The Romance of the Japanese Revolution', *Blackw.*, vol. cxv, (1874), p. 700.
92. Lord Redesdale, *Memories*, vol. II, p. 471.
93. Stanley Lane-Poole and Frederick Victor Dickins, *The Life of Sir Harry Parkes* (London & New York, 1894), vol. II. p. 358.
94. Baron de Hübner, *Promenade autour du monde –1871* (Paris, 1873), vol. I, p. 439: 'Ce livre vient de paraître à Londres, et un exemplaire est arrivé à la légation. On se l'arrache, et on a raison.'
95. ' "Ours" in Japan', *Fraser.*, vol. iii, new series (1871), pp. 555–62.
96. Ibid., p. 555.
97. Richard Mounteney Jephson and Edward Pennell Elmhurst, *Our Life in Japan* (London, 1869).
98. ' "Ours" in Japan', *Fraser.*, vol. iii, new series, p. 558.
99. Ibid., p. 557.
100. Ibid., p. 558.
101. Ibid.
102. Ibid., p. 559.
103. Ibid., p. 558.
104. Ibid., pp. 561–2.
105. Ibid., p. 562.
106. W. Elwin, 'Fortune and Huc', *Quar. Rev.*, vol. cii (1857), pp. 126–65; R. Fortune, *Two Visits to the Tea Countries of China and the British Tea Plantations in the Himalaya* (3rd edn, London, 1853); Fortune, *A Residence among the Chinese: Inland, on the Coast, and at Sea* (London, 1857); J. F. Davis, *China: a General Description of that Empire and its Inhabitants* (London, 1857); Huc, *L'Empire chinois*, 2nd edn. (Paris, 1854).
107. Elwin, *Quar. Rev.*, vol. cii. p. 128.
108. Ibid., p. 163.
109. Elwin, *Quar. Rev.*, vol. cii, p. 163.
110. 'Tales of Old Japan', *Saturday Rev.*, vol. xxxi (1871), pp. 317–18.
111. Antti Amatus Aarne, *The Types of the Folktale. A Classification and Bibliography*, trans. and enlarged Stith Thompson (Helsinki, 1928; 2nd rev., Helsinki, 1961).
112. Mitford, *Fort. Rev.*, vol. vii, new series, p. 668.
113. Ibid., p. 506.
114. Mitford, *Cornhill.*, vol. xxv, p. 313.
115. J. Ruskin, *Time and Tide* (London, 1867), pp. 26–7: Ruskin to Dixon, 28 Feburary 1867.
116. Lord Redesdale, *Memories*, vol. II, p. 637.

6 'The Strange History of This Strange Country'

1. See, for example, Nomura Kanetarô, *Tokugawa jidai no keizai shisô* (Economic Thought in the Tokugawa Era) (Tokyo, 1939), p. 451; Donald Keene, *The Japanese Discovery of Europe: 1720–1830* (revised and expanded edn, Stanford, 1969), p. 60.
2. Honda Rimei, 'Seiiki monogatari' (Tales of the West), vol. III (1788), Seikadô Bunko (Tokyo), MS.; for a detailed analysis of Honda's logic, see Yokoyama Toshio, 'Konippon Kamusasuka to Rodonsai Rimei (Rodonsai Honda Rimei and his Old Japan Kamusasuka)', *Zinbun Gakuhô* (Kyoto), vol. xlii (1976), pp. 59–101.
3. A. B. Mitford, 'Wanderings in Japan – II', *Cornhill*, vol. xxv (1872), p. 319.
4. Alcock, 'Reform in Japan', *Edin. Rev.*, vol. cxxxvi (1872), p. 252.
5. Alcock, 'Japan as It Was and Is', *Quar. Rev.*, vol. cxxxvii (1874), p. 195.
6. They were to be labelled 'globe-trotters' from the turn of the 1870s.
7. D. Wedderburn, 'Modern Japan', *Fort. Rev.*, vol. xxiii, new series (1878), p. 417.
8. Ibid.
9. R. Alcock, 'Old and New Japan: A Decade of Japanese Progress', *Contem. Rev.*, vol. xxxviii (1880), p. 848.
10. C. Lanman, *The Japanese in America* (New York and London, 1872).
11. Alcock, *Edin. Rev.*, vol. cxxxvi, p. 259.
12. Ibid.
13. F. Marshall 'Japan', *Blackw.*, vol. cxii (1872), pp. 387–8.
14. Alcock, *Quar. Rev.*, vol. cxxxvii, p. 203.
15. S. Mossman, *New Japan, the Land of the Rising Sun* (London, 1873); F. O. Adams, *The History of Japan from the Earliest Period to the Present Time*, (London, 1874), vol. I: to the year 1864; trans. J. F. Lowder, *The Legacy of Iyeyas (deified as Gongen Sama), a Posthumous Manuscript in One Hundred Chapters* (London, 1868).
16. Wedderburn, *Fort. Rev.*, vol. xxiii, new series, p. 417.
17. W. G. Aston, 'Japan', *Macmillan.*, vol. xxvi (1872), pp. 495–6. *Wellesley Index* identifies the author as William S. Ayton, interpreter to the Japanese Ambassador, 1872, on the basis of Alexander Macmillan's letter to George Grove dated 14 September 1872. However, this was a misreading on the part of the authors of the index. The postscript in the letter reads clearly as follows: 'William G. Aston, Esq., 20 Lower Belgrave Street, Eaton Square, SW'. See BL, Addit. MSS. 55392 (Macmillan Archive), fol. 936: Macmillan to Grove, 14 September 1872. Thanks are due to Mr A. E. Parker, Senior Conservation Officer of the British Library, for his endeavours to read this half-faded letter, using the most up-to-date equipment available in the Department of Manuscripts. Aston's title at that time was Interpreter and Translator of the Legation at Tokyo.
18. Aston, *Macmillan.*, vol. xxvi, p. 496.
19. Ibid.
20. Ibid.
21. See, for example, A. I. Shand, 'The Romance of Japanese Revolution',

Blackw., vol. cxv (1874), p. 708.
22. Marshall, *Blackw.*, vol. cxii, pp. 369, 376 and 377.
23. Alcock, *Quar. Rev.*, vol. cxxxvii, p. 205. Iwakura had been expelled from the Court and placed in confinement in his estate during 1862–7.
24. Ibid., p. 206. The Heir Apparent, Prince Mutsuhito, was enthroned at the age of fourteen in 1867.
25. C. W. Dilke, 'English Influence in Japan', *Fort. Rev.*, vol. xx, new series (1876), pp. 423–43. This article was reprinted in his book *Greater Britain*, 8th edn (London, 1885).
26. Dilke, *Fort. Rev.*, vol. xx, new series, p. 433.
27. Shand, *Blackw.*, vol, cxv, p. 708.
28. C. G. Leland, 'A New Dialect; or, Yokohama Pidgin', *New Quar. Mag.*, vol. ii, new series (1878), p. 114.
29. D. Wedderburn, 'Modern Japan II', *Fort. Rev.*, vol. xxiii, new series (1878), p. 536.
30. Shand, *Blackw.*, vol. cxv, p. 700.
31. Ibid.
32. *Commercial Reports from H.M.'s Consuls in Japan 1870–1871, presented to both Houses of Parliament by Command of Her Majesty August 1871* (London, 1871), p. 21: 'Annual report by Russell Robertson, Vice-Consul at Kanagawa'.
33. H. Reeve, 'Baron Hübner's *Trip round the World*', *Edin. Rev.*, vol. cxxxviii (1873), pp. 73–4.
34. 'Japanese Art at Vienna', *The Times*, 20 May 1873, p. 10.
35. M. D. W. Wyatt, 'Orientalism in European Industry', *Macmillan.*, vol. xxi (1870). pp. 551–6.
36. Wedderburn, *Fort. Rev.*, vol. xxiii, new series, p. 417.
37. Abraham Hayward, 'A Ramble round the World', *Quar. Rev.*, vol. cxliii (1877), p. 238.
38. H. Reeve, 'Baron Hübner's *Trip round the World*', *Edin. Rev.*, vol. cxxxvii (1873) pp. 65–94.
39. Alcock, *Quar. Rev.*, vol. cxxxvii, pp. 205–6.
40. Shand, *Blackw.*, vol. cxv, p. 709.
41. Hayward, *Quar. Rev.*, vol. cxliii, pp. 238–76.
42. See, for example, Alcock, *Edin. Rev.*, vol. cxxxvi, pp. 262–6; Aston *Macmillan's Magazine*, vol. xxvi, p. 497; Alcock, *Quar. Rev.*, vol. cxxxvii, pp. 199 and 208.
43. F. O. Adams, *The History of Japan from the Earliest Period to the Present Time*, vol. I: to the year 1864; vol. II: to the year 1871 (London, 1874–75).
44. S. Mossman, *New Japan, The Land of the Rising Sun: Its Annals during the Past Twenty Years, Recording the Remarkable Progress of the Japanese in Western Civilization* (London, 1873).
45. Alcock, *Contem. Rev.*, vol. xxxviii, p. 844.
46. E. J. Reed, *Japan: Its History, Tradition and Religions*, 2 vols (London, 1880).
47. I. L. Bird, *Unbeaten Tracks in Japan. An Account of Travels in the Interior Including Visits to the Aborigines of Yezo and the Shrines of*

Nikkô and Isé, 2 vols (London, 1880).
48. See Don Brown, 'On the Significance of the Asiatic Society of Japan', being the introduction of the reprint edition of *Transactions of the Asiatic Society of Japan* (1st series, vols i–l: 1872–1922), (Tokyo, 1965), index volume, pp. 4–7.
49. B. H. Chamberlain, 'The Death Stone: A Lyric Drama from the Japanese', *Cornhill.*, vol. xxxiv (1876), pp. 479–88.
50. B. H. Chamberlain, 'Japanese Miniature Odes', *Cornhill,* vol. xxxvi (1877), pp. 72–9.
51. H. Aidé, 'Jitsu-go-Kyo', *Cornhill.*, vol. xxxiv (1876), pp. 177–80. Regarding religion, see also 'The Mythology and Religious Worship of the Ancient Japanese', *Westmin. Rev.*, vol. liv, new series (1878), pp. 27–57.
52. R. L. Stevenson (R.L.S.) 'Yoshida-Torajiro', *Cornhill.*, vol. xli (1880), pp. 327–34.
53. Marshall, *Blackw.*, vol. cxii, pp. 369–88.
54. Gaikô Shiryô Kan (Tokyo), MS. 3-9-3-12: see the part entitled 'Marusharu'.
55. *Wellesly Index* states that Marshall died in 1915, on the basis of *Men-at-the-Bar*, but the Japanese Foreign Office records (MS. 3-9-3-12) contain telegrams concerning Marshall's death of 1905.
56. NLS, BP, MS. 4294, f. 138: Marshall to Blackwood, 18 July 1872.
57. Ibid.
58. NLS, BP, MS. 4294, f. 138: Marshall to Blackwood, 18 July 1872.
59. Ibid., f. 142: Marshall to Blackwood, 6 August 1872.
60. Ibid., f. 146: Marshall to Blackwood, 11 August 1872.
61. Ibid.
62. Reeve, *Edin. Rev.*, vol. cxxxviii, p. 84.
63. R. Alcock, 'The Foreign Relations of China', *Edin. Rev.*, vol. cxxxiii (1871), p. 180.
64. Marshall, *Blackw.*, vol. cxii, p. 379.
65. See the following manuscripts: 'Chokugo gonjô' (The Record of Preparations for His Imperial Majesty's Addresses); 'Chokugo roku' (The Record of His Imperial Majesty's Addresses), at Kunaichô Shoryôbu (The Imperial Household Agency, Archives and Mausolea Dept., Tokyo).
66. Reeve, *Edin. Rev.*, vol. cxxxviii, pp. 85–8.
67. Ibid., p. 86.
68. Ibid.
69. Ibid.
70. Ibid., p. 87.
71. Ibid.
72. Ibid.
73. Ibid., p. 88.
74. A. B. Mitford, 'A Ride Through Yedo', *Fort. Rev.*, vol. vii, new series (1870), p. 519.
75. Alcock, *Edin. Rev.*, vol. cxxxvi, p. 262.
76. Marshall, *Blackw.*, vol. cxii, p. 379.

77. Reeve, *Edin. Rev.*, vol. cxxxiii, p. 93.
78. NLS, BP, MS. 4308, ff. 130–1: Marshall to Blackwood, 20 and 21 September 1873.
79. Ibid., f. 136: Marshall to Blackwood, 5 October 1873.
80. Ibid., f. 132: Marshall to Blackwood, 21 September 1873.
81. Ibid., f. 131: Marshall to Blackwood, 21 September 1873; f. 136: Marshall to Blackwood, 5 October 1873.
82. F. Marshall, 'International Vanities (No. I) Ceremonial', *Blackw.*, vol. cxiv (1873), pp. 667–85; '(No. II): Forms', vol. cxv (1874), pp. 55–74; '(No. III) Titles', vol. cxv, pp. 172–93; '(No. IV) Decorations', vol. cxv, pp. 486–503; '(No. V) Emblems', vol. cxv, pp. 607–25; '(No. VI) Diplomatic Privileges', vol. cxvi (1874), pp. 346–64; '(No. VII) Alien Laws', vol. cxvi, pp. 450–66; '(No. VIII) Glory', vol. cxvi, pp. 723–40.
83. NLS, BP, MS. 4308, f. 165; Marshall to Blackwood, 12 December 1873.
84. See Marshall's published article, 'International Vanities (No. III) Titles', *Blackw.*, vol. cxv (1874), p. 192.
85. Ibid., p. 183.
86. NLS, BP, Acc. 5643, D8, pp. 424–5: Blackwood to Marshall, 12 January 1874.
87. Reeve, *Edin. Rev.*, vol. cxxxviii, p. 83; see also a similar opinion expressed in Shand, *Blackw.*, vol. cxv, pp. 711–12.
88. Alcock, *Quar. Rev.*, vol. cxxxvii, p. 206.
89. For example, see Shand, *Blackw.*, vol. cxv, p. 711; C. W. Dilke, *Fort. Rev.*, vol. xx, new series, p. 425.
90. Reeve, *Edin. Rev.*, vol cxxxviii, p. 88; see also Baron de Hübner, *Promenade autour du monde –1871*, 2nd edn (Paris, 1873), vol. II, p. 9. Von Hübner used the form 'de Hübner' for his French publications.
91. Marshall, *Blackw.*, vol. cxii, p. 383.
92. Alcock, *Quar. Rev.*, vol. cxxxvii, p. 217.
93. Alcock, *Contem. Rev.*, vol. xxxviii, p. 830.
94. Ibid., pp. 829–30.
95. Ibid., pp. 844–9.
96. F. V. Dickins, 'Recent Travels in Japan', *Quar. Rev.*, vol. cl (1880), p. 307.
97. The John Murray Archives, unclassified letters, Dickins to Murray, 15 August 1880; see I. L. Bird, 'A Chapter on Japanese Public Affairs', *Unbeaten Tracks in Japan* (London, 1880), vol. II, pp. 311–47.
98. See, for example, Alcock, *Quar. Rev.*, vol. cxxxvii, p. 215; Dilke, *Fort. Rev.*, vol. xx, new series, p. 434; Wedderburn, *Fort. Rev.*, vol. xxiii, new series, p. 428; Alcock, *Contem. Rev.*, vol. xxxviii, pp. 847–8.
99. Marshall, *Blackw.*, vol. cxii, p. 380.
100. NLS, BP, MS. 4294, ff. 158–9: Marshall to Blackwood, 22 August 1872; Ibid., Acc. 5643, D8, pp. 184–5; Blackwood to Delane, 26 August 1872.
101. 'Japan', *The Times*, 5 September 1872, p. 8.
102. BL, Addit. MSS. 55392 (Macmillan Archive), f. 936: Macmillan to Grove, 14 September 1872.
103. Aston, *Macmillan.*, vol. xxvi, p. 497.
104. See, for example, Alcock, *Quar. Rev.*, vol. cxxxvii, pp. 212–15; Wedderburn, *Fort. Rev.*, vol. xxiii, new series, p. 536; Alcock, *Contem. Rev.*,

vol. xxxviii, pp. 845–6.
105. Alcock, *Edin. Rev.*, vol. cxxvi, p. 256.
106. Alcock, *Contem. Rev.*, vol. xxxviii, p. 850.
107. Buddhist sects had dominated most Shinto shrines throughout the Edo period, directly exercising some of the Shogun's administrative power.
108. Alcock, *Edin. Rev.*, vol. cxxxvi, p. 249.
109. Reeve, *Edin. Rev.*, vol. cxxxviii, p. 80.
110. A. Humbert, *Le Japon illustré* (Paris, 1870). This book was translated by Mrs Frances Cashel Hoey into English: *Japan and the Japanese Illustrated*, trans. Hoey, and Henry Walter Bates (ed.) (London, 1874).
111. Reeve, 'Sir Rutherford Alcock's Japan', *Edin. Rev.*, vol. cxvii (1863), pp. 523–4.
112. Reeve, *Edin. Rev.*, vol. cxxxviii, p. 80.
113. Dilke, *Fort. Rev.*, vol. xx, new series, p. 437.
114. Vol. viii, new series (1872) onwards.
115. Mitford, *Fort. Rev.*, vol. vii, new series, pp. 517–8.
116. Alcock, *Edin. Rev.*, vol. cxxxvi, p. 265.
117. Alcock, *Quar. Rev.*, vol. cxxxvii, p. 217.
118. See T. Yokoyama, 'Shin koku e no michi', p. 79.
119. R. K. Douglas, 'Formosa', *Cornhill.*, vol. xxx (1874), p. 448.
120. C. A. G. Bridge, 'A Glimpse of the Korea', *Fort. Rev.*, vol. xix, new series (1876), p. 102.
121. *The Times*, 28 December 1876, p. 6; A. Hayward 'A Ramble round the World', *Quar. Rev.*, vol. cxliii (1877), p. 270.
122. Wedderburn, *Fort. Rev.*, vol. xxxiii, new series, p. 530.
123. Alcock, *Contem. Rev.*, vol. xxxviii, pp. 843–4.
124. Wedderburn, *Fort. Rev.*, vol. xxiii, new series, p. 428. Wedderburn seems to imply Parkes's measure taken after the Kyoto incident of March 1868, in which the Minister was attacked unsuccessfully by two samurai on his way to the Court. One of these was killed on the spot, and the other was, at Parkes' demand, stripped off his samurai rank and beheaded. Their heads were duly exhibited to the public, to Parkes' satisfaction. See Oka Yoshitake, *Reimei Ki no Meiji Nippon* (Meiji Japan in its dawn), (Tokyo, 1964), pp. 33–40. Attacks of this kind, however, were recorded in later years.
125. Wedderburn, *Fort. Rev.*, vol. xxiii, new series, p. 428.
126. Marshall, *Blackw.*, vol. cxii. p. 382.
127. Ibid.
128. Alcock, *Quar. Rev.*, vol. cxxxvii, p. 208. This paper seems to have been one of the papers issued by W. D. Howell who was then authorised to publish British Consular reports, summaries of the meetings of the Asiatic Society of Japan and the Japanese government's official information for foreigners. See Endô Moto'o and Shimomura Fujio (eds) *Kokushi Bunken Kaisetsu Zoku* (Commentaries on printed sources for Japanese history – Part II) (Tokyo, 1965), pp. 434–6.
129. Ibid., p. 209.
130. Alcock, *Contem. Rev.*, vol. xxxviii, p. 847.
131. A. B. Mitford, 'Wanderings in Japan, II', *Cornhill.*, vol. xxv (1872), p. 319.

7 The Expanding Gulf

1. A. I. Shand, 'The Romance of Japanese Revolution', *Blackw.*, vol. cxv (1874), pp. 696–712.
2. NLS, BP, MS. 4310, f. 183: Shand to Blackwood, 17 April 1873.
3. NLS, BP, MS. 4325, f. 21: Shand to Blackwood, 10 March 1874.
4. Ibid., ff. 21–2.
5. NLS, BP, MS. 4325, ff. 32–4: Shand to Blackwood, 20 April 1874.
6. Ibid.
7. Shand, *Blackw.*, vol. cxv, 696. The Belle Jardinière and the Bon Diable were ready-to-wear tailors mainly for the fashionable Paris *bourgeoisie*. See T. Zeldin, *France 1848–1945*, vol. II (Oxford, 1977), p. 443.
8. Shand, *Blackw.*, vol. cxv, p. 696.
9. Ibid.
10. Ibid., p. 697.
11. Ibid.
12. Shand, *Blackw.*, vol. cxv, p. 697.
13. Ibid.
14. Ibid.
15. NLS, BP, MS. 4325, f. 42: Shand to Blackwood, 12 May 1874.
16. See NLS, BP, Acc. 5634, D8, p. 485: Blackwood to Marshall, 16 April 1874; MS. 4325, f. 32: Shand to Blackwood, 20 April 1874; ibid., f 36: Shand to Blackwood, 4 May 1874.
17. Ibid., f. 42: Shand to Blackwood, 12 May 1874.
18. NLS, BP, MS. 4322, f. 169: Marshall to Blackwood, 17 May 1874.
19. Ibid.
20. Ibid., f. 167: Marshall to Shand, 14 May 1874.
21. *The Illustrated London News*, 7 April and 19 May 1866; 1 August 1868; 16 June 1872; 8 November 1873; 6 March 1875; 7 April 1877.
22. A. B. Mitford, 'A Ride through Yeddo', *Fort. Rev.*, vol. vii, new series (1870), pp. 506 and 516.
23. E. H. House, 'A Day in a Japanese Theatre', *Cornhill.*, vol. xxvi (1872), p. 343.
24. C. A. G. Bridge, 'The City of Kiyôto', *Fraser.*, vol. xvii, new series (1878), p. 66.
25. C. W. Dilke, 'English Influence in Japan', *Fort. Rev.*, vol. xx, new series (1876), p. 426.
26. Ibid.
27. Ibid., p. 427.
28. R. Alcock, 'Reform in Japan', *Edin. Rev.*, vol. cxxxvi (1872), p. 270.
29. W. G. Aston, 'Japan', *Macmillan.*, vol. xxvi (1872), p. 496.
30. Ibid.
31. F. Marshall, 'Japan', *Blackw.*, vol. cxii, p. 388.
32. Shand, *Blackw.*, vol. cxv, p. 712.
33. Marshall, *Blackw.*, vol. cxii, p. 388.
34. R. Alcock, 'Japan as it was and is', *Quar. Rev.*, vol. cxxxvii (1874), pp. 207–8.
35. Ibid., p. 207.
36. Ibid., p. 208.

37. Alcock, *Edin. Rev.*, vol. cxxxvi, pp. 253–6.
38. Alcock, *Quar. Rev.*, vol. cxxxvii, p. 211.
39. Marshall, *Blackw.*, vol. cxii, p. 388.
40. A. Hayward, 'A Ramble round the World', *Quar. Rev.*, vol. cxliii, p. 267.
41. D. Wedderburn, 'Modern Japan II', *Fort. Rev.*, vol. xxiii, new series (1878), p. 536.
42. R. Alcock, 'Old and New Japan: a Decade of Japanese Progress', *Contem. Rev.*, vol. xxxviii (1880), p. 850.
43. See, for example, Alcock, *Edin. Rev.*, vol. cxxxvi, pp. 250, 253 and 268; Aston, *Macmillan.*, vol. xxvi, pp. 496–7.
44. C. W. Dilke, 'English Influence in Japan', *Fort. Rev.*, vol. xx, new series (1876), p. 427.
45. Ibid., p. 430.
46. D. Wedderburn, 'Modern Japan', *Fort. Rev.*, vol. xxiii, new series (1878), p. 419.
47. Alcock, *Quar. Rev.*, vol. cxxxvii, p. 211.
48. Ibid., p. 204.
49. Ibid., p. 203.
50. Ibid., p. 204; Adams, *History of Japan*, vol. I (1874), pp. 106–7.
51. Ibid.
52. Wedderburn, *Fort. Rev.*, vol. xxiii, p. 417.
53. Marshall, *Blackw.*, vol. cxii, p. 373.
54. Ibid., p. 374.
55. Ibid., p. 375.
56. Ibid., p. 377.
57. Marshall, *Blackw.*, vol. cxii, p. 378. One wonders to what extent Marshall was influenced by Sameshima Naonobu in formulating this theory. Sameshima died young in Paris in 1880, leaving little of his personal writings, so one cannot give a ready answer to this question.
58. Alcock, *Contem. Rev.*, vol. xxxviii, pp. 834–7.
59. Ibid., p. 832.
60. Ibid.
61. Ibid.
62. Dilke, *Fort. Rev.*, vol. xx, new series, p. 437.
63. Ibid., pp. 437–8.
64. Alcock, *Quar. Rev.*, vol. cxxxvii, p. 216.
65. Aston, *Macmillan.*, vol. xxvi, p. 497.
66. Ibid.
67. Ibid.
68. Lord Elgin, *Letters and Journals of James, Eighth Earl of Elgin, Governor of Jamaica, Governor General of Canada, Envoy to China, Viceroy of India*, T. Walrond (ed.) (London, 1872).
69. H. Reeve, 'Letters and Journals of Lord Elgin', *Edin. Rev.*, vol. cxxxvii (1873), p. 39.
70. H. Reeve, *Edin. Rev.*, vol. cxxxvii, p. 39.
71. Ibid.
72. Ibid.
73. Marshall, *Blackw.*, vol. cxii (1872), p. 386.

74. Aston, *Macmillan.*, vol. xxvi, p. 498.
75. Ibid.
76. Alcock, *Edin. Rev.*, vol. cxxxvi, p. 268.
77. Ibid., p. 269.
78. NLS, BP, MS. 4322, ff. 124–5: Marshall to Blackwood, 1 January 1874.
79. Ibid., f. 126: Marshall to Blackwood, 7 January 1874.
80. Ibid., f. 130: Marshall to Blackwood, 14 January 1874.
81. Ibid., f. 134: Marshall to Blackwood, 15 January 1874.
82. Ibid., f. 136: Marshall to Blackwood, 21 January 1874.
83. NLS, BP, Acc. 5643, D8, p. 442: Blackwood to Marshall, 17 February 1874.
84. Ibid.
85. NLS, BP, MS. 4322, f. 147: Marshall to Blackwood, 19 Feburary 1874. See also ibid., f. 164: Marshall to Blackwood, 17 April 1874, in which Marshall wrote that 'Justice Abroad' would appear in the *Fortnightly Review* on 1 May.
86. F. Marshall, 'Justice Abroad', *Fort. Rev.*, vol. xvi, new series (1874), pp. 133–45.
87. Ibid., p. 133.
88. Ibid., pp. 142–5.

8 Victorian Travellers in the Japanese 'Elf-land'

1. R. Alcock, 'Old and New Japan: A Decade of Japanese Progress', *Contem. Rev.*, vol. xxxviii (1880), p. 828.
2. D. Wedderburn, 'Modern Japan', *Fort. Rev.*, vol. xxiii, new series (1878), p. 418.
3. Ibid.
4. C. W. Dilke, 'English Influence in Japan', *Fort. Rev.*, vol. xx, new series (1876), p. 441.
5. Ibid.
6. C. A. G. Bridge, 'The Mediterranean of Japan', *Fort. Rev.*, vol. xviii, new series (1875), pp. 214–5.
7. Dilke, *Fort. Rev.*, vol. xx, new series, p. 441.
8. C. A. G. Bridge, 'The City of Kiyôto', *Fraser*, vol. xvii, new series (1878), p. 61.
9. Ibid.
10. Ibid. In the interest of accuracy, it should be noted that Japanese women and children in rice farming areas intensively laboured in the field in the planting and harvesting seasons.
11. H. Reeve, 'Baron Hübner's *Trip round the World*', *Edin. Rev.*, vol. cxxxviii (1873), p. 89.
12. Bridge, *Fraser.*, vol. xvii, new series, p. 64.
13. Ibid.
14. 'Hakurankwai kakari shirabesho, Daigogô (The Document, No. 5 Provided by the Bureau of the Exhibition)', February 1872, *Kyotofu hyakunen no shiryô* (Documents of the One-hundred Years of Kyoto Prefecture), The Kyoto Prefectural Archives (ed.) (Kyoto, 1972), vol. II, pp. 54–5: 'kinjitsu yori taninzû nyûkô subeshi kono toki ni atatte

yaban hiretsu no soshiri wo ukeru tei nite wa hitori Kyoto no chijoku nomi narazu onkokujoku tomo iu bekereba'.
15. Wedderburn, 'Modern Japan II', *Fort. Rev.*, vol. xxiii, new series (1878), p. 422.
16. Ibid., p. 423.
17. Ibid.
18. Ibid.
19. Bridge, *Fort. Rev.*, vol. xviii, new series, pp. 210–1.
20. Wedderburn, *Fort. Rev.*, vol. xx, new series, p. 418.
21. Ibid., p. 419.
22. Ibid.
23. For example, ibid., p. 422.
24. R. Alcock, 'Japan and the Japanese', *Edin. Rev.*, vol. cxiii (1861), pp. 42 and 59–63.
25. Wedderburn, *Fort. Rev.*, vol. xxiii, new series, pp. 541–2.
26. Alcock, *Contem. Rev.*, vol. xxxviii, pp. 830–1.
27. Bridge, *Fort. Rev.*, vol. xviii, new series, p. 207.
28. Ibid., p. 205.
29. Ibid.
30. See C. W. Brooks, *Japanese Wrecks, Stranded and Picked Up Adrift in the North Pacific Ocean, Ethnologically Considered* (reprint edn, San Francisco, 1876).
31. Wedderburn, *Fort. Rev.*, vol. xxiii, new series, pp. 539–40.
32. Ibid., p. 539.
33. Ibid., p. 541.
34. Le Baron de Hübner [von Hübner], *Promenade autour du monde –1871* (2nd edn, Paris, 1873) vol. I, p. 394; *A Ramble round the World*, Mary Elizabeth Herbert (trans.) (London, 1874), vol. I, p. 365–6.
35. Bridge, *Fraser.*, vol. xvii, new series, p. 59.
36. Dilke, *Fort. Rev.*, vol. xx, new series, p. 442.
37. Ibid., p. 443.
38. Reeve, *Edin. Rev.*, vol. cxxxviii, p. 78; Le Baron de Hübner, *Promenade autour du monde –1871* (2nd edn., Paris, 1873), vol. I, p. 371.
39. R. L. S[tevenson] 'Yoshida-Torajiro', *Cornhill.*, vol. xli (1880), p. 334. Yoshida had hidden himself aboard Commodore Perry's ship in the hopes of visiting America. He was, however, discovered before the departure, and the Japanese authorities arrested him, for it was then illegal to leave Japan. Stevenson obtained information about Yoshida from Masaki Taizô in Edinburgh in 1879. Masaki held the position of Supervisor of the Japanese Students in Britain during the period 1876 to 81.
40. Ibid.
41. Dilke, *Fort. Rev.*, vol. xx, new series, p. 443.
42. Reeve, *Edin. Rev.*, vol. cxxxviii, p. 77; *Le Baron de Hübner*, vol. I, p. 369.
43. S. Osborn, 'A Cruise in Japanese Waters – Part II', *Blackw.*, vol. lxxv (1859), p. 60.
44. Alcock, *Contem. Rev.*, vol. xxxviii, pp. 832–3.
45. See Richard Jenkyns, *The Victorians and Ancient Greece* (Oxford,

1980), pp. 1–20.
46. Bridge, *Fort. Rev.*, vol. xviii, new series, p. 208.
47. Ibid., p. 209.
48. Ibid.
49. Ibid., p. 212.
50. Bridge, *Fraser.*, vol. xvii, new series, pp. 59–60.
51. Ibid., p. 68. This was the *Miyako Odori* which had recently started for the visitors to the Kyoto Exhibition in 1872. See *Kyoto no rekishi* (History of Kyoto), Kyoto Municipal Government (ed.) (vol. V, 1975), p. 129.
52. Wedderburn, *Fort. Rev.*, vol. xxiii, new series, p. 420.
53. Ibid.
54. Bridge, *Fort. Rev.*, vol. xviii, new series, p. 210.
55. Bridge, *Fraser.*, vol. xvii, new series, p. 60.
56. Ibid.
57. Ibid.
58. Ibid., p. 70.
59. J. H. Bridge, 'Is Our Cause in China Just?', *Fort. Rev.*, vol. xviii, new series (1875), p. 648.
60. Ibid.
61. C. W. Dilke, 'English Influence in China', *Macmillan.*, vol. xxxiv (1876), p. 562.
62. Wedderburn, *Fort. Rev.*, vol. xxiii, new series, p. 532.
63. R. Alcock, 'The Future of Eastern Asia', *Macmillan.*, vol. xxx (1874), p. 447.
64. Ibid., p. 448.
65. Wedderburn, *Fort. Rev.*, vol. xxiii, new series, p. 425.
66. Dilke, *Fort. Rev.*, vol. xx, new series, pp. 431–2.
67. R[udolph] L[indau], ' "Fred": A Tale from Japan', *Blackw.*, vol. cxxxiv (1878), pp. 475–9. During the latter half of the 1870s, the number of copies printed of this magazine was reduced to about 6000 (NLS, BP, Acc. 5644, F.6).
68. NLS, BP, MS. 4378, f. 107: Lindau to Blackwood, 9 September, 1878.
69. NLS, BP, Acc. 5643, D. 10, p. 497: Blackwood to Lindau, 16 September 1878.
70. Mrs Gerald Porter, *Annals of a Publishing House, John Blackwood* (Edinburgh and London, 1898), p. 416.
71. M. D. Wyatt, 'Orientalism in European Industry', *Macmillan.*, vol. xxi (1870), pp. 553–4.
72. A. I. Shand, 'The Romance of Japanese Revolution', *Blackw.*, vol. cxv (1874), p. 699.
73. Ibid.
74. Dilke, *Fort. Rev.*, vol. xx, new series, p. 435.
75. Ibid.
76. Bridge, *Fraser.*, vol. xvii, new series, p. 65.
77. Ibid.
78. Ibid., p. 66.
79. Ibid.
80. Wedderburn, *Fort. Rev.*, vol. xxiii, new series, p. 542.

81. Ibid.
82. Bridge, *Fraser*, vol. xvii, new series, p. 62.
83. Ibid., p. 70. Similarly, while Dilke was in Japan, he spent a long time in the theatre in order to see 'the true Old Japan'. Stephen Gwynn and Getrude Tuckwell, *The Life of the Rt. Hon. Sir Charles W. Dilke* (London, 1917), vol. I, pp. 194–5.
84. Bridge, *Fraser.*, vol. xvii, new series, p. 62.
85. Alcock, *Contem. Rev.*, vol. xxxviii, p. 840.
86. Ibid., p. 828.

Conclusion

1. R. Dawson, *The Chinese Chameleon, an Analysis of European Conceptions of Chinese Civilization* (London, 1967), p. 173.
2. NLS, BP, MS. 4294, ff. 112–13: Marshall to Blackwood, 18 February 1872.
3. Frank Ledlie Moore, *Handbook of Gilbert and Sullivan* (New York, 1962) p. 70.
4. Gloucestershire Record Office, The Redesdale Papers, D 2002/c, 44/1: Gilbert to Mitford, 17 March 1885.
5. F. V. Dickins, *Quar. Rev.*, vol. cl, pp. 309–10.
6. A. B. Mitford, *The Attache at Peking* (London, 1900), Preface, pp. vii–ix.

Select Bibliography

Reference books for biographical information and indexes to periodical literature are mentioned only in the notes, and are not listed here. Manuscript sources and printed sources which are of interest only to specialists, are dealt with in the same way.

MANUSCRIPT SOURCES

THE BRITISH LIBRARY, Additional Manuscripts, 55392 (Macmillan Archive).
GAIKO SHIRYÔ KAN (The Archives of the Japanese Ministry of Foreign Affairs), MS. 3-9-3-12, 'Zaigai Kôkan gaikokujin koyô zakken (Miscellaneous Documents Relating to Employment of Foreigners at Japanese Diplomatic Establishments Abroad)'.
THE GLOUCESTERSHIRE RECORD OFFICE, The Redesdale Papers, D2002.
THE JOHN MURRAY ARCHIVES, 50 Albemarle Street, London, Unclassified Letters from S. Osborn and F. V. Dickins.
KOKKAI TOSHOKAN (The Diet Library, Tokyo), MS. 808/8, 'Igirisu ikken (A Record of England)'.
THE NATIONAL LIBRARY OF SCOTLAND, Edinburgh, The Blackwood Papers, MSS. 4133, 4135, 4141, 4152, 4155, 4294, 4308, 4310, 4322, 4325 and 4378; Acc. 5643, D2–D10; Acc. 5644, F4–F10.
THE PUBLIC RECORD OFFICE, The Foreign Office Papers, Series 46 (Japan), vols. 5, 9, 16, 92.
THE UNIVERSITY OF READING, The Longman's Archive, Box Longman, II; Divide Ledger, 7D, 11D; Impression Book, Nos 14 and 15.

PRINTED SOURCES

Major sources cited

ADAMS, FRANCIS OTTIWELL, *The History of Japan from the Earliest Period to the Present Time*, 2 vols, (London, 1874–5).
AIDÉ, HAMILTON, 'Jitsu-go-kiyô', *Cornhill.*, vol. xxxiv (1876), pp. 177–80.
ALCOCK, RUTHERFORD, 'Japan and the Japanese', *Edin. Rev.*, vol. cxiii (1861), pp. 37–73.
ALCOCK, RUTHERFORD, *International Exhibition, 1862 Catalogue of Works of Industry and Art, Sent from Japan* (London, 1862).
ALCOCK, RUTHERFORD, *The Capital of the Tycoon: A Narrative of a Three Years' Residence in Japan*, 2 vols, (London, 1863).
ALCOCK, RUTHERFORD, 'China and Japan', *Edin. Rev.*, vol. cxxii

(1865), pp. 175–202.
ALCOCK, RUTHERFORD, 'The Foreign Relations of China', *Edin. Rev.*, vol. cxxxiii (1871), pp. 176–206.
ALCOCK, RUTHERFORD, 'Reform in Japan', *Edin. Rev.*, vol. cxxxvi (1872), pp. 244–69.
ALCOCK, RUTHERFORD, 'Japan as It Was and Is', *Quar. Rev.*, vol. cxxxvii (1874), pp. 189–218.
ALCOCK, RUTHERFORD, 'The Future of Eastern Asia', *Macmillan.*, vol. xxx (1874), pp. 435–48.
ALCOCK, RUTHERFORD, 'The Relations of Western Powers with the East', *Fort. Rev.*, vol. xix, new series (1876), pp. 46–66.
ALCOCK, RUTHERFORD, 'The Chinese Empire and Its Foreign Relations', *Fort. Rev.*, vol. xix, new series (1876), pp. 652–70.
ALCOCK, RUTHERFORD, 'Old and New Japan: A Decade of Japanese Progress', *Contem. Rev.*, vol. xxxviii (1880), pp. 827–50.
ASTON, WILLIAM GEORGE, 'Japan', *Macmillan.*, vol. xxvi (1872), pp. 493–8.
AYTOUN, WILLIAM EDMONDSTOUNE, 'American Explorations: China and Japan', *Blackw.*, vol. lxxxi (1857), pp. 702–18.
BIRD, ISABELLA LUCY (MRS BISHOP), *Unbeaten Tracks in Japan, An Account of Travels in the Interior, Including Visits to the Aborigines of Yezo and the Shrines of Nikkô and Isé*, 2 vols, (London, 1880).
BRIDGE, CYPRIAN ARTHUR GEORGE, 'The Mediterranean of Japan', *Fort. Rev.*, vol. xviii, new series (1875), pp. 205–16.
BRIDGE, CYPRIAN ARTHUR GEORGE, 'A Glimpse of the Korea', *Fort. Rev.*, vol. xix, new series (1876), pp. 96–102.
BRIDGE, CYPRIAN ARTHUR GEORGE, 'An Excursion in Formosa', *Fort. Rev.*, vol. xx, new series (1876), pp. 214–22.
BRIDGE, CYPRIAN ARTHUR GEORGE, 'The City of Kiyôto', *Fraser*, vol. xvii, new series (1878), pp. 58–70.
BRIDGES, JOHN HENRY, 'Is Our Cause in China Just?', *Fort. Rev.*, vol. xviii, new series (1875), pp. 642–63.
BUSK, MRS WILLIAMS, 'Manners and Customs of the Japanese. From Recent Dutch Accounts of Japan, and the German of Dr von Siebold', *Asiatic Jour.* vol. xxix, new series (1839), pp. 181–99 and 274–90; vol. xxx (1839), pp. 32–42, 93–104, 185–95 and 265–75; vol. xxxi (1840), pp. 5–17, 108–17; vol. xxxii (1840), 240–51.
BUSK, MRS WILLIAMS, *Manners and Customs of the Japanese. From Recent Dutch Accounts of Japan, and the German of Dr von Siebold*, reprint edn, (London, 1841); new edn (London, 1852).
CHAMBERLAIN, BASIL HALL, 'The Death-Stone: A Lyric Drama from the Japanese', *Cornhill.*, vol. xxxiv (1876), pp. 479–88.
CHAMBERLAIN, BASIL HALL, 'Japanese Miniature Odes', *Cornhill.*, vol. xxxvi (1877), pp. 72–9.
DE HÜBNER (VON HÜBNER), JOSEPH ALEXANDER, *Promenade autour du monde–1871*, 2 vols (Paris, 1873).
DE HÜBNER (VON HÜBNER), JOSEPH ALEXANDER, *A Ramble round the World*, trans. Mary Elizabeth Herbert (London, 1874).
DICKINS, FREDERIC VICTOR, 'Recent Travels in Japan', *Quar. Rev.*,

vol. cl (1880), pp. 305–36.
DILKE, CHARLES WENTWORTH, 'English Influence in Japan', *Fort. Rev.*, vol. xx, new series (1876), pp. 424–43.
DOUGLAS, ROBERT KENNAWAY, 'Formosa', *Cornhill.*, vol. xxx (1874), pp. 448–53.
DRUMMOND-DAVIES, FRANCIS MAURICE, 'Japan', *Westmin. Rev.*, vol. xvii, new series (1860), pp. 508–40.
'LORD ELGIN'S MISSION', *Bentley's Miscellany*, vol. xlvii (1860), pp. 136–43.
ELGIN AND KINCARDINE, LORD, JAMES BRUCE, *Letters and Journals of James, Eighth Earl of Elgin, Governor of Jamaica, Governor General of Canada, Envoy to China, Viceroy of India*, Theodore Walrond (ed.) (London, 1872).
ELWIN, WHITWELL, 'Travels in China – Fortune and Huc', *Quar. Rev.*, vol. cii (1857), pp. 126–65.
'EXPEDITION OF AN AMERICAN SQUADRON TO THE CHINA SEAS AND JAPAN', *New Quar. Rev.*, vol. v (1856), pp. 376–81.
FORTUNE, ROBERT, *Yedo and Peking, a Narrative of a Journey to the Capitals of Japan and China* (London, 1863).
GOLOWNIN, WASILY MIKHAILOWICH, *Narrative of My Captivity in Japan, during the Years 1811, 1812 & 1813; with Observations on the Country and the People*, 2 vols, (London, 1818).
GOLOWNIN, WASILY MIKHAILOWICH, *Recollections of Japan, Comprising a Particular Account of the Religion, Language, Government, Laws and Manners of the People with Observations on the Geography, Climate, Population & Productions of the Country* (London, 1819).
GOLOWNIN, WASILY MIKHAILOWICH, *Memoirs of a Captivity in Japan, during the Years 1811, 1812, and 1813; with Observations on the Country and the People*, 3 vols, 2nd edn (London, 1824).
GOLOWNIN, WASILY MIKHAILOWICH, *Japan and the Japanese*, 'S.R.' (ed.), 2 vols, new and revised edns, (London, 1852).
HABERSHAM, A. W., *My Last Cruise; or, Where We Went, and What We Saw; being an Account of Visits to the Malay and Loo-Choo Islands, & C.* (Philadelphia and London, 1857).
HAYWARD, ABRAHAM, 'A Ramble round the World', *Quar. Rev.*, vol. cxliii (1877), pp. 238–76.
HOUSE, EDWARD HOWARD, 'A Day in a Japanese Theatre', *Cornhill.*, vol. xxvi (1872), pp. 341–56.
HUMBERT, AIMÉ, *Le Japon illustré*, 2 vols (Paris, 1870).
HUMBERT, AIMÉ, *Japan and the Japanese Illustrated*, (tr. Mrs Frances Cashel Hoey), Henry Walter Bates (ed.) (London, 1874).
ISHIN SHI GAKKAI (ED.), *Bakumatsu ishin gaikô shiryô shûsei* (Collected Documents Relating to Japanese Diplomacy during the Late Tokugawa and Restoration Period) vol. III (Tokyo, 1943).
'JAPAN', *New Monthly Maga.*, vol. xcv (1852), pp. 95–102.
'JAPAN AND THE JAPANESE', *North Brit. Rev.*, vol. xxxi (1859), pp. 424–46.
'THE JAPANESE MARTYRS', *Frasers.*, vol. lxvii (1863), pp. 396–406.
THE JAPAN SOCIETY OF LONDON, *Bulletin of the Japan Society of*

London, vol. xviii (London 1956).
JEPHSON, RICHARD MOUNTENY AND ELMHIRST, EDWARD PENNELL, *Our Life in Japan* (London, 1869).
KAEMPFER, ENGELBERT, *The History of Japan, Giving an Account of the Ancient and Present State and Government of that Empire: of its Temples, Palaces, Castles and Other Buildings; of its Metals, Minerals, Trees, Plants, Animals, Birds and Fishes; of the Chronology and Succession of the Emperors, Ecclesiastical and Secular; of the Original Descent, Religions, Customs, and Manufactures of the Natives, and of their Trade and Commerce with the Dutch and Chinese, Together with a Description of the Kingdom of Siam*, (tr. John Gasper Scheuchzer), 2 vols, (London, 1727).
KAEMPFER, ENGELBERT, 'Account of Japan', *Universal Library of Standard Authors* (Edinburgh and London, 1852), vol. I.
KAEMPFER, ENGELBERT, 'Account of Japan', *Universal Library of Standard Authors* (London, 1853), vol. I.
KAEMPFER, ENGELBERT, 'Account of Japan', *Popular Voyages and Travels* (Glasgow and London, c. 1853).
KATSU, KAISHÛ, *Rikugun Rekishi* (History of the Japanese Army), reprint edn of edn of 1889 (Tokyo, 1967), vol. I.
KNOX, ALEXANDER ANDREW, 'Japan', *Edin. Rev.*, vol. xcvi (1852), pp. 348–83.
KURACHI, TADASHI, *Kobe-jiken to Taki Zenzaburô* (The Kobe Incident and Taki Zenzaburô), (Okayama, 1938).
KYOTOFU, SHIRYÔKAN, (The Kyoto Prefectural Archive) (ed.), *Kyotofu hyakunen no shiryô* (Documents of the One-hundred Years of Kyoto Prefecture), vol. II (Kyoto, 1972).
KYOTO SHIYAKUSHO (The Kyoto Municipal Government) (ed.), *Kyoto no rekishi* (History of Kyoto), vol. v (Kyoto, 1975).
LANMAN, CHARLES, *The Japanese in America* (New York and London, 1872).
LELAND, CHARLES GODFREY, 'A New Dialect; or, Yokohama Pidgin', *New Quar. Maga.*, vol. ii, new series (1879) pp. 114–24.
L[INDAU], R[UDOLPH], ' "Fred": A Tale from Japan', *Blackw.*, vol. cxxiv, (1878) pp. 475–79.
L[INDO], M[ARK] P[RAGER], 'Japan and its Intercourse with Foreign Nations', *Fraser.*, vol. li (1855), pp. 145–56.
L[INDO], M[ARK] P[RAGER], 'Our New Treaty with Japan', *Fraser.*, vol. lviii (1858), pp. 650–8.
MACDONALD, JOHN, 'From Yeddo to London with the Japanese Ambassadors', *Cornhill.*, vol. vii (1863), pp. 603–20.
MACFARLANE, CHARLES, *Japan: An Account, Geographical and Historical* (London, 1852).
MARSHALL, FREDERIC, 'Japan', *Blackw.*, vol. cxii (1872), pp. 369–88.
MARSHALL, FREDERIC, 'International Vanities (No. I): Ceremonial', *Blackw.*, vol. cxiv (1873), pp. 667–85; '(No. II): Forms', vol. cxv (1874), pp. 55–74; '(No. III): Titles', vol. cxv, pp. 172–93; '(No. IV): Decorations', vol. cxv, pp. 486–503; '(No. V): Emblems', vol. cxv, pp. 607–25; '(No. VI): Diplomatic Privileges', vol. cxvi (1874), pp. 346–64; '(No. VII): Alien Laws', vol. cxvi, pp. 450–66; '(No. VIII): Glory', vol. cxvi, pp. 723–40.

MARSHALL, FREDERIC, 'Justice Abroad', *Fort. Rev.*, vol. xvi, new series (1874), pp. 133–45.
MARTIN, MISS, 'Japanese Social Life', *House. Words*, vol. xix (1859), pp. 237–40.
MARTIN, MISS, 'Japan Traits', *House. Words*, vol. xix (1859), pp. 561–5.
MAYERS, WILLIAM FREDERIC, 'A Chinese Commissioner's Foreign Tour', *Cornhill.*, vol. xxi (1870), pp. 578–94.
MITFORD, ALGERNON BERTRAM, 'A Japanese Sermon', *Cornhill.*, vol. xx (1869), pp. 196–206.
MITFORD, ALGERNON BERTRAM, 'Another Japanese Sermon', *Cornhill.*, vol. xx (1869), pp. 356–62.
MITFORD, ALGERNON BERTRAM, 'The Execution by Hara-Kiri', *Cornhill.*, vol. xx (1869), pp. 549–54.
MITFORD, ALGERNON BERTRAM, 'A Ride through Yedo', *Fort. Rev.*, vol. vii, new series (1870).
MITFORD, ALGERNON BERTRAM, 'Tales of Old Japan, No. I – The Forty-seven Rônins', *Fort. Rev.*, vol. vii, new series (1870), pp. 668–84.
MITFORD, ALGERNON BERTRAM, 'Tales of Old Japan, No. II – The Loves of Gompachi and Komurasaki', *Fort. Rev.*, vol. viii, new series (1870), pp. 138–54.
MITFORD, ALGERNON BERTRAM, 'Missionaries and Mandarins', *Macmillan.*, vol. xxiii (1870), pp. 171–6.
MITFORD, ALGERNON BERTRAM, *Tales of Old Japan*, 2 vols (London, 1871).
MITFORD, ALGERNON BERTRAM, 'Wanderings in Japan – I', *Cornhill.*, vol. xxv (1872), pp. 196–213.
MITFORD, ALGERNON BERTRAM, 'Wanderings in Japan – II' *Cornhill.*, vol. xxv (1872), pp. 302–21.
MITFORD, ALGERNON BETRAM FREEMAN-, *Attache at Peking* (London, 1900).
MITFORD, ALGERNON BERTRAM FREEMAN- (LORD REDESDALE), *Memories*, 2 vols, (London, 1915).
MITFORD, ALGERNON BERTRAM FREEMAN- (LORD REDESDALE), *Further Memories*, Edmund William Gosse (ed.) (London, 1917).
MONTANUS, ARNOLDUS, *Atlas Japannensis, being remarkable addresses by way of embassy from the East-India Company of the United Provinces, to the Emperor of Japan, containing a description of their . . . territories, cities, temples and fortresses; their religions, laws, and customs . . . Englished by J. Ogilby* (London, 1670).
MONTANUS, ARNOLDUS, *Ambassades mémorables de la Compagnie des Indes Orientales des Provinces Unies vers les Empereurs du Japon, contenant plusieurs choses remarquables arrivées pendant le voyage des ambassadeurs et de plus la description . . . des Japonais*, trans. from Dutch (Amsterdam, 1680).
MORLEY, HENRY, 'Our Phantom Ship: Japan', *House. Words*, vol. iii (1851), pp. 160–7.
MORLEY, HENRY, 'Far East', *House, Words*, vol. xiii (1856), pp. 154–7.
MORLEY, JOHN, 'Home and Foreign Affairs', *Fort. Rev.*, vol. xx, new series (1876), pp. 131–44.

MOSSMAN, SAMUEL, *New Japan, the Land of the Rising Sun; its Annals during the Past Twenty Years, Recording the Remarkable Progress of the Japanese in Western Civilization* (London, 1873).

MOUNSEY, AUGUSTUS HENRY, *The Satsuma Rebellion: An Episode of Modern Japanese History* (London, 1879).

MURATA, FUMIO, *Seiyô bunken roku* (Records of My Experiences in the West) (Hiroshima, 1869–70).

'The Mythology and Religious Worship of the Ancient Japanese', *Westmin. Rev.*, vol. civ, new series (1878), pp. 27–57.

NAIKAKU KIROKU KYOKU (The Cabinet Records Bureau) (ed.), *Hôki bunrui taizen* (The Complete Classified Collection of Laws and Regulations), vol. I – foreign affairs (Tokyo, 1891).

NAKAI, ÔSHÛ, *Man'yû kitei* (Records of My Wanderings outside Japan) (Tokyo, 1876).

OLIPHANT, LAURENCE, *Narrative of the Earl of Elgin's Mission to China and Japan in the Years 1857, '58, '59*, 2 vols, 1st and 2nd edns (Edinburgh and London, 1859 and 1860).

OLIPHANT, LAURENCE, 'Political Tragedies in Japan', *Blackw.*, vol. xci (1862), pp. 424–33.

OLIPHANT, LAURENCE, 'Sensation Diplomacy in Japan', *Blackw.*, vol. xciii (1863), pp. 397–413.

OLIPHANT, LAURENCE, 'The Moral and Political Revolution in Japan', *Blackw.*, vol. ci (1867), pp. 427–43.

OLIPHANT, MARGARET OLIPHANT WILSON, *Memoir of the Life of Laurence Oliphant and of Alice Oliphant, his Wife*, 2 vols (Edinburgh and London, 1891).

OSBORN, SHERARD, 'A Cruise in Japanese Waters', *Blackw.*, vol. lxxxiv (1858), pp. 635–46; vol. lxxxv (1859), pp. 49–70, 239–50, 393–412 and 532–45.

OSBORN, SHERARD *A Cruise in Japanese Waters*, 1st and 2nd edns (Edinburgh and London, 1859).

OSBORN, SHERARD, 'China and the War', *Quar. Rev.*, vol. cvii (1860), pp. 85–118.

OSBORN, SHERARD *Japanese Fragments* (London, 1861).

' "Ours" in Japan', *Fraser.*, vol. iii, new series, (1871), pp. 555–62.

PORTER, MRS GERALD *Annals of a Publishing House, John Blackwood* (Edinburgh and London, 1898).

REDESDALE, LORD – see Mitford

REED, EDWARD JAMES, *Japan: its History, Tradition and Religions*, 2 vols (London, 1880).

REEVE, HENRY, 'Lord Elgin's Mission to China and Japan', *Edin. Rev.*, vol. cxi (1860), pp. 96–118.

REEVE, HENRY, 'Sir Rutherford Alcock's *Japan*', *Edin. Rev.*, vol. cxvii (1863), pp. 517–40.

REEVE, HENRY, 'Letters and Journals of Lord Elgin', *Edin. Rev.*, vol. cxxxvii (1873), pp. 39–56.

REEVE, HENRY, 'Baron Hübner's *Trip round the World*', Edin. Rev., vol. cxxxviii (1873), pp. 65–94.

ROYAL GEOGRAPHICAL SOCIETY, THE, *Journal of the Royal Geo-*

graphical Society, vol. xx (1851).
RUNDALL, THOMAS, *Memorials of the Empire of Japon: in the XVI and XVII Centuries* (London, 1850).
RUSSELL, CHARLES WILLIAM, 'The Lama of Tibet', *Dubl. Rev.*, vol. xxxiii (1852), pp. 1–45.
RUSSELL, CHARLES WILLIAM, 'Japan', *Dubl. Rev.*, vol. xxxiii (1852), pp. 267–92.
RUSSELL, CHARLES WILLIAM, 'Oliphant's Japan', *Dubl. Rev.*, vol. xlviii (1860), pp. 401–22.
'S.', 'The American Expedition to Japan', *Lawson's Merchant's Magazine, Statist and Commercial Review*, vol. i, (1852), pp. 36–9.
SAITÔ, *Edo meisho zue* (Pictorial Guide to the Famous Spots of Edo) (Edo, 1834–36).
SATOW, ERNEST MASON, *A Diplomat in Japan (London, 1921)*.
SENDAI KYÔDOSHI HENSAN IINKAI, (Committee for the Local History of Sendai in Kagoshima Prefecture) (ed.), *Ishin sen'eki jûgunki* (Soldiers' Journals from Battles during the Restoration Period), (Sendai, 1974).
SHAND, ALEXANDER INNES, 'Vienna in Exhibition-Time', *Blackw.*, vol. cxiv (1873), pp. 442–58.
SHAND, ALEXANDER INNES, 'The Romance of Japanese Revolution', *Blackw.*, vol. cxv (1874), pp. 696–712.
SHAND, ALEXANDER INNES, 'Foreign Opinion on England in the East', *Blackw.*, vol. cxxiii (1878), pp. 734–54.
SHIN, YOO HAN, *Kai yû roku* (The Record of a Seaborne Journey), trans. Kan Je On, (Tokyo, 1974).
SMITH, GEORGE, *Ten Weeks in Japan* (London, 1861).
STEINMETZ, ANDREW, *Japan and Her People* (London, 1859).
STEPHEN, JAMES FITZJAMES, 'Japan', *Fraser.*, vol. lxix (1864), pp. 101–17.
S[TEVENSON], R[OBERT] L[OUIS], 'Yoshida-Torajiro', *Cornhill.*, vol. xli (1880), pp. 327–34.
TAKAHASHI KYÔICHI, *Uraga bugyô shi* (The History of the Uraga Magistrates) (Tokyo, 1974).
'TALES OF OLD JAPAN', *Saturday Rev.*, vol. xxxi (1871), pp. 317–18.
TERAKADO, SEIKEN, *Edo hanjô ki* (The Record of Flourishing Edo) (Edo, 1832–36).
THUNBERG, CHARLES PETER, *Travels in Europe, Africa, and Asia, Made between the Years 1770 and 1779*, 2nd edn, (London, 1795).
TREMENHEERE, JOHN HENRY, 'Japan', *Quar. Rev.*, vol. cxiv (1863), pp. 449–80.
TRONSON, JOHN M., *Personal Narrative of a Voyage to Japan, Kamtschatka, Siberia, Tartary, and Various Parts of Coast of China; in H.M.S. Barracouta* (London, 1859).
T[URNER], F[REDERICK] S[TORRS], 'Feudal China', *Cornhill.*, vol. xxx (1874), pp. 548–55.
UNESCO Higashi Ajia Bunka Kenkyûsho (UNESCO Research Centre for East-Asian Cultures) (ed.), *Shiryô oyatoi gaikokujin* (Data on the Foreign Employees in the Meiji Government) (Tokyo, 1975).

VELEY, MARGARET, 'A Japanese Fan', *Cornhill.*, vol. xxxiv (1876), pp. 379–84.
Vocabvlaro da Lingoa de Iapam (Nagasaki, 1603).
VON HÜBNER – see de Hübner
'A WONDERER ON A RAFT' 'What the Chinese Really Think of Europeans, by a Native Literate', *Fraser.*, vol. iii, new series (1871), pp. 395–406.
WATANABE, SHÛJIRÔ *Abe Masahiro jiseki* (The Record of Abe Masahiro) vol. I, (Tokyo, 1910).
WEDDERBURN, DAVID, 'Maoris and Kanakas', *Fort. Rev.*, vol. xxi, new series (1877), pp. 782–802.
WEDDERBURN, DAVID, 'Modern Japan', *Fort. Rev.*, vol. xxiii, new series (1878), pp. 417–28.
WEDDERBURN, DAVID, 'Modern Japan II', *Fort. Rev.*, vol. xxiii, new series (1878), pp. 529–42.
'WHAT WE KNOW ABOUT JAPAN', *Bentley's Miscellany*, vol. xxxi (1852), pp. 545–52.
WHITE, JAMES, 'Lord Elgin's Mission to China and Japan', *Blackw.*, vol. lxxxvii (1860), pp. 255–77.
WHITTINGHAM, PAUL B., *Notes on the Late Expedition against the Russian Settlements in Eastern Siberia; and of a Visit to Japan and to the Shores of Tartary, and of the Sea of Okhotsk* (London, 1856).
WILSON, ANDREW, 'The Inland Sea of Japan', *Blackw.*, vol. xc (1861), pp. 613–23.
WYATT, MATTHEW DIGBY, 'Orientalism in European Industry', *Macmillan.*, vol. xxi (1870), pp. 551–6.
YOKOYAMA, TOSHIO, 'Han kokka e no michi (Towards the Establishment of Han States)', Hayashiya Tatsusaburô (ed.) *Kasei bunka no kenkyû* (Studies of Japanese Culture in the Bunka and Bunsei Eras) (Tokyo, 1976).
YOKOYAMA, TOSHIO, 'Shin koku e no michi (Towards the Divine Country)', Hayashiya Tatsusahurô (ed.) *Bakumatsu bunka no kenkyû* (Studies of Japanese Culture in the Late Tokugawa Era) (Tokyo, 1978).

Other works consulted

ALCOCK, RUTHERFORD, *Elements of Japanese Grammar, for the Use of Beginners* (Shanghai, 1861).
ALCOCK, RUTHERFORD, *Familiar Dialogues in Japanese, with English and French Translation* (London, 1863).
ADBURGHAM, ALISON, *Liberty's, a Biography of a Shop* (London, 1975).
ALTICK, RICHARD, *The English Common Reader, a Social History of the Mass Reading Public 1800–1900* (Chicago, 1963).
ARTS COUNCIL OF GREAT BRITAIN, THE, '*From today painting is dead*', *The Beginning of Photography* (London, 1972).
ASTON, WILLIAM GEORGE, *A Grammar of the Japanese Written Language, with a Short Chrestomathy* (London, 1872).
ASTON, WILLIAM GEORGE, *A Short Grammar of the Japanese Spoken Language*, 2nd edn, (Belfast, 1871).
BEASLEY, WILLIAM GERALD, *Great Britain and the Opening of Japan*,

1834–1858 (London, 1951).
BOLT, CHRISTINE ANNE, *Victorian Attitudes to Race* (London and Toronto, 1971).
BOULDING, KENNETH EWART, *The Image* (Ann Arbor, 1956).
BRASSEY, THOMAS, 'Round the World in the "Sunbeam", V (Conclusion): Across the Pacific', *Nineteenth Century*, vol. iii (1878), pp. 667–86.
BRIDGE, CYPRIAN ARTHUR GEORGE, *Some Recollections* (London, 1918).
BROOKS, CHARLES WOLCOTT, *Japanese Wrecks, Stranded and Picked up adrift in the North Pacific Ocean, Ethnologically Considered . . .* (San Francisco, 1876).
BROWN, DON, 'On the Significance of the Asiatic Society of Japan': introduction to the reprint edn of *Transactions of the Asiatic Society of Japan* (1st series, vols. i–l, 1872–1922) (Tokyo, 1965), index volume.
BROWN, S. R., *Colloquial Japanese, or Conversational Sentences and Dialogues in English and Japanese . . .* (Shanghai, 1863).
'The Centenary of "The Quarterly Review" ', *Quar. Rev.*, vol. ccx (1909), pp. 731–74; vol. ccxi (1909), pp. 279–324.
CHURCH MISSIONARY SOCIETY, THE, (ed.) The *Church Missionary Intelligencer and Record*, vol. viii, new series (London, 1872) – onwards.
COOK, MARK, *Perceiving Others, the Psychology of Interpersonal Perception* (London and New York, 1979).
DANIELS, GORDON, 'Contemporary British Assessments of Bakumatsu Japan: Major Books and Reviews', Ian Nish (ed.) *Bakumatsu and Meiji Studies in Japan's Economic and Social History/International Studies 1981/2* (London, 1982).
DAVIS, JOHN FRANCIS, *China: A General Description of that Empire and its Inhabitants; with the History of Foreign Intercourse down to the Events which Produced the Dissolution of 1857 . . .*, 2 vols (London, 1857).
DAWSON, RAYMOND, *The Chinese Chameleon, an Analysis of European Conceptions of Chinese Civilization* (London, 1967).
DE CHARLEVOIX, PIERRE FRANÇOIS XAVIER, *Histoire et description generale du Japon*, 9 vols (Paris, 1736).
DE FONBLANQUE, EDWARD BARRINGTON, *Niphon and Pe-che-li; or, Two Years in Japan and Northern China* (London, 1862).
DILKE, CHARLES WENTWORTH, *Greater Britain*, 8th edn (London, 1885).
DOUGLAS, ROBERT KENNAWAY, 'The Marriage of the Emperor of China', *Cornhill.*, vol. xxvii (1873). pp. 82–8.
EIDELBERG, MARTIN, 'Bracquemond, Delâtre and the Discovery of Japanese Prints', *Burlington Magazine*, vol. cxxiii (1981).
ELLEGÅRD, ALVAR, 'Public Opinion and the Press: Reactions to Darwinism', *Journal of the History of Ideas.* vol. xix (1958), pp. 379–87.
EVERETT, EDWIN MALLARD, *The Party of Humanity, The Fortnightly Review and its Contributors 1865–1874* (New York, 1971).
FAIRBANK, JOHN KING, *China Perceived, Images and Politics in Chinese American Relations* (London, 1976).
FORTUNE, ROBERT, *Two Visits to the Tea Countries of China and the British Tea Plantations in Himalaya . . .*, 2 vols (London, 1853).

Select Bibliography

FORTUNE, ROBERT, *A Residence among the Chinese; Inland, on the Coast, and at Sea* . . . (London, 1857).
FOX, GRACE, *Britain and Japan, 1858–1883* (Oxford, 1969).
FUJIOKA, YOSHINARU, *Image to ningen* (Image and Man), (Tokyo, 1973).
GATENBY, EDWARD VIVIAN, 'The Influence of Japan on English Language and Literature', *Transactions and Proceedings of Japan Society*, vol. xxxiv (1936–37), pp. 37–64.
GWYNN, STEPHEN AND TUCKWELL, GERTRUDE, *The Life of the Rt. Hon. Sir Charles W. Dilke*, 2 vols (London, 1917).
HALL, IVAN PARKER, *Mori Arinori* (Cambridge, Mass., 1973).
HAWKS, FRANCIS LISTER, *Narrative of the Expedition of an American Squadron to the China Seas and Japan, Performed in the Years 1852, 1853 and 1854 under the Command of Commodore M. C. Perry* . . . *by Order of the United States*, 3 vols (Washington, 1856).
HENDERSON, PHILIP, *The Life of Laurence Oliphant, Traveller, Diplomat and Mystic* (London, 1956).
HODGSON, CHRISTOPHER PEMBERTON, *A Residence at Nagasaki and Hakodate in 1859–1860* (London, 1861).
HOUGHTON, WALTER EDWARDS, *The Victorian Frame of Mind: 1830–1870* (New Haven, 1957).
HUC, ÉVARISTE RÉGIS, *L'Empire chinois* . . ., 2 vols, 2nd edn (Paris, 1854).
HUXLEY, LEONARD, *The House of Smith Elder* (London, 1923), chs XIV and XXIV: concerning the publication of *Cornhill*.
IMPEY, OLIVER, *Chinoiserie, the Impact of Oriental Styles on Western Art and Decoration* (London, 1977).
IRIE, AKIRA (ED.), *Mutual Images, Essays in American Japanese Relations* (Cambridge, Mass., 1975).
ISAACS, HAROLD R., *Scratches on Our Minds. American Image of China and India* (New York, 1958).
ISHII, TAKASHI, *Meiji ishin no kokusaiteki kankyô* (The International Conditions for the Meiji Restoration), enlarged edn (Tokyo, 1966).
ISHIZUKI, MINORU, *Kindai nihon no kaigai ryûgaku shi* (History of Overseas Studies of Modern Japanese Students) (Kyoto, 1972).
IVES, COLTA FELLER, *The Great Wave: The Influence of Japanese Woodcuts on French Prints* (New York, 1974).
JENKYNS, RICHARD, *The Victorians and Ancient Greece* (Oxford, 1980).
KIERNAN, VICTOR GORDON, *The Lords of Human Kind, European Attitudes towards the Outside World in the Imperial Age* (London, 1969).
KURATA, YOSHIHIRO, *1885-nen London Nihonjin mura* (The Japanese Village in London – 1885) (Tokyo, 1983).
LANE-POOLE, STANLEY AND DICKINS, FREDERIC VICTOR, *The Life of Sir Harry Parkes*, 2 vols (London and New York, 1894).
LEHMANN, JEAN-PIERRE *The Image of Japan: From Feudal Isolation to World Power, 1850–1905* (London, 1978).
LEHMANN, JEAN-PIERRE (ed.), 'Britain and Japan – Mutual Images', *Proceedings of the British Association for Japanese Studies*, vol. v – Part One (1980), pp. 149–204.

'M.', 'The "Fortnightly" – A Retrospect', *Fort. Rev.*, vol. lxix, new series (1901), pp. 104–17.
MACLEOD, N., *Japan and the Lost Tribes of Israel* (Nagasaki, 1879).
MASUDA, TAKESHI, *Bakumatsuki no eikokujin* (An Englishman of the Late Tokugawa Period) (Tokyo, 1980).
MAX MÜLLER, FRIEDRICH, 'On the "Enormous Antiquity" of the East', *Nineteenth Century*, vol. xxix (1891), pp. 796–810.
MINOR, EARL, *The Japanese Tradition in British and American Literature* (Princeton, 1958).
MITFORD, ALGERNON BERTRAM FREEMAN-, *The Bamboo Garden* (London, 1896).
MITFORD, ALGERNON BERTRAM FREEMAN-, (LORD REDESDALE), *The Garter Mission to Japan* (London, 1906).
MITFORD, ALGERNON BERTRAM FREEMAN-, (LORD REDESDALE), *A Tragedy in Stone and Other Papers* (London, 1912).
NIHON NO EIGAKU HYAKUNEN HENSHÛBU (The Editorial Board of the Book as follows) *Nihon no eigaku hyakunen* (The Hundred Years of English Learning in Japan) (the Meiji vol.) (Tokyo, 1968).
NISH, IAN, *Japanese Foreign Policy 1869–1942, Kasumigaseki to Miyakezaka* (London, 1977).
OKA, YOSHITAKE, *Reimeiki no Meiji Nippon* (The Meiji Japan in its Dawn) (Tokyo, 1966).
PALMER, AARON HAIGHT, *Documents and Facts Illustrating the Origin of the Mission to Japan* (Washington, 1857).
PASTON, GEORGE, *At John Murray's, Record of a Literary Circle 1843–1892* (London, 1932).
The *Phoenix, a Monthly Magazine for China, Japan & Eastern Asia* (London, 1870–73).
RAFFLES, THOMAS STAMFORD, *The History of Java*, 2 vols, (London, 1817), vol. ii.
REDESDALE, LORD – see Mitford
ROBINSON, RONALD AND GALLAGHER, JOHN WITH DENNY, ALICE, *Africa and the Victorians, the Official Mind of Imperialism*, 2nd edn (London, 1981); 1st edn published 1961.
ROSTOW, WALT WHITMAN, *British Economy of the Nineteenth Century*, reprint edn (oxford, 1961); 1st edn published 1948.
RUSKIN, JOHN, *Time and Tide* (London, 1867).
SAKATA, YOSHIO AND YOSHIDA, MITSUKUNI (eds), *Sekaishi no naka no Meiji Ishin* (The Meiji Restoration in World History) (Kyoto, 1973).
SATOW, ERNEST MASON, *An Austrian Diplomat in the Fifties* (The Rede Lecture Delivered in the Cambridge Senate-House on June 13, 1908) (Cambridge, 1908).
SCHENK, HANS GEORGE, *The Mind of the European Romantics: an Essay in Cultural History* (London, 1966).
SCOTT, JOHN WILLIAM ROBERTSON, *The Story of the Pall Mall Gazette, of its First Editor Frederic Greenwood, and of its Founder George Murray Smith* (London, 1950), ch X: 'Cornhill' under Eight Editors.
SHATTOCK, JOANNE AND WOLFF, MICHAEL (eds), *The Vicorian*

Periodical Press: Samplings and Soundings (Leicester and Toronto, 1982), chs I, VI and IX.
SMITH, ARTHUR H., *Chinese Characteristics*, 5th edn, revised (Edinburgh and London, 1900).
SUMMERS, JAMES (ed.), *The Chinese and Japanese Repository* (London), 1863–65).
SWIFT, JONATHAN, *Gulliver's Travels* (London, 1726), Parts II and III.
TANIGAWA, KEN'ICHI (ed.), *Nihon shomin seikatsu shiryô shûsei* (Collected Documents from the Lives of Japanese Common People), vol. XII (Tokyo, 1971).
TAYLOR, ANNE, *Laurence Oliphant, 1829–1888* (Oxford, 1982).
THE TIMES (ed.), *The History of The Times, the Tradition Established, 1841–1884* (London, 1939).
TREDREY, FRANK D., *The House of Blackwood, 1804–1954. The History of a Publishing Firm* (Edinburgh and London, 1954).
VENN, HENRY, *The Missionary Life and Labours of Francis Xavier, Taken from his Own Correspondence: with a Sketch of the General Results of Roman Catholic Missions among the Heathen* (London, 1862).
VICTORIA AND ALBERT MUSEUM, *The International Exhibition of 1862* (London, 1962).
VON SIEBOLD, PHILIPP FRANZ BALTHASAR, *Nippon: Archive zur Beschreibung von Japan . . .*, 20 vols, (Leiden, 1832–52).
WALLACE, DONALD MACKENZIE, 'The Territorial Expansion of Russia', *Fort. Rev.*, vol. xx, new series (1876), pp. 145–66.
WEISBERG, GABRIEL P., 'Japonisme: Early Sources and the French Printmaker 1854–1882', in G. P. Weisberg, Phillip Dennis Cate, Gerald Needham, Martin Eidelberg and William R. Johnston, *Japonisme, Japanese Influence on French Art 1854–1910*, reprint edn (London, 1975).
WILKINSON, ENDYMION, *Gokai* [misunderstanding], *Europe versus Japan* (Tokyo, 1981).
YOKOYAMA, TOSHIO, 'Mitford and Murata – Two Critical Minds on Popular Images between Britain and Japan in the Early Meiji Period', *Proceedings of the British Association for Japanese Studies*, V–Part One (1980), pp. 155–63.
YOKOYAMA, TOSHIO, 'Victoriaki Igirisu ni okeru Nihonzô keisei ni tsuite no oboegaki (Some Notes on the Formation of Japanese Images in Victorian England) – part one & two', *Zinbun Gakuhô* (Kyoto), vol. xlviii (1980), pp. 1–24; vol. 1 (1981), pp. 55–83.
YOKOYAMA, TOSHIO, 'Fushigi no Yôroppa' (F. Marshall's Discovery of 'the Strange Europe'), Yoshida Mitsukuni (ed.) *Jûkyûseiki Nihon no jôhô to shakaihendô* (Information and Social Change in 19th Century Japan) (Kyoto, 1985).
YOSHIDA, MITSUKUNI, *Ryôyô no me* (Eastern Eyes and Western Eyes) (Tokyo, 1978).
ZELDIN, THEODORE, *France 1848–1945*, 2 vols (Oxford, 1973 and 1977).
ZUSHORYÔ (THE IMPERIAL ARCHIVES OF JAPAN), *Bakumatsu no kyûtei* (The Court towards the End of the Tokugawa Period) (Tokyo, 1922).

Index

Aberdeen, 36–7, 61
Adams, F. O., 111, 117, 121, 136, 141
Adams, William, 4, 17, 26, 54, 155
Admiralty, 31, 33, 41–2
Agri-Horticultural Society of India, 75
Aidé, Hamilton, 118
Ainsworth, W. H., 17
Akashi, 152
Alcock, Sir Rutherford, ix (1859, 63), Chapter 4, 168, 170, 172, 174
   appointed Minister to Japan, 63
   attitudes to Kaempfer, 70–1, 82, 155–6
   on contemporary writers on Japan, 125–6
   idea of progress, 128
   on the issue of treaty revision, 146
   on Japan in the late 1870s, 160, 163, 167
   on Japanese revolution, 109–12, 116–18, 120, 122, 125–6, 128–32, 138–44, 149–50
   journey from Nagasaki to Edo, 69–70
   knowledge of Japanese language, 98
   compared with Mitford, 100, 104
   Mitford's criticism of, 98
Aldershot, 76
Alieutian Islands, 156
Alps, 156
Amazon, HMS, 63
American
   diplomacy, 139
   Expedition to Japan, *see* Perry's Expedition
   officers in Hakodate, 64
   Revolution, 139
   whalers, 18
Americans, British attitudes to the, 17–9, 27–8

amiability, 6–7, 23, 47, 79, 162, 174
analogy, 16, 50, 71, 100, 174
ancient Graeco-Roman world, 159–60
Andô Hiroshige, *see* Hiroshige
Angelis, Father de, 8
Anglo-Japanese alliance, possibility of, 164
Anglo-Japanese Convention, viii (1854), 20, 27, 31–2
Anglo-Japanese Treaty, ix (1858), 20, 50, 71, 77
Anglo-Satsuma War, *see* bombardment of Kagoshima
anti-Christian policy, abandoned, x (1872), 128–9
anti-foreign movements, ix (1862), 68–9, 76, 78, 89, 112, 172, Plate 13
anti-Shogunate movement, xxii, 71
Apollo, 161
aptitude, 139
Arabian Nights, The, 42, 44, 48, 125
Arcadia, 162
Archer, Frederic Scott, 189n.2
Ariosto, Ludovico, 13
Armstrong guns, 76
Arrow War, viii (1856), 20
Asakusa, 54, 62, 97
Ashington, Mrs, 21–31, 34
Asiatic Journal, 3
Asiatic Society of Japan, x (1872), 107, 168
Asiatics, 8, 58, 77
Aston, W. G., 107, 111, 118, 149, 168, 172
   criticised Marshall, 127–8
   on the issue of treaty revision, 146
   on the Iwakura Mission, 144
   on Japanese revolution, 138
Atami, 151
Atkinson, Hoffman, 113

Index

Aytoun, William, 20, 51, 55

Babylon, 15, 51
bath, 25, 49, 103, 161, Plate 17
beggars, 23, 53, 71, 152
Bentley's Miscellany, 2
Bible, 13, 49, 101
Bird, Isabella, xi (1880), 117, 125–6, 173, 175
Birmingham, 162, 166
Bismarck, xxi
Birmingham, 76
Bizen, 88–90
Black Current, 156
Black, John Reddie, 116–17
Blackwood, John, Chapter 2, 48, 65, 68, 123–4, 127, 134, 136, 171, 174
  declined Marshall's 'Justice Abroad', 146–8
  friend of Marshall, 119
  friend of Shand, 104
  last years of, 164
Blackwood, William, 29, 30, 32, 36–7, 66
Blackwood's Magazine, 20, Chapter 2, 51, 68, 70, 74, 78–9, 104, 111, 116, 118, 123–5, 127–8, 134, 142, 145–7, 168, 171
  became less concerned with Japan, 164
  general character of, xxiii
  ledger of, 206n. 67
  Marshall's first article in, 119
  number of copies printed, 29, 44
blue and white China, 94
Blue Books, 33, 35–6, 120
bombardment of Kagoshima (Satsuma) and Shimonoseki (Chôshû), ix (1863, 4), xxi, 68, 76, 83–5, 112, 137, 163
Bombay, 77
boots, 162
Borgia, 86
botanical specimens of Japan, 75
bowing, 155, 171, 173
boxing games, 91
Bracquemond, Felix, viii (1856), 75
Brahmin, 25, 135

Bridge, Sir Cyprian A. G., 131, 137, 152–4, 157, 160–2, 165–6, 173
Bridges, John Henry, 163
British
  anxiety, 48, 84–5, 138, 163, 166–8, 171, 175
  Association for the Advancement of Science, 61
  census paper, 62
  centres of trade, 144
  community in Japan, 68
  factories, 144
  Legation in Edo (Tokyo), 66, 69, 71, 105, 111, 117, 121
  Legation, attack on, ix (1862), 66, 68, Plate 13
  lower classes, 106
  machinery, 144
  Museum, 130
  navigators, 60
  Parliament, 69, 84
  scholarship on Japan, xx, 116–18, 168
  security in the Far East, 163
  upper classes, 59
Brittany, 107
Brooks, Charles Wolcott, 156
Buddhism, 11–12, 88, 129
Buddhist, 129
  temples, destruction of, 128
bunmei-kaika, 107
Busk, Mrs William, 3–5, 8–10, 13–14

Cambridge, 118
Canton, 35
Cantonese, 52
Capital of the Tycoon by Alcock, ix (1863), 68–74, 78, 85
  number of copies printed, 70
Cartwright, William, 147
Catholic, 12, 14, 86
ceremonial rules, 15
Ceylon, 12
chalêts, 24
Chamberlain, Basil Hall, 105, 107, 118, 150, 168
Charlevoix, Pierre François Xavier de, 4, 46, 60
chastity, 7, 8–9, 86, 103

Index

children, 154
China, 32, 34, 88, 120, 130, 152, 163, 172
  British relations with, 1
  different from Japan, 24, 156–7
  Elwin's image of, 106
  European ideas about, 170
  images about 1860, 50–1, 58
  as a market, xxii
  Mitford's memoirs of his days in, 175
  Oliphant's stay in, 37
  Osborn's criticism of the British system in, 28
China and the Chinese, 52, 59
China Mail, the, 2, 79
Chinaman, White's view of, 44, 50
Chinese
  abroad, 135
  anti-progressive, 163
  city, 156
  Classics, 101
  cultural influence on Japan, 156
  different from the Japanese, 14–15, 44, 156
  Elwin's idea of, 106
  goods to Vienna, 115
  high officials, 25, 58
  life in country side, 106
  as a money changer, 15
  prison, 35
Chinese and Japanese Repository, 117
chitôn, 161
chivalry, 8–9, 13, 26
Chôshû (chôshiu), 76, 121, 137
christianity, 11, 93
  and civilisation, 87
  and commerce, 85, 170
  Japan re-opened to, 128–9
  reintroduction to Japan, 7, 52, 57
Christians, extirpation of, 17, 47
Christie, Manson and Woods, 76
Church Missionary Intelligencer and Record, 129
Cincinnatus, 161
Circassian, 57
Circumnavigation, *see* round-the-world tours
civil war after Meiji Restoration, 83, 88
civilisation, 87, 128, 170–1
  Britain's mission of, 163
  in Japan, 15, 25, 45, 60–1, 77, 79, 107, 166
  Eastern, 4, 175
  Drummond-Davies's idea of, 60
  Knox's idea of, 18–9
  modern Western, 83, 150, 152, 162–5, 168
  Reeve's idea of, 145
  Wedderburn's idea of, 166
  Western, 23, 86
civility, 23, 26, 46, 60, 63, 154
class-consciousness, 62–3
classical world, 159–62
cleanliness, 23, 25, 79, 153, 155–6
clichés, 173–4
Cocks, Richard, 4, 24
Columbus, Christopher, 1
Communism, 139
Confacianism, 11–12, 68, 88
constititional monarchy, 82
consular jurisdiction, 145–8
contradictory features of Japan, 80, 174
  see also paradoxical
Cook, Edward Dutton, 95
Cooke, Wingrove, 31–2, 35, 41, 43
coolies of Japan, 155
Cornhill Magazine, ix (1860), 88–9, 92–3, 96–8, 102, 111, 118, 158
  its editorial documents, 95, 194n. 33
  sales of the first issue of, 76
corruption, 103–4, 140, 146
Corsican mountaineer, 9
Council of State, 10, 14, 70, 73, 138
courtesans, 70, 98, 103
courtesy, 6, 8, 9, 19, 26, 51, 80, 159, 166
Crawfurd, Oswald, 113
cremation, 161
Crimean War, viii (1853), 20, 32, 34
cruelty, 9, 46–7, 78
Cruise in Japanese Waters, A, by Osborn, 38, 53
  number of copies printed, 31
  publication ledger of, 33, 41

Index

Crystal Palace, 19

Daguerre, L. J. M., 189n. 2
Dai Nihon, 154
Daibutsu (Daiboudhs), 129, Plate 23
daimyo, 73, 76, 97, 132, 143, 151, 160
daimyo-domains, 53, 75,
  abolition of, x (1871), xxii, 112, 134, 142, 151
Darwin, Charles, ix (1859), 92
Davis, Sir John Francis, 106
Dawson, Raymond, 170–1
decency, 162
de Fonblanque, Edward Barrington, 68, 71
de Hübner, *see* Hübner
deified heroes, 14
Dejima, 17
Delane, John, 4, 40, 127, 134
Delft, 166
Depression, Great, xi (1874), xxi, 164, 171
Devon, 24, 156
Dickens, Charles, 1, 180n. 107
Dickins, F. V., 117, 126, 175
dignity, 8, 58, 85, 90, 135
Dilke, Sir Charles Wentworth, x (1868), 112, 129, 143, 149, 151–2, 158–9, 163–5, 171, 173, 207n. 83
  sympathetic with Shimazu Hisamitsu, 137–8, 140
Diósy, Arthur, 113
Dixon, Thomas, 108
dockyards, 111, 144
Dodona, 160
Dorian youths, 161
Douglas, Robert Kennaway, 130
Draconian severity of Japanese law, 78
drawing-room, 67, 157
Drummons, James, 4, 8
Drummond-Davies, F. M., 48, 57, 60
Dunfermline, 37
Dublin Review, 2, 12, 46
Dutch, 1, 16, 17, 27, 70
  factory at nagasaki, 3, 5, 64
  language, 51
  trade, 75

earthquakes, 69, 78
East, distrust of England in the, 49
Eastern civilisation, *see* civilisation
Eastern design, 165
Edinburgh, 21, 37
  Duke of, 98
Edinburgh Review, 39, 46, 60, 69, 100, 110, 116, 121, 159, 164
  general character of, 4, 11,
  number of copies printed in 1852, 177n. 15
  editorship, xxiii, Chapter 2, 173–4, 180n. 107
Edo (Jedo, Yedo, Tokyo), 19, 60, 69, 74, 83, 86, 96–7, 101, 109, 151
  authorities' decrees when Lord Elgin landed, 54
  Bay of, 63
  Mitford's descriptions of, 97
  street scenes in, 50, 67
Edo hanjô ki, 97–8
Edo meisho zue, 97–8
education, 15, 90–1, 94, 132–3
Education, Japanese Ministry of, 101, 133
Education Act in Britain, x (1870), xxi
Education Law in Japan, General, x (1872), 132
educational system of Prussia, 15
Egawa, Tarozaemon, 63
elf-land, 150, 158, 175
Elgin, Lord (James Bruce), 20–2, 27, 33–6, 42, 44, 51, 54, 58, 64–5, 68, 120, 125, 172, 183n. 78
  acknowledged as a daimyo, 62–3
  participation in making Oliphant's *Narrative*, 36, 38
  letters of, 144
  Reeve's view of, 145
Elgin's Mission, *see* Lord Elgin's Mission
Elwin, Whitwell, 39, 43, 106
Emperor of China, 122
Emperor of Japan, xxii, 71, 100, 104, 122, 124
  see also Mikado
Empson, William, 4
English newspapers in Japan, 74,

116–8, 134
Enomoto, Takeaki, 143
equality, 79, 139
  see also levelling
espionage system, see Shogunate
Established Church, 14
Eton, 88, 91
European
  desks and chairs in Japan, 162
  residents, xx, 65, 140
Eves of Japan, 25
evolution, 60
Examiner, 40
excursions, 96
execution, 88–9, 91, 105
Exhibition (Exposition)
  of art and industries in Kyoto (1874), 151, 153, 165
  Great, viii (1851), 19
  of Japanese applied art in London, viii (1854), 75
  in Knightsbridge (Japanese Village), (1885), xix–xx
  London International, ix (1862), 75–6, 108, 115, Plates 7, 8
  Paris Universal, x (1867), 76, 115, Plate 18
  Paris Universal, xi (1878)
  Vienna Universal, xi (1873), 115, 134, 165, Plate 22
exhibitions (expositions), international, xxiii, 165
exoticism, 94–5
extraterritoriality, 164
  see also treaty revision

factual accuracy, xxii, 33, 36, 44–5, 55–6, 136, 143, 150, 172, 174
  see also realism
fairy-land, 23, 45
fairy tale, 44
famine, 53
Far East, 117
Farmer and Rogers, 75
Fertility of Japanese soil, 23
Fghono-Kami, see Higo
fires, 69, 78
Flemish burgher, 13
folk-tales, 104, 107

Fonblanque, see de Fonblanque
Foreign Office, 20, 42, 65, 69, 84–5, 88, 163
Foreign Office Papers, 92
foreigners' travels outside the treaty limits, 151
formalism, 166
Formosa, xi (1870), 130
Fortnightly Review, 95–6, 131, 148, 164
Fortune, Robert, 71, 75, 106
'Forty-seven Ronins', 95
foulness in China, 52, 156
Fox-hunting, 105
fragmentation of images of Japan, 75, 77, 80
France, 116, 171
Franco-Prussian War, x (1870), 164
Fraser's Magazine, 51, 72, 81, 87, 105
Free Church of Scotland, 49
free trade, xxi
French
  compared with the Japanese, 138
  Revolution, 139
Froude, James Anthony, 87
frugality, 79
  see also Japanese sumptuary laws
Fujisawa, 101
Fujiyama, see Mt Fuji
Fukuchi, Gen'ichirô, xix
Fukuoka, 131
Furious, HMS, 21, 27, 31

Gaikokujin naichi ryokô, 151
gentleman, 90–1, 93–4, 96, 131, 138, 155, 159, 173
gentleness, 6, 8–9, 58, 155, 166
gentry, xxiii, 95
George Eliot, 21, 95
German Empire, x (1871)
Germany, xxi, 107, 171
  see also Prussia
Gilbert and Sullivan, xi (1885), xx, 87
Gilbert, W. S., xix–xx, 172–3
Glasgow, 37
globe-trotters, 198n. 6, Plate 24
  see also round-the-world tours
Gobi Desert, king of, 148
gold, 63–4

Golownin, Wasily M., 3–5, 8–9, 12, 14
good breeding, 47, 58–9, 154, 166
gôshi, 104
Gotô, Shôjirô, 93
grace, 25, 56–8, 80, 159
Graeco-Roman world, ancient, 159–61
graphic, 24, 28, 70
Great Depression, *see* Depression
Great Exhibition, *see* Exhibition
Greater Britain by Dilke, 112
Greece
 ancient, 99, 159–60
 modern, 25
Greek sculpture, 159
Greeks, 14
Greenock, 37–8
Grey, third Earl, 84
grotesqueness, 82, 157, Plates 9, 10, 11
Grove, George, 127
guidebook, 97
Gulliver's Travels, 44
gun-boat policy, 17

Habersham, A. W., 51, 55
Hagi, 131
Hakodate, 48, 57–8, 64, 67
Hakone, 97, 151
Hansard, Albert W., 116
happy country, 155, 173
happy despatch, 81, 89, 96, 112–13, 131, 173
happy Japanese, 11, 23, 26, 79
hara-kiri, *see seppuku*
harlot of Yokohama, 103
Harris, Thomas Lake, 83–4
Hawaii, 156
Hawks, Francis Lister, 60
Hayward, Abraham, 116, 140
Hegt, M. J. B. Noordhoek, 116
Henry Colburn, 3
Herbert, Lady Mary Elizabeth, 116–17
hero-worship, 99, 161
heroism, 96
Highlands of Scotland, 24
Higo, Lord, 97

Hindu, 135
Hirata school, 128
Hiroshige, 38, 157
History of Japan by F. O. Adams, 141
History of Japan by Kaempfer, 3
Hizen, 121
Hodgson, C. P., 68, 71
Hokusai, viii (1856), 38, 75, 157
'holier-than-thou' attitude, 84
homogeneity of mankind, 99, 101–2, 104, 106
Honda, Rimei, 109–10
Hong Kong, 115, 150
horse-racing, 105
hot springs, 151
Household Words, 4, 20, 22, 48, 50, 180n. 107
House, E. H., 102, 137
Howell, W. D., 117, 201n. 128
Hübner, Joseph Alexander von (de), xi (1873), 116, 125, 129, 134, 151–2, 157–9, 174
 met the Mikado, 121–2
Huc, Évariste Régis, 2, 106
Humbert, Aimé, 129
humour, Japanese sense of, 26, 155
humorousness of things Japanese, 80, 82, 157–8
Huxley, Thomas, ix (1863), 92
Hyôgo (Kobe), 73–4, 86, 88–9

ichiko, 100
idolatry, 99, 129
Ii, Naosuke, 70
Illustrated London News, 76, 117, 137
illustrations, 38, 180n. 113
Imabari, 152, 154, 161
imitation, 135–7, 139–40, 144, 165–6, 171
imitative character, 23, 64–5, 107, 175
immutability, 6–7, 47, 177n. 24
Imperial University, 105, 133
incontinence, *see* licentiousness
India, 12, 15, 24, 49, 79
Indian Army, 29
Indian 'Mutiny', viii (1857), 20
indifference to death, 80
indifference to religion, 11, 129
industrialised Britain, 162

Inland Sea of Japan, 79, 160
inner life, 88, 96, 118, 170
intelligence, 8, 25, 58, 144
intemperance, 78
interior of Japan, 69, 75, 146, 150–1
international exhibitions (expositions), *see* exhibition
international law, 82
'International Vanities' by Marshall, 123
Ireland, 15, 107
Isaiah, 87
Isle of Wight, 24, 43
Itagaki, Taisuke, 121
Ivanhoe, 15
Iwakura Mission, x (1871), 110–11, 115, 119, 144
Iwakura, Tomomi, 112, 121, 124, 127, 130, 152
Iwase, Tadanari, 26, 58
Izu, 97

Jack and the Beanstalk, 113
James I, King of England, 24
Japan
  different from China, 24, 156–7
  as the England of the Pacific, 15
  as a market, xxii, 51
Japan Society, London, 113
Japan Commercial News, 84, 116
Japan Express, 116
Japan Gazette, 117
Japan Herald, 116–17, 122
Japan Mail, 117
Japan Punch, 117
Japan Times, 93, 116
Japan Weekly Paper, 132, 140
Japanese
  army, 107, 111, 130
  art, 38, 108, 166
  art and industry, 46, 75, 153
  arts and crafts, 47, 57, 79, 82, 115, 157–8, 165–6
  athletes, 162
  Board of Revenue and Customs, 111
  Buddhist temple, Plate 1
  budget table, 127
  carpenter, 81

castles, 23, 53, 151
children, 46, 49, 152, 154–5, 204n. 10, Plate 5
different from the Chinese, 14–5, 44, 156
Christians, 17, 47, 81
climate, 23–4, 50
clothing habits, 52, 157
comedians, 102
Commissioners, 26, 59, 64
common people, 64
conjurers, 98
coolies, 155
country folk, 53, 58, 150, 154, 161, 172, 204n. 10
countryside, 68, 71, Chapter 8
Court, 121–2, 125 (*see also* Kyoto Court)
court dress, Plate 10
craftsmen, 166
damsels, *see* Japanese maidens
dance, 161, Plate 25
design, 82
diviners, 100
dogs, 155
drama, *see* Japanese theatre
dwarfed shrubs, 154
Expedition to Formosa, xi (1874), 130
fan, 173
farmers, 52, 161
food habits, 53
fortune-tellers, 98
gardens, 23, 43, 57, 79, 152, 154, Plate 4
gentlemen, 90, 94, 131, 138, 159, 173
girls, 103, 153 (*see also* Japanese maidens)
goldfish, 154
goods to Europe, xxiii, 75
government, xxii, 89, 116
government, financial conditions of, 126–8
government, press censorship of, 117
governmental system, 9–11, 14, 71
hair styles, 157
higher classes, 25–6, 122

highways, 151
horticulture, 75
housing, 53
ideas of honour, 96
intellectuals, 12, 19, 51, 91, 98, 118, 168, 170
ivory carving, 57
jugglers, 108
junks, 156, 160
–Korean Treaty, xi (1876), 130–1
lacquerwares, 58, 75, 157, 162
ladies, 2, 8, 57, 60, 153, Plate 2 (*see also* Japanese women)
language, knowledge of, 69–70, 91, 96, 98, 104, 107, 154
Legation in Paris, 119, 146
Legation in Washington, 110
legends, 97, 99
love for flowers, 154
love of the picturesque, 152
maidens, 23, 48–9, 152–4
manners and customs, 6–9, 47, 70, 100
marriage, 13
married women's teeth and eyebrows, 2, 8, 56, 68
matted flooring, 162
men, 8, 46
merchants, 52, 54, 187n. 48
metal work, 58
middle and lower classes, 98
military class, 78, 91, 98 (*see also* samurai)
Ministry of Education, 102, 133
Ministry of Foreign Affairs, 118
music, 59
natural products, 47, 75
natural scenery, 24, 37, 47–8, 79, 108
navy, 111
New Year, 97
nobles, 47–8, 121, 137, 165
office buildings, 162
officials, 25–6, 58, 62, 78, 140, 172
performing monkeys, 98
political system, 70, 100
porcelain, 75, 157
prints, 75, 82, 157
prostitutes, 102 (*see also* prostitution)
racial origin, 14, 24–5, 49, 51–2, 159, 186n. 32
religions, 11–12, 70, 78, 80, 96
revolution, 110–2, 118, 121–2, 124, 129, 134–5, 139–43
roads, 18
screen, 155, 173
sermon, 88, 101, Plate 15
sensitivity to criticism, 61, 65
silk, 79
smiling, and laughing, 158–9
social classes, 62, 70, 104, 175
soldiers, 107, Plate 19
street entertainment, 50
students in Europe, 76, 140, 205n. 39
sumptuary laws, 52
swords, 79, 130, 187n. 48
tailor, 81
tea-gardens, 43, 49, Plate 4 (*see also* Japanese gardens)
tea-houses, 23, 48, 68, 70, 154
theatre, 62, 98, 102, 207n. 83, Plate 25
treaty ports, 145
tribunal, 78, 146
village, 152, 154, 171, Plate 3
village girls, 157
villagers, 153, 172
visitors to Europe, xxiii, 75, 134 (*see also* Japanese students)
warriors, *see* samurai
way of thought, 96
wife, 8
women, 7–8, 25, 46, 53, 86, 103–4, 155, 161–2, Plate 18 (*see also* Japanese ladies)
woodblock patterns, 75
Japonisme, 94, 136, Plate 22
Jesuits, 4, 16, 155
jinrikisha, 155, Plate 24
Jitsugokyô, 118
John Murray, 3, 30, 39, 75, 126
John Murray Archives, 194n. 33
Jonah's Gourd, 113
judicial quality in accounts of Japan, 134, 136, 174
see also factual accuracy

Index

'Justice Abroad' by Marshall, 146–8

Kabuki, *see* Japanese theatre
Kaempfer, Engelbert, 3–5, 7, 9–11, 23, 46, 54, 60, 82, 129, 157, 168
   Alcock's attitudes to, 70, 100, 155–6, 172
   stay in Japan, 185n. 7
   history of Japan, 3
   on the life of the Mikado, 9, 73
   theory of Japanese double sovreignty, 9, 68, 71–2
   theory of Semitic origin of the Japanese, 14–15, 25, 51
Kaga, Prince of, 73
Kegan Paul, 113
Kagoshima, *see* bombardment
Kaiseisho, 84
kaishaku, 90–1
Kamakura, 97–9, 129
Kamakura Shogun, 98
Kamchatka, 109
Kami, 12, 14
Kanagawa, *see* Yokohama
Kanakas, 25
Kanghwa Island Incident, 130
Katsu, Kaishû, 63
Katsushika, Hokusai, *see* Hokusai
Kido, Takayoshi, 121, 124, 130
Kikuchi, Dairoku, 118
Kinglake, A. W., 21
King's College, London, 117
Knight-errant, 13, 96
Knox, Alexander, Chapter 1, 23, 60, 170, 173
Kobe, 151–2, 157
Kobe Incident, x (1868), 88
Kojima, Matajirô, 64
Korea, 66, 130
Korean Mission to Japan (1719), 53
Kûkai, 118
Kumamoto, 131
Kunisada, 38
Kuse Yamato no Kami, 73
Kyoto, 10, 53, 68, 71–3, 151–3, 165
Kyoto ceramics, 166
Kyoto Court, 71, 73, 89, 152–3, 178n. 61
Kyoto Incident, 201n. 124

Kyûô Dôwa, 88, 101

Labelais Club, 113
Lama of Tibet, 14
language for describing Japan, xxiii, 13–16, 49, 112–13, 174
Lanman, Charles, 110
laticlave, 161
Lawson's Merchant's Magazine, 2
Lay, Horatio Nelson, 117
Lee, Daniel, 75
Leland, C. G., 113
levelling of Japanese society, xxii, 129, 139
Lewes, George Henry, 95
Lewis Carroll, 159
liberality, 19
Liberty, Arthur, 75
Liberty's, 75
licentiousness, 47, 65, 78, 80, 102
lighthouses, 111
Lilliput, 44
Lindau, Rudolph, 164
Lindo, Mark Prager, 51, 62–3
linguists, 111, 117
Liverpool, 76
London, 109
London International Exhibition, *see* Exhibition
Longman, 70
Lord Elgin's Mission, viii (1857), 21, 28–9, 34–5, 41, 47, 50, 60, 62, 172
Louis XVIII, King of France, 14
Lowder, J. F., 111

MacDonald, John, 76
MacFarlane, Charles, 4, 6, 8–9, 12
Machi Bugyô, 54
Machiavelli, 86
Macmillan, Alexander, 127
Macmillan & Co., 104
Macmillan's Magazine, 111, 127, 145, 163, 172
'Maga', 185n. 115
Malays, 157, 186n. 32
Manchester, 75
maps of Japan, 38–9, 187n. 48
Marco Polo, 1

Margary, Augustus Raymond, 163
Mariner, HMS, 63
Maron, Hermann, 71
Marshall, Frederic, 122, 124–6, 132, 136–9, 142, 145, 168, 170–2, 174
  criticised by Aston, 127–8
  employed by Sameshima, 118–9
  'International Vanities' by, 123
  'Japan', 119–20
  'Justice Abroad' by, 146–8
  In Paris, 110
Masaki, Taizô, 118, 205n. 39
Massachusetts, 166
Mathison, Charles Mitchell, 63
Max Müller, Friedrich, x (1868), 92
Mayfair, 65
Meiji government, *see* Japanese government
Meiji Restoration, *see* Restoration
mendacity, 74, 78
Merovingian Dynasty, 14, 100
mésalliances, 9, 103
metaphors, xix, 16, 50, 82, 100–1, 159, 161, 174
Metternich, Prince, 116
Middle Ages, 13, 71, 82, 100, 125, 152
Middle Kingdom, 156–7
Midlands, 162
Mikado, 10, 14, 71–3, 82, 111–12, 123–4, 133, 143, 165, 173, Plate 21
  Kaempfer's account of the, 9
  Mitford's idea of the, 100
  Hübner met the, 121–2
Mikado, The, x (1885), xix–xx, 87, 173
Mill, John Stuart, xxii, 95
Minamiza Theatre, Plate 25
Minamoto, Yoritomo, *see* Yoritomo
mint, 111
mirror image, 61, 63, 65, 105, 169
Mitford, Algernon Bertram (Freeman-), (Lord Redesdale), x (1871), 87, Chapter 5, 109, 118, 129, 134, 137, 170, 173, 175
  criticised Alcock, 98
  defence of Japanese morality, 103

fluency in Japanese, 91, 96
Mito, 66, 68
Mitsukuri, Teiichirô, 84
Miyako Odori, 161, Plate 25
Mizuno, Tadakuni, 62
modernity, 162
Mongolians, 157, 186n. 32
morality, xxi, 80, 84, 103, 128
Morley, Henry, 1–2, 4, 15, 20, 22, 48, 50, 58–9, 73
Morley, John (Viscount Morley), 95, 148
Mossman, Samuel, 111, 117, 125, 134, 136, 143–4, 149, 174
Mounsey, A. H., 117, 126
Mount Fuji, 24, 157
Mount Ôyama, 99
Murata, Fumio, xxii
mushuku, 62

Nagasaki, 1, 4, 16–7, 22–3, 25, 44, 49, 52, 59, 61–2, 67, 83, 151, 156
Nagoya, 53
Nakai, Oshû, xxii
Nakasendô, 154
Napoleon Bonaparte, 14
Napoleon, Louis, viii (1851), 41
Narrative of Lord Elgin's Mission by Oliphant, ix (1859), 34–45, 59, 61, 65, 71, 78
  number of copies printed, 39
  publication ledger of, 40, 66
  reviews of, 46–8, 50, 59
Nathaniel Cooke, 3–4, 7
national character, xv, 7
national education, *see* education
National Library of Scotland, xxiii, 194n. 33
nationalism, xv, xxi, 175
nationality, xv, 175
Neale, Edward St John, 84
Nebuchadnezzar, 124
Nepal, 34
netsuke, 82
New Japan, 107, 109, 128, 133, 135, 137, 140, 144–5, 150, 159, 162, 167–8, 170
New Monthly Magazine and Humorist, 2, 17–8

New Quarterly Review, 20, 113
Newcastle, 76
Newgate prison, 93
New York Courier and Inquirer, 18
Nihonbashi, Plate 16
Niigata, 73–4, 86
9th Regiment, 105
nishikigi, 13, 179n. 89
Noh, 98, 118
non-Christian world, 92
  see also Graeco-Roman world
North British Review, 49, 52, 55, 57

obedience, 8, 46, 139
Ôkubo, Toshimichi, 124, 130
Ôkuma, Shigenobu, 121, 127
Okuyama, 98
Old Japan, 87, 109, 150, 152–4, 160, 162, 164, 168, 207n. 83
Oliphant, Laurence, ix (1859), 21, 28–47, 50, 52, 56, 59–61, 65–6, 68, 70, 73–4, 76, 79–80, 83, 86, 155, 167, 173–4
  Alcock criticised, 71, 125
  Blackwood's payment to, 40–1
  Reeve criticised, 78
  well-known writer, 34
Oliphant, Margaret, 21
open-mindedness, xxi, 92, 102, 123, 171
opium trade, 163
Opium War, viii (1840), 19, 180n. 105
Oriental character, 83
Orientals, 77, 135
  see also Asiatics
originality, 107, 171, 175
Osaka, 53, 74, 86, 151–2, 157
Osborn, Sherard, Chapter 2, 47, 49–56 60–2, 71, 173
Our Life in Japan, 105
Oxford, 88, 91–2
oyatoi gaikokujin, 125–7

Pacific liner service, 114
pagan, 99
Pall Mall East, 75
paradoxical features of Japan, 13, 23, 80–1
Paris, 75, 110, 116, 135

Paris Commune, x (1871), 106, 119, 139
Parkes, Sir Harry, ix (1865), 92, 105, 107, 131
pavilions, 94
Peking, ix (1860), 109
Peking Court, 33, 36
Peloponnesus, 25
Perry, Commodore, xxi, 18, 51, 53–4, 64, 71, 112
Perry's Expedition to Japan, viii (1853), 2, 4, 51, 53
  British attitudes towards, 17–19
Philippines, 156
Phoenix, 118
photographic accuracy, 67, 70, 100, 170
photographic realism, 77, 86
picturesqueness, 24, 55, 152, 157
plants from Japan, 76
pliancy, 143
political economy, 86
politeness, 26, 85, 154–5, 166
  see also civility
Polynesians, 157
Popes, 9
population, 16, 180n. 111
Portsmouth, 76
Portuguese, 70
poverty, 26, 71, 79, 152
pre-Raphaelites, 160
precision, see factual accuracy
progress, 60, 125, 128, 162
Promenade autour du monde by Hübner, xi (1873), 116
prosperity, 23, 25, 79
prostitution, 8, 39, 79, 98, 103
proverbs, 101
Prussia, 15
public bath-houses, see bath
public opinion, 93, 147
public works, 111, 126–7
publication in Japan, 132
punctilliousness, 17, 90

Quakers of the East, 26
Quarterly Review, 39, 42, 71, 106, 116, 126, 139, 141, 164
Quebec, 48

Index

radicalism of Japanese government, 138, 140
Raffles, Sir Thomas Stamford, 4
railway, x (1869, 71), 111, 162, Plate 21
realism, 67, 71, 77, 82, 86–7, 149–50, 170, 173
  see also factual accuracy
Redesdale, Lord, *see* Mitford
Reed, Sir Edward, 117, 125–6, 140
Reeve, Henry, 39, 114, 116, 120, 122, 124, 129, 133, 153, 158–9, 168, 173–4
  under Alcock's influence, 70, 72–3, 78–81, 84, 86
  idea of Japan about 1860, 46, 52, 58–9, 62–3, 65
  review of Lord Elgin's letters, 144–6
refinement, 56, 64, 105–6
resident writers on Japan, 68, 167–8, 172
respectability, 103, 162
Restoration of the Imperial Rule, x (1868), xxii, 87–8, 170
Revue des Deux Mondes, 164
rhetoric, *see* language
rice-riots, 83
Richard Griffin, 3
Richardson, Lennox, 163
Rickerby, Charles, 93, 116
rickshaws, 155, Plate 24
Rokko hills, 157
Roman galleys, 160
'Romance of Japanese Revolution' by Shand, 168
rônin, 66, 91, 94–5
round-the-world tours, 108, 112, 115–16, 150, 167, Plate 24
Royal Engineers, 48
Royal Geographical Society, 110
Royal Navy, 19, 27, 36, 38, 68, 118, 131, 152
Roza Francisco S. da, 116
ruffians, 91
Rundall, Thomas, 60
rural Japan, *see* Japanese countryside
Ruskin, John, 108
Russel, Charles, Chapter 1, 23, 46, 50, 65, 73, 173
Rusell, Lord John, 42, 63, 65, 84–5
Russia, 32, 84, 106
Russians, 26, 62, 78

Saigô, Takamori, 121, 130–1
St Petersburg, 113, 143
Saitô family, 97
Sameshima, Naonobu, 119–20, 125, 127, 145–6, 174, 203n. 57
samurai, 52, 62, 71, 88–95, 105, 129, 132, 137, 151–2, 155, 167, 173, 187n. 48, 201n. 124
  banned from bearing swords, 130
  insurrections of, 131
San Francisco, 108, 114, 156
Sanjô, Sanetomi, 121–2
Saris, John, 4, 17
Saruwaka-chô, 98
satire, 83, 86–7, 123–4, 173–4
Satow, Ernest, 92–3, 107, 117–8, 121–2, 168
Satsuma, 121
  Prince of, 86, 137
  Rebellion, xi (1877), 131, 139
  wares, 166
Saturday Review, 72, 106, 171
Savoy Theatre, xix, 173
schools in Japan, 132–3, 153, 173
Schoyer, Raphael, 116
Scotch Puritan, 9
Scott, Sir Walter, 15
Scottish country societies, 38
screw-schooner, 26
secularism, 11, 92
seclusion policy of the Shogunate, xxi, 7, 18, 23
self-disembowelment, 10, 83, 89, 91, 96
  see also seppuku
Self Help by Smiles, xxii
sensationalism, 31, 41
sensuality, 53
seppuku (hari-kiri), 2, 10, 81, 83, 88–9, 91–2, 96, 131, 173, Plate 14
Seward, William Henry, 121
Seymour, Sir Michael, 41–2
Shakespeare, 13

Index

Shand, Alexander Innes, 112–3, 116, 138, 149, 158, 165, 168, 173–5
    Marshall's attitude towards, 136
    met Japanese in Vienna, 134–6
    praise of Mitford, 104
Shanghai, viii (1843), 50, 150
Sheffield, 79
Shen Tien, 101
Shibata, Kyûô, 88, 101
Shimazu, Hisamitsu, 137, 163
Shimoda, 23, 63
Shikoku, 152
Shimonoseki, *see* bombardment
Shin, Yoo Han, 53
Shinagawa, 47
Shingaku, 88
Shinkoku, xxii
Shintoism, 11, 14, 88, 97, 99, 128
Shogun, x (1867), 9, 14, 25–6, 53, 97–8, 141, 143, 163, 187n. 48
    Kaempfer's theory of the, 9–10, 71
    Mission to Europe, ix (1862), 76, Plate 7
    no attribute of sovereignty, 71
Shogunate, 62, 71, 73, 100, 142–3, 152, 167
    espionage system of the, 141
    short-term visitors to Japan, 167, 172–3
    see also travellers
Siebold, Philipp Franz von, 3, 8
similies, 16, 100–1, 113, 174
    see also language
Sinicisation of Japanese images, 180n. 113
slavery, 15
Smiles, Samuel, xxii
Smith, Elder & Co., 194n. 33
Smith, Rev George, 68, 71
Smith, George, the publisher, 76, 95
Socialism, 139
Spain, 107
Spaniards, 70
Sparta, 160, 162
Speke, John Hanning, 21
Staffordshire, 166
Stanley, Lord, 92
steam navigation, 56, 120
steamer, 65
Stephen, Sir James Fitzjames, 72, 74, 77–9, 84, 87, 174
stereoscope, 67
Stevenson, Robert Louis, 118, 158–9, 166
Stirling, Sir James, 20, 27, 31–2, 37
strikes, 171
Student Interpreters, 69
Su Chou, 50
Suez Canal, x (1869)
suicide, 78, 89
    see also seppuku
Sullivan, Authur, xix
Summers, James, 117–8
Sumô wrestling, Plate 12
superstition, 15, 46, 99, 129
swashbucklers, 91
Swift, Jonathan, 1
Swiss Consul, 164

tagata, 161
Taiping Rebellion, viii (1850)
Taki, Zenzaburô, 88–95, 172
Talbot, W. H. F., 189n. 2
Tales of Old Japan by Mitford, x (1871), 104–5, 134
Taoism, 88
tariff autonomy, 145
    see also treaty revision
taste, 26, 50, 57–8, 64, 162, 165–6
tea-houses, *see* Japanese tea-houses
technology of communications, 172
telegraph, x (1871), 111, 120
Tempô Reforms, viii (1841), 53, 62, 103, 172
Tengu, 99
Terakado, Seiken, 97
terra incognita, 2, 54–5
Thackeray, ix (1860), 21, 76
theatre, *see* Japanese theatre
Thunberg, Charles Peter, 5, 7, 8, 70, 78
Tibet, 3, 171
Tientsin, 36
Tientsin Treaty, ix (1858), 35, 41, 50
Times, The, xx, 2, 4, 21, 24, 33, 40, 43, 65, 76, 92, 127, 131, 148
    coverage of Japan, 115
    correspondents, 34–35, 42, 134
    titles, 123–4
Titsingh, 46

Index

toasting, 64, 105
toga, 161
Tokugawa Inspectors, 54
Tokugawa government, 53, 84,
  see also Shogunate
Tokugawa regime, see Shogunate
Tokugawa Shogun, see Shogun
Tokyo, see Edo
Tory, 123, 137
Tosa, 121
tourists, see travellers
Tôzenji Incident, see British Legation
Tractarians, 12
travel books, 54
travellers to Japan, 152, 154–5, 157, 160, 167, 172, 175
treaty-limits, 151
treaty ports of Japan, 67, 69, 150–1
treaty revision, 87, 119, 144–8, 164
Tremenheere, John Henry, 71–3, 76, 79–80, 84–6, 174
Tronson, John M., 49, 52, 55, 57, 60
Troubridge, Edward Norwich, 63
Tsushima, 66
Turks, 6
Tycoon, see Shogun
Tycoon, title of, 190n. 27
Tyrian Astarte, 160

Unbeaten Tracks in Japan by Isabella Bird, xi (1880), 126
unchangeableness, see immutability
Universal Library by Blackwood, 3
Universal Library by Cooke, 4, 7
Uraga, 63–4
urbanity, 51, 62, 166
  see also civilisation
Utagawa Kunisada, see Kunisada

vaccination, 86
Vatican, 81, 116,
Venetian Oligarchy, 14
Venus, 161
vicarious responsibility, 167
Victoria, Queen of Great Britain, 25
Vienna, 116
Vienna Universal Exhibition, see Exhibition
von Hübner, see Hübner

'W. N. S.', 23–4
Wade, Thomas, 36
waka, 118
Walrond, Theodore, 144
Wedderburn, Sir David, 110, 113, 115, 131, 140–1, 149–52, 154–7, 161–4, 173
Wellesley Index, 176n. 8, 197n. 17, 199n. 55
Western advisers, xxii, 125–7
Western art, 166
Western civilisation, see civilisation
Westernisation, 107, 126, 133, 144, 165, 167, 168, 171–2
Westminster Review, 48, 57
White, James, 43–4, 48, 51–2, 173
Whittingham, Bernard, 48, 58
William Blackwood & Sons, xxiii, 21, 28, 30, 56
  see also Blackwood
Williams, Henry, 31
willow-pattern china plates, 94
Wilson, Andrew, 79
Wilson, Sir Thomas, 23–4
Wirgman, Charles, 117
Wiseman, Nicholas, 2
Woolwich, 76
Worcester porcelain, Plate 22
Wyatt, Sir Matthew Digby, 115, 165

Xavier, St Francis, 7, 11, 18, 46, 54

Yedo, see Edo
Yokohama (Kanagawa), 65, 83–4, 114, 118, 151, 158, 164
Yokohama pidgin, 113
Yokohama press, 74, 116–8, 134
Yoritomo, the first Shogun, 72, 98–9
Yorkshire, 101
Yoshida, Shôin (Torajirô), 118, 158–9, 166
Yoshida, Temple of, 158–9
Yoshiwara, 103
Young Japan, 140
Yunnan, 163

Zanbô ritsu, 117
Zôjôji, 97

toasting, 64, 105
toga, 161
Tokugawa Inspectors, 54
Tokugawa government, 53, 84,
    see also Shogunate
Tokugawa regime, see Shogunate
Tokugawa Shogun, see Shogun
Tokyo, see Edo
Tory, 123, 137
Tosa, 121
tourists, see travellers
Tôzenji Incident, see British Legation
Tractarians, 12
travel books, 54
travellers to Japan, 152, 154–5, 157, 160, 167, 172, 175
treaty-limits, 151
treaty ports of Japan, 67, 69, 150–1
treaty revision, 87, 119, 144–8, 164
Tremenheere, John Henry, 71–3, 76, 79–80, 84–6, 174
Tronson, John M., 49, 52, 55, 57, 60
Troubridge, Edward Norwich, 63
Tsushima, 66
Turks, 6
Tycoon, see Shogun
Tycoon, title of, 190n. 27
Tyrian Astarte, 160

Unbeaten Tracks in Japan by Isabella Bird, xi (1880), 126
unchangeableness, see immutability
Universal Library by Blackwood, 3
Universal Library by Cooke, 4, 7
Uraga, 63–4
urbanity, 51, 62, 166
    see also civilisation
Utagawa Kunisada, see Kunisada

vaccination, 86
Vatican, 81, 116,
Venetian Oligarchy, 14
Venus, 161
vicarious responsibility, 167
Victoria, Queen of Great Britain, 25
Vienna, 116
Vienna Universal Exhibition, see Exhibition
von Hübner, see Hübner

'W. N. S.', 23–4
Wade, Thomas, 36
waka, 118
Walrond, Theodore, 144
Wedderburn, Sir David, 110, 113, 115, 131, 140–1, 149–52, 154–7, 161–4, 173
Wellesley Index, 176n. 8, 197n. 17, 199n. 55
Western advisers, xxii, 125–7
Western art, 166
Western civilisation, see civilisation
Westernisation, 107, 126, 133, 144, 165, 167, 168, 171–2
Westminster Review, 48, 57
White, James, 43–4, 48, 51–2, 173
Whittingham, Bernard, 48, 58
William Blackwood & Sons, xxiii, 21, 28, 30, 56
    see also Blackwood
Williams, Henry, 31
willow-pattern china plates, 94
Wilson, Andrew, 79
Wilson, Sir Thomas, 23–4
Wirgman, Charles, 117
Wiseman, Nicholas, 2
Woolwich, 76
Worcester porcelain, Plate 22
Wyatt, Sir Matthew Digby, 115, 165

Xavier, St Francis, 7, 11, 18, 46, 54

Yedo, see Edo
Yokohama (Kanagawa), 65, 83–4, 114, 118, 151, 158, 164
Yokohama pidgin, 113
Yokohama press, 74, 116–8, 134
Yoritomo, the first Shogun, 72, 98–9
Yorkshire, 101
Yoshida, Shôin (Torajirô), 118, 158–9, 166
Yoshida, Temple of, 158–9
Yoshiwara, 103
Young Japan, 140
Yunnan, 163

Zanbô ritsu, 117
Zôjôji, 97